D1521767

CONSTITUTIONAL COURTS AND DEMOCRATIC VALUES

VÍCTOR FERRERES COMELLA

Constitutional Courts
AND Democratic Values

A EUROPEAN PERSPECTIVE

YALE UNIVERSITY PRESS   NEW HAVEN & LONDON

Set in FontShop Scala and Scala Sans by Duke & Company, Devon, Pennsylvania.
Printed in the United States of America.

Library of Congress Control Number: 2009904635
ISBN 978-0-300-14867-1 (paperback : alk. paper)

A catalogue record for this book is available from the British Library.

This paper meets the requirements of ANSI/NISO Z39.48-1992 (Permanence of Paper).

10 9 8 7 6 5 4 3 2 1

To Owen Fiss

CONTENTS

ACKNOWLEDGMENTS

I BEGAN TO THINK about the ideas advanced in this book in 1992, when I undertook to write a doctoral dissertation at Yale Law School on the American debate concerning the democratic legitimacy of judicial review. I benefited enormously from the intellectual guidance and personal encouragement of my supervisor, Owen Fiss. His passion for justice, his intellectual rigor, his generosity, and his good practical sense have always been a source of inspiration for me. The book is accordingly dedicated to him. I also learned a lot from Bruce Ackerman and Anthony Kronman, the other members of my JSD committee, as well as Mirjan Damaška and the late Carlos Nino, whose comments were always remarkably useful and sharp. That dissertation, which I finished in 1996, was the starting point of a larger project about the historical origins, the rationale, and the potential advantages of the European model of constitutional review.

Writing this book has involved a long process. During the years, I have had the privilege of teaching at institutions that offered an excellent environment for intellectual discussion and research. In 1994 I joined the department of constitutional law at Universitat Pompeu Fabra in Barcelona. I am indebted to Marc Carrillo and Carles Viver for their invaluable support. Later, in 2001, I became a faculty member of the Escuela Judicial, where young judges in Spain are educated and trained. The library services of the Escuela, under the direction of Cristina González, were admirably helpful. In both places, I met wonderful colleagues whose enthusiasm for my projects has been a great blessing.

There is nothing like teaching courses on the topics one is researching. I have been extraordinarily lucky to have had the opportunity to do so in different places. In 1992 I was invited by the Universidad de Puerto Rico in Río Piedras to teach a course on judicial review from a comparative perspective. I am deeply grateful to the faculty for their hospitality and their interest in my work. In 2001, 2003, and 2007, I visited New York University School of Law, where I offered a course on European constitutionalism, as well as a seminar on constitutional theory, which I had the privilege to teach with Larry Sager (in 2001) and with Mattias Kumm (in 2003 and 2007). The University of Texas was another institution that generously opened its doors to me. I was there in 2005, teaching a course on European law and co-teaching a constitutional seminar, again with Larry Sager. It is difficult to exaggerate the enormous progress I made through these experiences. I am very grateful to both Larry and Mattias for the many illuminating and fascinating conversations we engaged in. Moreover, the students that took our classes—many of whom wrote excellent papers (which I still have!)—were active participants in the discussions. The same is true of the students who took my courses in the summer programs offered in Barcelona by the University of Miami (in 2002, 2004, and 2006) and by the Universidad de Puerto Rico (in 2003–2008). Many thanks to them all.

The ideas I take up in the book figured in many formal presentations at Universitat Pompeu Fabra (Barcelona), Universitat de Barcelona, Universitat Autònoma de Barcelona, Universidad Carlos III (Madrid), Centro de Estudios Políticos y Constitucionales (Madrid), Universidad de Buenos Aires, Universidad de Córdoba (Argentina), Universidad de Santiago de Chile, New York University, the University of Texas, Washington University in St. Louis, the University of Maine, Cornell University, Cardozo School of Law, Instituto Tecnológico Autónomo de México (ITAM), Universidad Nacional Autónoma de México (UNAM), Escuela Libre de Derecho (Mexico), Centro de Investigación y Docencia Económicas (CIDE), Universidad Autónoma Metropolitana–Azcapotzalco (Mexico), Università di Pisa, Università degli Studi di Siena, Université Paris X Nanterre, Université Paris 1 Panthéon Sorbonne, and Humboldt-Universität zu Berlin, as well as at a conference on legislatures and constitutionalism that was held in Banff, Alberta, in July 2004. I greatly benefited from the stimulating comments I received from members of those audiences.

Many people have been very generous in reading earlier drafts of this book or drafts of previous writings that established the intellectual foundations for it. (Some of the ideas in this book were anticipated in an underdeveloped form in two articles: "The European Model of Constitutional Review of Legislation: Toward Decentralization?" *International Journal of Constitutional Law* 2 (2004): 461–491, and "The Consequences of Centralizing Constitutional Review in a Special Court: Some Thoughts on Judicial Activism," *Texas Law Review* 82 (2004): 1705–1736. I need to mention, in particular, Bruce Ackerman, Marian Ahumada, Pedro Cruz Villalón, Luis María Díez-Picazo, Owen Fiss, Barry Friedman, Roberto Gargarella, Ernesto Garzón Valdés, Dieter Grimm, Mattias Kumm, Mitchel Lasser, Luis Javier Mieres, José Juan Moreso, Rick Pildes, Luis Rodríguez Abascal, Michel Rosenfeld, Carlos Rosenkrantz, Francisco Rubio Llorente, Larry Sager, Alejandro Saiz Arnaiz, Daniel Sarmiento, Aida Torres, and Michel Troper. All of them have saved me from many errors and have suggested various ways to improve my arguments. They are not to be held responsible, however, for any flaws in this book. I am also grateful to the anonymous readers of Yale University Press, whose suggestions and criticisms were crucial in helping me transform the original manuscript into a more interesting book. Michael O'Malley, Alex Larson, Jack Borrebach, and Karen Schoen made the editorial process a wonderful experience. It has been a real pleasure to work with them.

Finally, my wife, Maite, and my kids, Irene, Laura, and Marc, have been extremely patient with me during all these years, as my work was slowly finding its way. Without their love, this book would not have seen the light of day.

IF WE LOOK AT the legal landscape of contemporary Europe, we will be struck by the institutional salience of constitutional courts. Most European countries have established such bodies to guarantee the supremacy of the constitution over parliamentary enactments. Within the European Union, in particular, the vast majority of countries have opted for this kind of arrangement.

In so doing, Europe has radically departed from the model of judicial review that has existed in the United States since *Marbury v. Madison* was decided in 1803.[1] Instead of allowing all judges, in the context of ordinary legal disputes, to set aside legislation that is allegedly inconsistent with the constitution, most European nations have preferred to assign the task of legislative review to a special tribunal. Europe is clearly associated with the "centralized" or "concentrated" model of constitutional justice, whereas the United States exemplifies the "decentralized" or "diffuse" model.[2]

There are, of course, many variations within the centralized model, as we will see in chapter 1. Each particular version has its own advantages and disadvantages. The defining feature, however, is the existence of a dualist structure within the judiciary. The constitutional court occupies its own space, which is different from that of regular courts ("ordinary courts"). Why this separation? If the constitution is part of the law, and if it belongs to courts to say what the law is, shouldn't all judges be empowered to disregard unconstitutional legislation, as the *Marbury* decision famously concluded? Why have most European nations resisted this conclusion? Why have they thought it necessary to set up a special court with the exclusive authority to determine the constitutionality of statutes?

The answers that have traditionally been given are either unpersuasive or of limited value. One theory, which I examine in chapter 2, invokes the principle of separation of powers. The French revolutionaries of 1789, it is asserted, espoused a conception of this principle that differed radically from that of the Americans. The role of judges was conceived more narrowly in revolutionary France than in the United States, making it impossible in France for judges to be granted the power to review the constitutionality of legislation. Given the general influence of French revolutionary ideas in continental Europe, an alternative arrangement had to be found in order to guarantee the supremacy of the constitution over ordinary law. Constitutional courts, which are not part of the ordinary judiciary, emerged as the institution in charge of this task.

This account is fine as a historical narrative, but it is not convincing at the normative level, as we will see. If we want to come up with a fresh justification for the European model, we need to look elsewhere. For these purposes, a second theory is usually offered, one that appeals to the value of legal certainty. The claim here is that a decentralized system of judicial review would not work well in European countries that belong to the civil-law culture. If legal certainty is to be safeguarded, it is better to concentrate constitutional review in a single court. As I argue in chapter 3, this line of defense is basically correct when properly qualified. Legal certainty, however, is not the only value that informs the centralized system. Other values have also been taken into account, and rightly so. The particular version of the centralized model that European countries have constructed is one that sacrifices legal certainty to a certain extent in order to accommodate other considerations.

More needs to be said, therefore, to support the European preference for constitutional courts. That is the purpose of part 2 of the book, where I start with the foundational question, What reasons do we have to expect that fundamental rights will be better protected if we include them in a constitution that is hard to amend and entrust courts with its interpretation? In chapter 4 I sketch a relatively abstract answer to this question, in light of which I then go on to discuss the potential strengths of the centralized model. Are constitutional tribunals promising candidates to perform legislative review? In what respects may they be better than regular courts? What advantages does the European model exhibit when judged from the standpoint of a foundational theory of constitutional review? Throughout chapters 5, 6, and 7, I explore the potential virtues of the model, as well as the possible risks it incorporates. I claim that constitutional courts are better equipped than ordinary courts to treat the constitution as a special kind of law, one that is deeply connected to abstract principles of political morality. Constitutional courts' contribution to the debates that develop in society, moreover, is likely to be significant, since they have to operate in an area of high public visibility. Constitutional courts, I also maintain, cannot be passive when they review legislation: they cannot easily abstain from ruling on constitutional matters they might otherwise wish to avoid; nor can they be extremely deferential toward the governmental majority. Despite some dangers, this tendency toward activism is not a trait we should condemn.

After having elaborated these arguments, with which I hope to strengthen the case in favor of the establishment and maintenance of a centralized model of judicial review in European civil-law countries, I then proceed to discuss the "democratic objection." What can be said in response to those critics who claim that it is not right for courts to be authorized to invalidate democratically enacted legislation? When it comes to this criticism, are there any specific advantages to constitutional courts? I address these questions in chapters 8 and 9.

Finally, in part 3 I direct attention to the potential sources of "crisis" of the centralized model. Despite the triumph of constitutional courts in Europe, there are forces, both internal and external to the domestic legal systems, that are undermining the courts' power, or that may potentially do so. The internal pressures derive from the principle that requires ordinary judges to interpret legislation in light of the constitution. Those judges are not entitled to disregard the statute that is applicable to a given case—only the constitutional court is empowered to do that. But they are expected to read the relevant statute in a way that makes it cohere with constitutional values. This division of labor between the constitutional court and ordinary courts is not easy to define in practice: When is it that an ordinary judge is still "interpreting" a legislative provision instead of "correcting" it in the name of constitutional values? In chapter 10 I address this question and suggest some adjustments to the centralized model to make it more efficient.

The external sources of the crisis are connected to supranational events. Constitutional courts have clearly lost the monopoly they were conferred in the past: they are no longer the only courts that can strike down parliamentary legislation in the name of higher norms. Ordinary judges are now required to disregard national legislation that clashes with the law of the European Community. They can do so directly, without first asking the national constitutional court to intervene. Similarly, in many countries, ordinary judges are entitled to refuse to apply national legislation if they find it inconsistent with the European Convention on Human Rights. Should these developments be criticized? How deeply do they affect the centralized model? Do they endanger its underlying values? These are important questions to address if we are to develop a complete picture of the role of constitutional courts in Europe, and I do so in chapters 11 and 12.

These are the main themes of the book. Inevitably, I must generalize to make my points—I have to transcend some details in order to capture the structural features of the centralized model, the most important reasons for having embraced it, the potential advantages that are connected to it, and the transformations that are afoot. Throughout the discussion, I hope to show that the classical defense of the European model needs to be enriched in light of modern conditions.

PART ONE THE TRIUMPH OF AN IDEA

CHAPTER ONE

The Rise of Constitutional Courts

A SUCCESSFUL STORY

Let's go back to 1920. It is very unlikely that the framers of the constitutions of the new republics of Czechoslovakia and Austria imagined that the institution they had just created (a constitutional court) would be so popular nowadays. Before the Second World War, only Lichtenstein (in 1921) and Spain (in 1931) had decided to establish such a court. The other countries in Europe remained impervious to the invention.[1]

During that period, a particularly powerful voice, that of Hans Kelsen, could be heard in support of the new system. This important legal philosopher (who lived from 1881 to 1973) was very influential in the construction of the Austrian Constitutional Court—where he served as a judge from 1921 to 1930. Of course, Kelsen did not invent the constitutional court out of nothing; others had come up with similar ideas before, and some institutions served as precedents.[2] But there is no doubt that he deserves enormous credit for its introduction and for its theoretical defense. He wrote extensively in favor of subjecting legislation to some type of judicial review and in favor of the centralized model, in particular, as opposed to the American alternative.[3] It is very useful to examine Kelsen's ideas in order to understand the intellectual sources of the European model—which is often called "Kelsenian."

After the Second World War, things started to change in a dramatic way. Italy (in 1947), Germany (in 1949), and France (in 1958) enacted new constitutions whose protection against ordinary legislation was entrusted to a constitutional tribunal. After their transitions to democracy, Portugal (in 1982) and Spain (in 1978) introduced such a court in their new constitutions too.[4] Belgium and Luxemburg joined the club as well (in 1980 and 1996, respectively). And after the fall of communism, almost all Central and Eastern European countries followed suit.[5]

In particular, eighteen out of the twenty-seven states that currently belong to the European Union—Austria, Belgium, Bulgaria, Czech Republic, France, Germany, Hungary, Italy, Latvia, Lithuania, Luxembourg, Malta, Poland, Portugal, Romania, Slovakia, Slovenia, and Spain—have created constitutional courts, a figure that shows the extent to which there is a strong preference for such institutions in the region. Only three countries within the European Union have adopted a system of judicial review similar to that of the United States: Sweden, Finland, and Denmark. In practice, though, courts in these Nordic countries very rarely find a statute unconstitutional.[6]

Of the six remaining countries within the European Union, four—Ireland,[7] Greece,[8] Cyprus,[9] and Estonia[10]—have adopted systems that are difficult to classify because they combine features of the American and the European models in different ways. The other two countries, the Netherlands and the United Kingdom, are exceptional in that they have no system of constitutional review of legislation. The Constitution of the Kingdom of the Netherlands explicitly prohibits judges from setting aside legislation on constitutional grounds.[11] Judges lack that capacity in the United Kingdom as well. The Human Rights Act 1998, which came into force in October 2000, has empowered certain U.K. superior courts to declare that a given statute is incompatible with any of the human rights that are enumerated in the act. (The act incorporates the European Convention on Human Rights into the domestic legal system.) Such a judicial declaration, however, does not mean that the statute is invalidated or set aside. Courts must still enforce it. The effect of a declaration of incompatibility is mainly political: the British parliament is expected to modify a law that a court has found to violate a human right, but it may elect not to do so. Parliament is still sovereign.[12]

The centralized model, which is clearly dominant within the European Union, has also had some influence in other regions. In Latin

America, for example, some countries have gradually departed from the American model that was originally established in the nineteenth century and have moved toward a mixed system that includes some components of the centralized model.[13] The system is mixed in that all courts are usually empowered to exercise constitutional review in the course of ordinary adjudication, but in addition, legislation can be formally invalidated by a specific body. For these purposes, some countries (Peru, Guatemala, Chile, Ecuador, Bolivia, Colombia) have introduced constitutional courts, whereas others (Costa Rica, El Salvador, Honduras, Nicaragua, Paraguay, Venezuela) have created a special constitutional chamber within the existing supreme court. We also find constitutional courts in other parts of the world (in South Korea, Indonesia, Thailand, South Africa, Egypt, and Turkey, for example).

Actually, there are so many nations that have established constitutional tribunals that a wide variety of types has emerged. We need to transcend the particular traits of the different national systems, however, in order to understand the deep principles and tendencies of the centralized model. For these purposes, my discussion is anchored by a group of eight countries of Western Europe (Austria, Belgium, France, Germany, Italy, Luxembourg, Portugal, and Spain), though I sometimes offer information about other nations, especially those of Central and Eastern Europe.[14]

THE BASIC FEATURES OF THE EUROPEAN MODEL

Before we embark upon a discussion about the rationale of the European model, we need to identify its main characteristics. We must briefly consider three questions: (1) Over what matters does the constitutional court have jurisdiction? (2) Who is authorized to ask the court to review the constitutionality of a statute? (3) What are the effects of the court's decisions? The answers to these questions will give us the technical infrastructure we need for the topics discussed throughout the remainder of the book.

Functions of the Constitutional Court

As already explained, what defines the European model is the existence of a special institution—the constitutional court—in charge of assessing the constitutionality of legislation. This institution is granted a monopoly in this field: no other court—not even the supreme court—is entitled to disregard a parliamentary statute on its own authority. In many countries, ordinary judges, as we will see shortly, are allowed to stay the proceedings of a given case in order to make an application to the constitutional court for the annulment of a statute that they think is inconsistent with the constitution. They are not authorized, however, to disregard the statutory provision themselves.[15]

Two qualifications about the constitutional court's monopoly should be mentioned, however. First, in some countries, ordinary judges may set aside a legislative provision that was enacted *before* the constitution entered into force. In those countries, therefore, it is only post-constitution legislation that falls under the exclusive control of the constitutional court.[16] Second, in Portugal, a constitutional tribunal has been created, but ordinary judges are also empowered to exercise legislative review.[17] It must be noted, however, that the tribunal must intervene whenever a lower court has ruled that a law is unconstitutional. (The public prosecutors' office has the duty to lodge an appeal in such a case.) This means that, in practice, the system is relatively centralized: only the constitutional tribunal has the final authority to set aside a statute in a particular lawsuit.[18]

Now, constitutional courts differ as to the relative prominence of legislative review within their portfolio of responsibilities. Constitutional courts are sometimes given jurisdiction to supervise the regularity of elections and referenda, for example, or to verify the legality of political parties or to enforce the criminal law against high governmental authorities or to protect fundamental rights against administrative and judicial decisions. Most of these tasks are still "constitutional" in that they require the interpretation and enforcement of constitutional provisions, but others are not: they merely involve ordinary law. We can say that a constitutional court is not "pure" when, apart from reviewing legislation, it has some other functions. The more important those other functions are, the larger the workload they generate, and the closer they are conceptually to the enforcement of ordinary law, the less pure the constitutional court is.

We can thus locate constitutional courts along a spectrum of purity. At one extreme, we find absolutely pure constitutional courts, whose only job is to review legislation for its constitutionality (Belgium and Luxembourg).[19] In the middle, we find courts that perform some additional tasks, although their main activity is still legislative review (France, Italy, and Portugal).[20] At the other end of the spectrum, courts have jurisdiction over so many different matters that it would be wrong to say that, in terms of everyday practice, their most important function is to determine the constitutionality of legislation (Germany, Austria, and Spain).[21]

Access to the Court

Let us now turn to the issue of standing. Various procedures have been established in different European countries to submit claims to the constitutional court that a particular statute is unconstitutional. One type of procedure is initiated through *constitutional challenges,* which are usually brought by public institutions, such as the executive, the ombudsman, the general prosecutor, the parliament, or a qualified minority of the parliament. In some countries, private individuals are also allowed to bring such challenges. Through this type of procedure, legislative provisions are attacked directly and in the abstract—the procedure is not tied to any specific controversy. Normally, the challenge must be filed after the statute has been promulgated. In some jurisdictions, however, preventive (a priori) review is permitted: statutes can be attacked before they are promulgated.[22]

A second way to get to the court is through so-called *constitutional questions,* which are initiated in the course of ordinary adjudication. When regular judges handling specific disputes believe that the applicable statute is unconstitutional, or have doubts about its validity, they stay the proceedings and certify the issue to the constitutional court.[23] The latter will simply declare whether the statute is valid. It is then for the ordinary judges who raised the question to decide the specific controversies in light of the answer provided by the constitutional court.[24]

In some countries (Spain, Germany, and Austria), there is a third way to invoke the jurisdiction of the constitutional court. Individuals can file a *constitutional complaint* alleging that one of their fundamental rights has been violated by public authorities.[25] In most cases in which the complaint is justified, the breach of the fundamental right stems from an incorrect interpretation or application of the relevant statute or body of law. But sometimes it is the statute itself that is at fault. In such instances, the constitutional court will review the statute and determine its validity.

A fourth type of procedure exists in Portugal. As already explained, the Portuguese system is exceptional in that regular courts are permitted to disregard legislation they find unconstitutional. Their rulings can then be appealed to the Constitutional Court by the parties to the case (or by the public prosecutor). The Constitutional Court's jurisdiction is limited, however: it can decide only whether the lower court got it right when it disregarded, or upheld, the pertinent piece of legislation.

So there are variations within the European model. Obviously, a constitutional tribunal is more or less detached from the ordinary judiciary, depending on the type of procedures that can be used to attack a statute. In the context of abstract challenges, the tribunal is not linked to the regular courts. In contrast, there is such a link when ordinary judges raise constitutional questions. The link is even stronger when the constitutional tribunal has jurisdiction to review decisions rendered by ordinary judges, as in the complaints procedure or in the appeals procedure of Portugal. The dualist structure that characterizes the European model can thus be more or less rigid.

This, of course, has implications for how "abstract" or how "concrete" the system of legislative review is. The general tendency in Western Europe is for constitutional courts to scrutinize the laws in the context of specific cases—through constitutional questions, individual complaints, or appeals of the Portuguese sort. Abstract review initiated by means of constitutional challenges is less frequent in practice.[26] Until very recently, France represented the most prominent exception to this general pattern, for abstract review brought by public institutions was the only kind of review that the French Constitutional Council could engage in. An important constitutional amendment of July 23, 2008, however, has deeply transformed the French system. Ordinary judges are now empowered to certify questions to the Constitutional Council, if the applicable law is attacked on the grounds that it violates one of the constitutionally guaranteed rights or liberties.[27] (Such questions, however, must be filtered by the Court of Cassation, the highest court of ordinary jurisdiction, or the Council of State, the highest administrative court.) Abstract review is thus combined with concrete review. It is likely that in the near future, a great number of statutes will be tested by the French Constitutional Council in the context of questions raised by ordinary judges, as has happened in other European countries. The general practice in Central and Eastern Europe, in contrast, seems to more strongly center around abstract review. According to Wojciech Sadurski, abstract review, which has been established in all the countries in that region, is widely used, whereas concrete review initiated by regular courts is rarely practiced.[28]

Effects of the Court's Decisions

Finally, what about the effects of the decisions handed down by the constitutional court? In general, when the court declares that a statute is unconstitutional, its decision is binding on everyone. It produces *"erga omnes* effects," as the expression goes. The statute is effectively repealed, and no court or governmental organ is allowed to apply it.[29] Kelsen used to say that the constitutional court acts as a "negative legislature" when it strikes down a law, for it does something similar to what the parliament does when it repeals a law.[30]

When the court upholds a statute, in contrast, one may still challenge that statute in the future by bringing new objections in subsequent proceedings.[31] Of course, if the court reviews the statute not only in light of the specific grounds that the challengers have adduced in their briefs but also in light of additional reasons that the court articulates *sua sponte,* its conclusion that the statute is constitutional is harder to revisit in the future.[32] Still, there is always some room for further judicial examination, whereas if the statute is invalidated, that's the end of the story. (A new statute with the same provisions would have to be passed by the legislature in order for the constitutional court to have the opportunity to take a second look at the underlying issue.)[33]

It is important to note, however, that constitutional courts quite often hand down "intermediate" decisions that identify the constitutional defects of a given statute but do not immediately invalidate it. Courts, for example, sometimes suspend the effects of their decisions declaring a law unconstitutional in order to give the parliament enough time to repair the defects. In other cases, they issue a "reconstructive" decision that directly amends the defective statute to make it comport with the constitution. These and other techniques have been crafted to satisfy practical needs. Experience has shown that the dichotomy between striking down statutes, on the one hand, and fully upholding their constitutionality, on the other, is unacceptably rigid.[34]

With this preliminary characterization of the European model, we have the technical background we need for the discussion in the next chapters. So let us now proceed to the question concerning the rationale of the model. Why should a country establish a special tribunal to assess the constitutionality of legislation instead of entrusting this function to ordinary courts, as is the case in the American system?

CHAPTER TWO

Historical Background

THE PRINCIPLE OF SEPARATION OF POWERS

IN ORDER TO EXPLAIN, at least in part, the European inclination toward constitutional courts, scholars often note that a specific conception of the principle of separation of powers emerged in continental Europe as a result of the French Revolution of 1789. Under this conception, which was very influential in many countries, judges were to have a restricted role. Determining the validity of legislation was not a power to be allocated to them. To guarantee the supremacy of the constitution over ordinary law, alternative institutions had to be conceived. Constitutional courts finally emerged as the appropriate bodies for the task.

As I will argue, this historical narrative is fine, but if we want to construct a modern justification of the European preference for constitutional tribunals, we should forget about the principle of separation of powers as traditionally understood. We should instead assess the potential advantages and disadvantages of such tribunals in a more straightforward and pragmatic way, without being constrained at the normative level by the historical accidents that led to a particular understanding of separation of powers. History is important in explaining the birth of institutions, but we should transcend it when we try to find good reasons to maintain or reform the institutions we have.

THE FRENCH REVOLUTION AND THE PRINCIPLE OF SEPARATION OF POWERS

The historical narrative is as follows: Both the American and the French revolutionaries at the end of the eighteenth century explicitly invoked the principle of separation of powers. The constitutions that were adopted on both sides of the Atlantic were supposed to respect that principle. The specific content that was ascribed to the idea of separation of powers, however, was remarkably different, especially when it came to the role of the judiciary vis-à-vis popularly elected assemblies.

Americans tended to trust judges as guardians of individual liberties and were prepared to grant them the power to check legislation under the U.S. Constitution, although the precise scope and the limits of that power were controversial. The problem of parliamentary tyranny was high on the constitutional agenda. Americans, after all, had rebelled against the British parliament, and the framers of the U.S. Constitution reacted, at least in part, against the legislative excesses that they found in the states after Independence. It is against this background that we must read Chief Justice John Marshall's famous holding in *Marbury v. Madison* that courts in the United States have the power of constitutional review. The whole political system was built on the idea of checks and balances, which is a particular rendering of the more abstract principle of separation of powers. As M. J. C. Vile explains, "The separation of powers, in itself, is not a sufficient basis for the establishment of a doctrine of judicial review." Something more is needed: the acceptance of the idea of *checks and balances* as essential barriers to the improper exercise of power. One branch can then interfere with the functions of another to the extent of invalidating its acts.[1]

The French revolutionaries, in contrast, relied on the legislature and the executive as the main engines of social transformation to liberate the people from feudal privileges. New codes would be enacted to protect individual rights and the principle of equality before the law. Thanks to codification, moreover, the law could be reduced to a precise, coherent, and complete body of written legislation so that the task of judges would be rather mechanical.[2] A modernized and meritocratic administration, in its turn, would be in charge of bringing society closer to the revolutionary ideals.[3]

To a considerable extent, this restrictive conception of the role of judges was a reaction against the abuses perpetrated during the ancien régime by the higher courts—the parlements—that had been set up in various French cities. Those courts had suspended the enforcement of royal decrees, whose aim was to modernize the law against old feudal privileges. The courts had done so in the name of traditional higher law (the so-called fundamental laws of the kingdom). As Mauro Cappelletti explains, judges were "almost always among the bitterest enemies of even the slightest liberal reform. They were the fiercest opponents of the Revolution, whose guillotine was soon to reap a rich harvest of their most honorable heads."[4]

In this historical context, then, separation of powers was understood differently than it was in the United States. Under the new scheme in France, judges would have a rather modest part to play. Judges were required to "address themselves to the legislative body" whenever they thought it "necessary to interpret a statute or to make a new one."[5] Through this mechanism—which was called référé législatif—the parliament would clarify the meaning of the applicable statute. It would provide judges with the "authentic interpretation" of the legislative text. In this regard, the French revolutionaries followed Montesquieu's idea that judges were to be "only the mouth that pronounces the words of the law, inanimate beings who can moderate neither its force nor its rigor."[6]

Actually, the French revolutionaries suspected that judges might be tempted to decide cases against the clear meaning of the law. Accordingly, they created the Court of Cassation.[7] This institution, which would quash judicial decisions that deviated from the law, was originally conceived as an appendix of parliament that would protect its laws against judicial erosion. Thus, the 1791 constitution provided that each year, a commission of eight members of the court would be sent to the legislative assembly to report the judgments made.[8]

Given the distrust with which the revolutionaries viewed the judiciary, it is not surprising that the latter was denied any power to check the actions of the executive and legislative branches. "Judicial functions," the law provided, "are distinct and will always remain separate from administrative functions." Therefore, "it shall be a criminal offence for judges of the ordinary courts to interfere in any manner whatsoever with the operation of the administration, nor shall they call administrators to account before them in respect of the exercise of their official functions."[9]

As a result, different institutions, separate from courts, had to emerge to make it possible for the legal validity of administrative acts to be checked. This task was gradually assumed by the Council of State, which was established by Napoleon in 1799, and by lower administrative tribunals that were created later.[10] These bodies were separate from the judicial branch. A division of labor between the ordinary judiciary and the "administrative tribunals" was thus introduced as a result of the restrictive conception of the role of the judiciary in a system of separation of powers.[11]

Similarly, judges were forbidden to assess the validity of statutes. The law provided that courts could not "interfere with the exercise of legislative powers or suspend the application of the laws."[12] This principle was soon understood to mean that judges could not set aside legislation on constitutional grounds.

It is important to emphasize that the French revolutionaries did not deny that the constitution is the supreme law of the land. The preamble to the 1789 Declaration of the Rights of Man and of the Citizen stated that rights were declared so that the acts of the legislature and of the executive could be compared with the goal of all political institutions—namely, the protection of rights. The declaration (which was later attached to the constitution of 1791) established direct limits on the legislature: article 5, for example, provided that the law could punish only those actions that were harmful to society, and article 8 prohibited penalties that were not strictly and evidently necessary. There is no doubt that the French revolutionaries wanted legislation to respect these constitutional principles. After all, they made the constitution more difficult to amend than ordinary legislation because they took it for granted that the constitution was supreme.[13] Their restrictive understanding of the role of judges, however, precluded judicial review of legislation. They relied on other types of constraints on the legislature, such as the executive veto. They had great confidence, moreover, in the watchful eyes of the citizenry as a guarantee that the constitution would be observed. To this effect, the 1791 constitution appealed to the general loyalty of public institutions, the vigilance of parents, the affection of young citizens, and the courage of the French people in general.[14]

When it was gradually felt that, quite apart from these general political checks on the legislature, some specific system of constitutional review was needed, ordinary courts were not relied upon. Other bodies were instead conceived. Thus, the French revolutionary Emmanuel-Joseph Sieyès soon proposed the creation of a "constitutional jury" (*jurie constitutionnaire*), a body of 108 members to be recruited from among political representatives. His proposal was rejected, however.[15] Later, in 1799 and in 1852, the Conservative Senate was established as a guardian of the constitution. This solution was not successful, though, for the Conservative Senate was under the complete political dependence of the emperor and therefore lacked the necessary institutional distance to evaluate the laws.[16]

In the twentieth century, the constitution of 1946 created yet another nonjudicial body, the Constitutional Committee, which was granted the authority to determine whether a law was contrary to the organic (that is, structural) part of the constitution and thus required a previous constitutional amendment in order for it to be validly enacted.[17] The present arrangement in France is part of this tradition. The 1958 constitution assigns the task of determining the validity of legislation to a special body, the Constitutional Council. Because this institution is not part of the judiciary, it is possible to maintain that the traditional principle of the Revolution is still honored: there is no *judicial* review of laws in France, since the institution responsible for review is emphatically not part of the judiciary.

This interpretation of the principle of separation of powers, under which it is not for ordinary judges to assess the constitutionality of statutes, has been adopted in a more extreme form in France than in other European countries. But it has nevertheless played a role historically in many of them, in one form or another. The wave of codification that swept Europe during the nineteenth century brought with it the assumption that the judiciary was to play a modest part in the governmental scheme. As Allan-Randolph Brewer-Carías puts it, "The traditions of parliamentary supremacy, on the one hand, and of separation of powers on the other, have been so powerful in Europe that they have prevented ordinary judicial bodies from any possibility of judging the constitutionality of legislation." The constitutional court, in contrast, is created at a later stage, as a fourth branch of government that is separate from the judiciary and whose specific task is to scrutinize parliamentary enactments. It is erected on a different institutional level, "above the traditional horizontal separation of powers—equally above the legislator, the executive and the courts—to ensure the supremacy of the Constitution with respect to them all."[18]

The establishment of a constitutional court, in short, seems to be the natural option in those countries that want to protect the constitution against the legislature but have traditionally entertained a relatively narrow conception of the role of (ordinary) judges under a system of separation of powers.

Now, if we move beyond this historical explanation and try to assess and justify the European model of constitutional review from a normative perspective, is there much we can get from the principle of separation of powers? In what follows, I argue that the answer is no.

THE LIMITED NORMATIVE RELEVANCE OF THE PRINCIPLE OF SEPARATION OF POWERS

Whether it was a good idea for European countries to create special constitutional courts to review the validity of laws is a question to be decided in a pragmatic spirit. The principle of separation of powers, as traditionally understood in Europe, should not distract us from a direct assessment of the advantages and disadvantages of these special institutions. That the French revolutionaries distrusted ordinary judges at the end of the eighteenth century is a historical fact that has great explanatory force in accounting for later events. But it is irrelevant when it comes to constructing a modern justification for the set of institutions that Europeans inherited from those revolutionaries.

Despite their important differences in several respects, ordinary courts and special constitutional tribunals are both "courts": they are relatively independent from the political branches; they normally render their decisions in the context of procedures initiated by others; and they justify those decisions by reference to a set of legal norms that they are in charge of interpreting and enforcing. If a special tribunal is instrumentally better than the ordinary judiciary for checking the validity of legislative provisions, we have a good reason to set it up. But the principle of separation of powers does not by itself dictate that this is the right choice. Why should such a principle proscribe legislative review by ordinary courts but license (or even require) legislative review by special constitutional tribunals?[19]

It is interesting to note, by the way, that some of the special bodies

that were created as a result of the French revolutionary distrust of ordinary courts have undergone a process of "judicialization." Thus, the
original notion that ordinary judges should not interpret the law but
should instead ask the parliament to do so was abandoned in 1804, when
the Napoleonic Code (Code civil des Français), was promulgated. The *référé législatif* was abolished, and from then on, judges would have to solve
the interpretive problems on their own. As a result, the Court of Cassation
became the institution in charge of interpreting statutes when they were
ambiguous. It was thus transformed into a modern supreme court.[20] In
the same vein, the Council of State and the administrative tribunals in
charge of reviewing administrative decisions are now regarded as courts,
albeit a special kind. Constitutional courts in Europe have undergone a
similar process of judicialization in many countries: they are strongly
linked to the regular courts and view themselves as part of the judiciary,
broadly conceived. Whether this is a development to be celebrated or, on
the contrary, criticized is a question to be considered in an instrumental
spirit: we have to examine how well the institutions perform their functions in their new forms. Discussing the issue in light of the principle of
separation of powers is not a fruitful strategy.

The principle of separation of powers is also unhelpful when it comes
to more specific matters. For example, at what stage should constitutional
review of a statute take place—before it is promulgated, or afterward? Both
a priori and a posteriori review have their own advantages and disadvantages. It is hard to see, however, what help we can get from the notion of
separation of powers to start answering this question. Gustavo Zagrebelsky, for instance, notes that a priori review by the French Constitutional
Council is in keeping with the classic understanding of the principle
of separation of powers that has prevailed in France, under which laws
should be immune from judicial review. Since the constitutional court
scrutinizes the laws *before* they are promulgated, that classic understanding can be maintained.[21] (Zagrebelsky's comment, of course, referred to
the system that existed in France until the recent reform of July 2008,
which has introduced a posteriori review.) This classic understanding,
however, seems a bit too formalistic. Even if a statute has not yet been
promulgated when the court ascertains its constitutionality, the parliamentary majority has already expressed its will, and this is the key fact.
It is not at all obvious why, given the principles of separation of powers

and parliamentary sovereignty, constitutional review by a court should be fine if it takes place a priori but should be condemned if it occurs a posteriori.

Or consider the question whether courts in charge of constitutional review should formally repeal statutes or should instead merely disregard them for purposes of deciding a specific case. This is again a technical question, the answer to which should not depend on a particular understanding of separation of powers. In this connection, there has been too much discussion, of a fruitless kind, as to how to characterize the action of a constitutional court when it strikes down a statute. In part, this is because one of Hans Kelsen's more or less felicitous metaphors—the constitutional court as a "negative legislature"—has been wrongly transformed into a touchstone of legitimacy (or illegitimacy). Let me explain.

As already noted, Kelsen used to say that what the court does when it invalidates a statute can be classified as part of the "legislative function."[22] The legislative function, he wrote, has two aspects: one is "positive," and the other is "negative." The positive function consists of enacting (or modifying) statutes, and it pertains to parliament exclusively. The negative function, instead, consists of repealing statutes. When the court examines a law and concludes that it offends the constitution, the court cancels that law with general effects. Since this outcome is similar to what parliament does when it repeals a law, Kelsen claimed that the "legislative power" (when it comes to repealing legal provisions) is now shared by two institutions: parliament and the court.

To a certain extent, this is a verbal pirouette, however. We should not take Kelsen's metaphor too seriously when defending or attacking the idea of setting up a constitutional court with the power to formally eliminate statutes. First, Kelsen himself was aware of the limited sense in which we can say that the constitutional court exercises a "legislative" function. We can analogize the court with the legislature only if we focus on the *effects* of the court's decisions: they are similar to the effects that the legislature produces when it repeals a statute. If we focus on the *grounds* of the court's decisions, however, there is a crucial difference between the two institutions. Whereas a parliament is free to act as it wills, within the limits prescribed by the constitution, the constitutional court is not. Whereas the parliament can freely repeal a statute, for any reason whatsoever, the court can invalidate a statute only if it concludes that it is unconstitutional. Kelsen himself regarded the court's function as "jurisdictional" when seen from this perspective. He acknowledged that the court enjoys some degree of discretion when it interprets the constitution, but he believed that what the court does, basically, is enforce the constitution. From this perspective, it is not really a "legislature," he asserted, but a "jurisdictional" body.[23]

Second, the opposition between the European and the American models, though relevant in various aspects, is not as categorical as the metaphor of a "negative legislature" seems to imply. It is true that (normally) constitutional courts in Europe can formally repeal a given statute, whereas American courts simply disregard it for purposes of deciding a specific controversy. Yet the impact of the decisions of the courts in the United States is not confined to the particular cases: they establish binding precedents for the future. The enforcement of statutes gets blocked as a result of the body of precedents laid down by such courts. In this regard, the judiciary in the United States acts as a "negative legislature" too.

So to say that a constitutional court of the Kelsenian type is a "negative legislature" is simply to use a metaphor of limited value. This label tells us nothing interesting about the legitimacy of the institution. It may have been an excellent idea for European countries to create such a court and give it the power to formally strike down statutes. The fact that it can be conceived as a "negative legislature," however, adds no value, even if this image seems to better fit a particular conception of separation of powers inherited from the past—under which "judicial" review was to be excluded.

And the opposite is also true, of course: the fact that the constitutional court can be said to be a "negative legislature" in a metaphorical sense should attract no special objection in the name of separation of powers. If a constitutional court is the right institution to establish for purposes of checking the validity of parliamentary enactments, we should not be worried about the fact that it could be classified as a "negative legislature." At the beginning of the twentieth century, for example, there was an important scholarly debate in France about the introduction of an American, decentralized, model of judicial review. Some prominent academic figures, working against the historical currents in France, advocated that model and condemned the idea of a special constitutional court.[24] Again, the principle of separation of powers occupied center stage. Interestingly, new implications were drawn from this principle, implications opposite to those that had been traditionally embraced in France. Some scholars, indeed, argued that constitutional review is perfectly acceptable when it is decentralized and concrete. It is legitimate, they claimed, for courts to be authorized to set aside statutes in particular cases (*refus d'application*), but it is not legitimate for a court to be empowered to formally repeal statutes (*annulation*). The former activity, they asserted, is of a judicial nature and thus acceptable under the principle of separation of powers, but the latter is not: it is a legislative function.

This thesis was clearly misguided, as Charles Eisenmann argued in the 1920s after visiting Vienna as a young student to write a doctoral dissertation (under Kelsen's supervision) on the new constitutional court in Austria. Eisenmann reasoned, quite rightly, that the choice between formal invalidation of a statute, on the one hand, and concrete nonapplication of a statute, on the other, is a technical question that cannot be decided on the basis of the principle of separation of powers. The difference has some relevance, but it does not amount to a categorical distinction between a "legislative" function and a "judicial" one.[25] We cannot automatically claim that if a given institution strikes down statutes, it is really a "legislative" body, whereas if it merely sets them aside for purposes of resolving disputes, it acts as a real "court." What matters is the sort of grounds—political or legal—on which the institution rests its decisions.

In sum, the principle of separation of powers and the metaphors it has sometimes generated are of no real value when it comes to justifying institutional choices of the kind we have examined. The historical understanding of this principle in Europe is certainly important in explaining the rise of special bodies like constitutional courts, but it gives us no justificatory reasons for their existence and for the particular details of their design. We should transcend historical inertia and judge institutional arrangements in a pragmatic spirit, in light of the ultimate goals that we seek and in light of other values that may operate as constraints.

In this pragmatic spirit, for example, Kelsen believed that, quite apart from any talk about separation of powers, there is an important consideration that speaks in favor of a centralized model of constitutional review: the need to protect legal certainty. As I explain in the next chapter, there is some truth to this argument, but it needs to be properly qualified.

CHAPTER THREE

A Traditional Justification

LEGAL CERTAINTY

ALL LEGAL SYSTEMS MUST try to satisfy the value of legal certainty to a sufficient extent. Both citizens and public officials need to be relatively sure what the law is. If a system of constitutional review of legislation is set up, it is important to design it in such a way that legal certainty is not impaired. Hans Kelsen, and others after him, have argued that the centralized model is much better in this respect. To what extent is this so? In the United States, for example, judicial review is decentralized, yet legal certainty seems to be sufficiently preserved. It is true that different lower courts reach opposite conclusions in many constitutional controversies, but as cases get litigated to the Supreme Court, precedents are established and uniformity is achieved. Is there any reason such an arrangement would not be feasible in continental Europe? Are there any features of the civil-law tradition that conspire against the introduction of an American-type decentralized system? Is centralization of legislative review really necessary to protect legal certainty?

THE CONSTRAINTS OF THE CIVIL-LAW TRADITION

It is often argued that it is not possible to adopt a decentralized system of judicial review in the European countries that belong to the civil-law family. Two main reasons are offered to support this claim.[1]

First, it is noted, quite rightly, that the judiciary in those countries is organized differently than it is in common-law jurisdictions: courts are specialized in different areas of the law, and there is more than one supreme court sitting at the apex. Typically, there is a division of labor between two supreme courts, one dealing with ordinary law (private and criminal law, basically) and the other with administrative law.[2] Under these circumstances, it is contended, a decentralized system of judicial review would not work well: a statute could be held constitutional by the courts that are grouped under one supreme court and unconstitutional by the others. As Kelsen wrote, referring to the situation that existed in 1920, "It must be [taken into account] that in Austria as well as in many other countries of the European continent there were other courts besides the ordinary courts, especially administrative courts which occasionally had to apply the same statutes as the ordinary courts. Hence a contradiction between administrative courts and ordinary courts was not at all precluded."[3] A decentralized system can be implemented, it seems, only if the judiciary is unified.[4]

There is a problem here, no doubt, but it should not be too difficult to come up with a solution for it: a special body could be assigned the task of settling the disagreements between the supreme courts. In Greece, for example, the Special Highest Court is in charge of resolving conflicts that arise between the various supreme courts with respect to the constitutionality of statutes.[5] Of course, some institutional inertia has to be overcome to establish such a new body, but this is nothing compared with the creation of a constitutional court.

The second and more important reason that is often given against the introduction of the diffuse model of constitutional review refers to the absence of the doctrine of precedent in the civil-law tradition. The rulings of the highest courts interpreting and applying the law are not binding on lower courts. The latter are legally entitled to deviate from those rulings if they disagree with them. Consequently, as Mauro Cappelletti argues, "since the principle of stare decisis is foreign to civil law judges, a system which allowed each judge to decide on the constitutionality of statutes could result in a law being disregarded as unconstitutional by some judges, while being held constitutional and applied by others."[6] Even if the supreme court ruled on the matter, it would have no authority to bind lower courts. Kelsen wrote that this was "the most important fact" that explained the preference for a centralized model in Austria.[7]

Now, it is true that in many European countries, the official under-standing is that lower-court judges are under no duty to follow the doc-trines established by the supreme court. Every judge is "independent": judges are bound by the law, but not by the supreme court's interpretation of the law. To a large extent, this conception of judicial independence is a consequence of the legal philosophy that inspired the French Revolution. As I mentioned earlier, the French revolutionaries thought it possible to reduce the law to a body of coherent, complete, and specific legislation so that the task of judges would be utterly mechanical. In that scenario, precedents would not be needed. This conception, however, makes no sense. Experience and mature reflection soon made it clear that such aspirations are impossible to fulfill. Inevitably, the law exhibits ambi-guities, gaps, and contradictions, and a supreme court has to unify the law's interpretation and application. Legal certainty would be destroyed if lower-court judges felt completely free to disregard the case law gener-ated by the highest courts.

Actually, lower courts in civil-law countries tend to respect the ex-isting case law in practice, even if they are not officially bound by it.[8] Judicial convergence is a universally felt need in any modern rational legal system—it is not idiosyncratic to the common-law world. But then why isn't the doctrine of precedent officially recognized in many civil-law countries? To a large extent, this is because judicial compliance with precedents can be achieved in other ways. In some countries, for example, the promotion of judges to the higher courts is decided, at least in part, by the supreme courts or by institutions that are close to them. As Mir-jan Damaška explains, if judges want to be promoted, they had better be respectful of what their senior colleagues sitting on the highest courts have held in their past decisions.[9] In addition, the highest courts can regularly quash the decisions of lower courts that deviate from existing precedents. Civil-law countries tend to have a "hierarchical" system in which a substantial portion of lower-court judgments are reexamined by the supreme courts, which lack the power to select the cases they will hear, whereas common-law countries tend to have a "coordinate" system under which complaints that reach the top of the judicial pyramid are exceptional.[10] In such a hierarchical context, it has not been necessary in civil-law countries to insist on the binding character of precedents. In common-law countries, in contrast, it has been imperative to do so. As

Mirjan Damaška puts it, "A judicial organization composed of loosely hierarchical judges may require a doctrine of binding precedent as an internal ideological stabilizer."[11]

There is thus a certain tension between the official theory in the civil law and the actual practice of courts: precedents are not a "source of law," but judges tend to follow them. In some European countries, moreover, there is an increasing willingness to accept the idea that precedents established by the highest courts are indeed formally binding.[12] More and more scholars, lawyers, and judges believe that the role of precedents has to be officially acknowledged in a more transparent way if legal certainty is to be protected in highly complex legal systems. Even if precedents are not a genuine "source of law," their authority vis-à-vis lower courts should be officially recognized. The Portuguese Constitutional Court, for example, has held that although the Supreme Court of Justice does not create general rules for citizens to obey, it does furnish doctrines that other judges may be legally required to follow—judicial independence notwithstanding.[13]

The upshot of all of this is that it is not impossible for civil-law countries to adopt a decentralized (American) system of judicial review. Legal certainty will not collapse, for the highest courts will determine whether statutes are constitutional and lower courts will tend to comply with those rulings. Allan-Randolph Brewer-Carías, for instance, explains that the American model of judicial review has been successfully implemented in some civil-law countries, such as Argentina, Mexico, Greece, Japan, and Switzerland.[14]

A persuasive defense of the centralized model in the name of legal certainty, therefore, should acknowledge that we are dealing with a question of degree. The civil-law tradition is compatible with a diffuse system of judicial review—legal certainty will not be in ruins. Legal certainty can be more or less strongly cherished, however. In this regard, perhaps the civil-law tradition has given special weight to it.[15] If the protection of legal certainty is to be maximized, the centralized model may be preferable. By establishing a constitutional court that can be reached as soon as a statute raises constitutional problems, the centralized model safeguards legal certainty in a very straightforward manner. The sooner the constitutional court speaks, the more quickly any legal doubts will be dispelled.

The constitutional court's decisions striking down a statute, moreover, have general effects. The procedure of review may be abstract or concrete, but the court will typically eliminate the statute from the legal system if it concludes that it is unconstitutional. The statute will be "written off the books."[16] The court, therefore, will not contradict itself in the future in connection with that particular law. Since the statute will have formally disappeared from the legal system, the court will not have the chance to review it again.[17]

Furthermore, the constitutional court, if properly designed, can devote all or an important part of its time and energy to the task of legislative review. Thus liberated from the burdens of ordinary adjudication, it is in a good position to construct a consistent jurisprudence in the field of constitutional review of statutes. The supreme courts in many European countries, in contrast, are often overwhelmed with cases and run the risk, consequently, of contradicting themselves.[18]

For these reasons, Kelsen was right in linking the centralized model to legal certainty. Although a diffuse system of judicial review could also work in civil-law countries, it would be less efficient than the centralized alternative.

IS LEGAL CERTAINTY THE OVERRIDING VALUE?

We should not accept all the particular techniques that Kelsen advocated in order to preserve legal certainty, however. Some of them have been embraced in several European countries, but others have been rejected, and rightly so, to accommodate other interests.

Kelsen, for example, was sympathetic to the possibility of setting a deadline for a statute to be brought to the constitutional court. Once the deadline had passed, the relevant statute could no longer be attacked. In this way, there would be a high level of certainty in the system.[19] The Czechoslovaks, for example, established such a deadline (of three years) when they created their constitutional court in 1920.[20] And the French followed a strategy that was even more radical until they changed the system in 2008: laws could be challenged only before they were promulgated (a priori review).

An important price is being paid under such an arrangement, however, for it usually takes some time for a law to reveal all its constitutional defects. If there is a deadline that must be complied with, a law will remain secure in the system if it is not initially challenged, despite the constitutional shortcomings that are later discovered. For this reason, many European countries have rejected preventive (a priori) review, and others have embraced it but only in combination with a posteriori review.[21] Legal certainty is not the overriding value they seek to serve.

Similarly, Kelsen rejected giving retroactive effect to the decisions of the constitutional court striking down statutes. The cases that were decided in the past, in conformity with the relevant statute, should not be reopened, he argued, in the name of legal certainty. Only future cases should benefit from a declaration of unconstitutionality.[22]

Constitutional courts in Europe, however, have evolved toward a flexible jurisprudence on this issue. Apart from the fact that equality under the law is affected when the court's decision is not retroactive, the injustice of maintaining the past effects of an unconstitutional statute may sometimes clearly outweigh the costs associated with disrupting past legal expectations. It is necessary, moreover, to reward the plaintiff who brings a constitutional complaint and to encourage ordinary judges to make applications to the constitutional court.[23] Most constitutional courts in Europe, therefore, think that pragmatic balancing is inevitable.[24]

Kelsen, moreover, maintained that the constitutional court should have the authority to postpone the effects of its decisions declaring a law unconstitutional. This would give the parliament enough time to enact a revised statute and prevent a "gap" in the legal system, which might create legal uncertainty. This technique was introduced in Austria in 1920 and has been accepted in other countries as well.[25]

The disadvantage of this technique is that a statute can be maintained in the legal system for a certain period of time despite the fact that it has been declared unconstitutional. This result may be more or less acceptable depending on the seriousness of the constitutional vice that the court has found, on the one hand, and the seriousness of the consequences that would be caused if a legal gap emerged, on the other. Some amount of balancing and flexibility is advisable. Legal certainty is not the only consideration.

Finally, Kelsen went so far in his desire to protect legal certainty that he also favored introducing the following mechanism, which seems to be the legal equivalent of the resurrection of the dead in theological thought: if a law is invalidated by the constitutional court, the legal provisions that were rescinded by that law become effective again (unless the judgment pronounces otherwise).[26] This technique guarantees that no legal gap will appear in the system after the court's decision. Such a gap would be "very undesirable," Kelsen wrote.[27]

The drawback of this solution (as Kelsen acknowledged) is that the resurrected statute may be an old statute that had been repealed a long time ago.[28] Some countries in Europe have introduced this mechanism, but with flexibility. The Portuguese Constitution, for example, explicitly provides that a declaration of unconstitutionality of a law shall cause the revalidation of the earlier laws. It empowers the court, however, to restrict this effect for "reasons of fairness or an exceptionally important public interest."[29] Other considerations, therefore, must be taken into account. Legal certainty is not the only value.

CONCLUSION

We find in Kelsen's work a plausible reason to favor the centralized model of constitutional review. There is indeed a relatively strong link between centralization and the protection of legal certainty. Though legal certainty would not collapse in a decentralized system, even if implemented in civil-law countries, there is no doubt that by concentrating review in a single court, we can secure legal certainty in a more efficient way. Some of the additional techniques that Kelsen advocated, however, have been rejected in various countries or have been accepted only in a qualified manner. In this way, the value of legal certainty has been partially sacrificed to other considerations, and rightly so.

The task, now, is to explore the advantages of the European model from a completely different normative angle. Let us go to the very foundations of constitutional review: Why do we want to subject parliamentary acts to some kind of judicial review, to begin with? What benefits do we expect? In particular, what entitles us to think that fundamental rights will be better safeguarded in this way? Are special constitutional tribunals more promising candidates than ordinary courts when it comes to legislative review? Legal certainty is simply a value that operates as a constraint. A political community establishes judicial review of legislation for other reasons. In light of these other reasons, what are the potential strengths of the European model?

PART TWO EXPLORING THE ADVANTAGES OF
CONSTITUTIONAL COURTS

CHAPTER FOUR

The Justification of Constitutional Review

THE SKETCH OF AN ARGUMENT

THE INSTITUTION OF judicial review of legislation is relatively easy to justify when it operates in the field of federalism. In politically decentralized polities, the laws enacted by the state legislative assemblies often clash with the laws of the federation. Since it is not reasonable to permit each level of government to decide the limits of its own authority, the intervention of an external institution like the judiciary seems justified. Constitutional review acquires "the utmost importance" in federal states, Hans Kelsen wrote.[1] Indeed, as in America, judicial review in many European nations emerged as a technical solution to the legislative collisions that decentralized political systems inevitably generate.[2]

In more modern times, however, judicial review came to play a key role in the domain of fundamental rights. In the post–Second World War period, in particular, constitutional courts in Europe were normally allocated important responsibilities in this field from the very beginning. This was so in Italy and Germany after the war, for example, in Spain and Portugal after their transitions to democracy in the 1970s, and in Central and Eastern Europe after the fall of communism in the 1990s. (In France and Belgium, however, things went differently, for the constitutional courts were initially given no jurisdiction in the area of rights—it was only later that they got it.)[3]

The establishment of a system of judicial review in the area of rights is more controversial, however, than in connection with federalism. Why should courts (whether regular courts or special constitutional tribunals) have the power to disqualify parliamentary enactments under a constitutional bill of rights? Shouldn't the legislature have the last say in these matters? In what follows, I present a sketch of a theory of judicial review in order to guide my inquiry in the next chapters.

THE SUPREMACY OF THE CONSTITUTIONAL BILL OF RIGHTS

The starting point for constructing such a theory is the assumption that a bill of rights expresses values that are widely shared in the political community. These values refer to particular requirements of justice that are regarded by most of the community's members as being of vital importance. A mixture of relatively specific rules and more abstract principles are typically included in the constitution. The more specific rules refer to aspects of justice that are strongly and widely believed to derive from the more abstract foundational principles. Such rules may figure in the constitution as a reaction against specific past violations, or to protect particular rights in a categorical way, against the risk of undermining them in the future through too many exceptions. In any case, the specific rules do not exhaust the requirements of justice that the constitution tries to satisfy.

The constitutional rules and principles may have been agreed upon after an extended process of popular deliberation at extraordinary moments, as Bruce Ackerman believes to be the case in the United States, for example.[4] Or they may be the product of a more elitist negotiation among political representatives, as in some transitions to democracy such as Spain's in 1977–1978. It is even possible that the framers of the constitution, under the pressure of external forces, reacted against widespread illiberal practices of the past, as in Germany after the Second World War or in many Central-Eastern European countries after the demise of communism. Whatever the specific circumstances that gave birth to the constitution, the rules and principles that it announces need to find a social base on which to stand.

In this regard, the situation in Europe between the First and Second World Wars was too divisive for a bill of rights to succeed, for the chasm between the Right and the Left was very wide. The Weimar constitution of 1919, for example, included a catalog of individual rights and social principles that reflected in a contradictory way the ideological programs of the various political parties. Its provisions conflicted with each other so deeply that it was impossible to start a tradition of interpretation under it. Kelsen shared Carl Schmitt's diagnosis that there was not enough political consensus for an assembly to hammer out an ambitious and coherent bill of rights. Kelsen was very impressed, in particular, by the impact of the Russian Revolution of 1917. The gap between the Left and the Right had expanded so much in that era that the only common ground that could be found in Europe, he believed, was the acceptance of a democratic legislative procedure through which different interests could be accommodated. For Kelsen, the politically charged bill of rights of the Weimar constitution was therefore a mistake—a more "procedural" constitution (like Austria's) was to be preferred.[5] If any substantive limits were to be imposed on the legislature, he asserted, they should be framed in very specific language. Abstract values like justice, liberty, and equality had to be excluded from the constitutional text.[6]

Things started to change after the Second World War, however. The defeat of Nazism and fascism created a more favorable environment for the passage of declarations of rights. New catalogs of rights were introduced in the constitutions that were then adopted, and an important international instrument was agreed upon: the European Convention on Human Rights. A stronger and wider moral consensus gradually emerged on which to build the new constitutionalism. Since the end of the cold war, moreover, the ideological clashes between the Right and the Left in Europe have diminished in intensity. In this political climate, Kelsen's pessimism over a constitution of substance is no longer justified. The abstract terms of a bill of rights are not meaningless, for the disagreements that may arise at the legislative level now take place within a stable framework of shared understandings.[7]

The fundamental rights enshrined in a constitution are not easy to honor, however. It is tempting for the political community at a particular moment, in connection with a specific problem, not to accept some of the costs that rights impose. Because of a lack of moral imagination, weakness of the will, impulsive passions in some extraordinary circumstances, or a mixture of these different shortcomings, a political community may fail to respect certain rights.[8] "It is easier to commit ourselves to sound moral principles at a comparatively abstract level," Lawrence Sager asserts, "than it is to live out those commitments in our day-to-day lives, when we have to pay the costs associated with the commitments." Moral progress "is often associated with broad forward reaches of principle, followed by much slower and more halting progress on the level of the concrete."[9]

The incorporation of a bill of rights in a constitution is a good strategy to force the different governmental institutions to take rights seriously when they exercise their powers. The legislature is more likely to be attentive to fundamental principles in the course of enacting ordinary law. The hope is that the community as a whole will act in a more self-critical way when it judges its practices and laws against the basic rights it cherishes.

This justification of the supremacy of the constitution does not presuppose that the framers were wiser than the present generation of citizens and their representatives. They were not: there is moral progress in increasingly inclusive democratic societies. The specific interpretations that prevailed at the founding moment, therefore, should not be favored over those that are constructed in the course of later public discussions. As history develops, constitutional meanings accumulate, and the more recent popular judgments as to the specific content of rights and liberties may be preferred to the original ones. The constitution has a "sedimentary" character in this regard, as Barry Friedman and Scott Smith have argued.[10]

THE ROLE OF COURTS

Now, why should courts—whether regular courts or special constitutional tribunals—have the power to review legislation? What conditions must be satisfied for us to have reason to believe that courts will do a better job than legislative assemblies when it comes to drawing the implications of the abstract principles that the constitution announces?

The first condition relates to what Alexander Bickel called "the leisure" and the "insulation" that judges must have "to follow the ways of the scholar in pursuing the ends of government."[11] Fundamental rights have to be given concrete meaning as they are applied to the various problems that a changing society poses. The doctrine to be generated under the constitution should form a consistent whole. The long-term consequences of the various possible interpretations must be taken into account: the operational rules must have a durable content. A certain environment of peace and quiet seems necessary to this deeply intellectual task.

The second condition is this: courts must exhibit a certain inclination to take constitutional values seriously. This disposition can be facilitated by institutional specialization. As Sager, referring to the responsibility of courts in the American system, explains, "The constitutional judiciary has a specialized role with regard to political choices. Judges are steeped in the tradition of constitutional discourse, and their job is pointed towards the evaluation of governmental conduct against the norms of the Constitution." The judiciary, Sager asserts, is in the rough position of a quality-control inspector examining some product for defects: its job is specialized.[12]

The third condition refers to the ethics of principled decision making. Courts must develop their constitutional interpretations in a consistent fashion. Internal coherence is indeed a virtue that we generally expect from judges. As Sager argues, "Judges are obliged by the protocols of adjudication to attend to comparatively general and comparatively durable principles—principles that apply to a variety of circumstances." This moves judges in the direction of objectivity. "Judges are affected in a variety of conflicting and diffuse ways by the cases before them. Judges are constrained to abide by principles that, by their temporal, geographic, or substantive reach, sprawl across areas of disinterest and interest on the judges' part. Were they otherwise inclined to choose principles that cut narrowly in favor of things they care about today, they would have to appreciate that those same principles could work powerfully against them tomorrow."[13] In a similar vein, Owen Fiss points out that there is a special feature of adjudication that makes it likely that courts will make a relevant contribution to the interpretation of the public values that the constitution announces: judges are compelled to address the claims that the parties make, and their answers must be supported by reasons. These reasons "must somehow transcend the personal, transient beliefs of the judge or the body politic as to what is right or just or what should be done. Something more is required to transform these personal beliefs into values worthy of the status 'constitutional' and all it implies—binding upon society as a whole, entitled to endure, not forever but long enough to give our public morality an inner coherence, and largely to be enforced by courts."[14] In other words, "judges must justify their decisions in terms that can be universalized." This is often called, following Herbert Wechsler, "the neutral principles requirement."[15]

So the relative leisure and insulation of the judiciary (in comparison with political representatives), the specialized character of their function, and the ethics of principled decision making that is associated with it, are the key conditions that need to be met for a system of judicial review to be ultimately justified. When discussing the strengths and weaknesses of the centralized European model of judicial review, therefore, we will have to evaluate the model from this perspective.

Courts, however, should exercise legislative review in a way that attracts the attention of citizens and their political representatives. Judicial discourse on the constitution cannot be detached from the moral discussions that develop in the broader public sphere. Courts may have more time to focus on constitutional principles, and they may be under the duty to elaborate a consistent jurisprudence, but they need to draw their ideas from the less formalized debates that take place in society at large. Constitutional principles, after all, are part of the community's collective morality. Conversely, citizens and their representatives should be attentive to what courts say, for their opinions can enrich collective deliberations. Judicial review, therefore, should be designed in ways that help enhance its public visibility. The European model needs to be assessed from this perspective, too.

What we certainly cannot expect, obviously, is that the judiciary will always get things right in constitutional matters. Actually, it would be too optimistic to expect that it will get them right very often. Historical experience should warn us against excessive optimism: even communities that have viewed themselves as strongly committed to certain fundamental rights have dismally failed to honor them in many respects, and neither the legislatures nor the courts seemed to be aware of it—or were not willing to do much about it. What we need is the expectation that courts are *less imperfect* than legislatures at the particular task we are considering. As in other contexts of institutional design, we are comparing imperfect organs and procedures.[16] The ultimate hope is that the presence of a judicial "forum of principle," as Ronald Dworkin calls it, will make it more likely that the political community as a whole will reach just outcomes in the domain of fundamental rights.[17]

The justification of judicial review that I have just sketched needs to be tested against the actual practice of courts in the various countries. Even if we have some structural ex ante reasons to believe that courts are likely to do a good job in this field, experience may prove us wrong. To assess whether judicial review is instrumentally good, we need to have some substantive theory that allows us to classify decisions as "right" or "wrong" from a political-moral point of view. Obviously, people will sometimes strongly disagree about this. In the abortion controversy, for instance, those who are pro-choice will celebrate decisions of courts that invalidate restrictive abortion laws, whereas their opponents will strongly condemn them. And the reverse will be true when courts invalidate abortion laws with the argument that they do not protect the fetus sufficiently. The case in favor of judicial review gets stronger or weaker depending on one's views on the underlying issues. In many cases, however, opinions are not so polarized. There is a certain consensus about the values on which a liberal democracy rests. From this perspective, has judicial review been a progressive institution or a regressive one? In the United States, liberals have generally deemed the Supreme Court to have been beneficial to the cause of fundamental rights in the modern period. Some voices have recently been heard, however, questioning this view.[18] In the European context, the liberal consensus is clearly supportive of the role of constitutional courts. Even scholars who are otherwise critical of judicial review on democratic grounds share the generalized opinion that, by and large, those courts have served the cause of rights, even if they have sometimes missed opportunities to overturn objectionable laws or have struck down laws that were perfectly acceptable or even commendable. For instance, Wojciech Sadurski, who is critical of the negative consequences of judicial review for the maintenance of a mature political culture, accepts this. Writing on the performance of constitutional courts in Central-Eastern Europe, he observes that such courts "have a positive score card when it comes to the protection of civil and political rights, regardless of the occasional bad decisions in which rights-restrictive laws have not been struck down or rights-protective laws have been invalidated."[19]

To be sure, there is a "countermajoritarian" objection that is often articulated against judicial review, an objection that must be reckoned with. Is judicial review democratic given its possible tension with majoritarian legislative decisions? I address this problem at a general level in chapter 8 and try to show, in chapter 9, some potential advantages of constitutional courts in this regard. But before we consider the democratic objection, we must examine both the virtues and the defects of the European model in light of the skeletal justification of judicial review that I have just offered. This is the purpose of the next three chapters.

CHAPTER FIVE

The Special Nature of Constitutional Discourse

IF WE WANT TO CREATE a forum of principle where fundamental rights are taken seriously, there are various things to be said in favor of the centralized model of judicial review. As I will try to highlight in this chapter, there are potential advantages to creating a special constitutional tribunal that is relatively detached from the ordinary judiciary. This is especially so in civil-law countries.

TIME FOR STUDY AND REFLECTION

Constitutional judges need to have a degree of "leisure" and "insulation" to reflect upon fundamental values, as Alexander Bickel put it. The centralized model offers an obvious advantage in this regard: the constitutional court can concentrate all its time and energy on checking the validity of parliamentary enactments. It is liberated from the task of ordinary adjudication.

In many European countries, as we know, ordinary judges are given the authority to trigger the process of review: when they have doubts about the validity of a statute that is relevant to a case they are handling, they can certify a question to the constitutional court. In this way, they contribute to the enterprise of legislative review. The final decision on the statute, however, is made by the constitutional court, which has more time to engage in a deep discussion of the fundamental issues involved.

This division of labor is an important advantage in civil-law countries, where all courts—including the ordinary supreme courts—are usually overwhelmed with work. As we saw in chapter 3, appeals are very frequent in the civil-law tradition, and the highest courts do not have discretionary jurisdiction. As a result, huge workloads are pushed to the upper levels of the judicial pyramid. It is not surprising that the supreme courts are composed of a large number of judges (sometimes more than one hundred), who are distributed in different panels or sections. A constitutional court, in contrast, if properly designed, is liberated from all these cases, and the number of judges can be smaller. Thus, there are fourteen judges on the constitutional court in Austria; twelve in Belgium; nine in France (plus any former president of the republic that wishes to join the court);[1] sixteen in Germany;[2] fifteen in Italy; nine in Luxembourg; thirteen in Portugal; and twelve in Spain.

This argument in favor of the centralized model, therefore, would be significantly weaker in most common-law countries, where the courts of appeals have means to control the flood of litigation that is brought to them, and the supreme court (which consists of a small number of judges) has discretionary jurisdiction to decide which cases to hear. The problem of time can then be addressed in a satisfactory manner. The Supreme Court of the United States, for example, can normally select its cases.[3] Lower courts are overloaded with work, but the highest court, at least, can make its way through the docket and focus on a few disputes in order to think carefully about the important issues they raise.

Even in such common-law countries, however, there is a potential problem. If the supreme court focuses too much on cases that give rise to constitutional issues, it leaves other fields of the law unattended. This is detrimental to its other function as the supreme interpreter of *ordinary* law. In the 1970s, for example, two commissions in the United States (the Freund Committee and the Hruska Commission) called for the creation of a "National Court of Appeals" to ease the burden of an increasing caseload on the Supreme Court and to enhance the uniformity of the law among the circuits. The more the Supreme Court acts as a "constitutional tribunal," the more it abandons its role as the "supreme court" in ordinary legal matters. This is especially troublesome in modern times, when ordinary law is increasingly complex. As Richard Posner explains, "With many areas of federal law becoming ever more complicated, the number of non-constitutional cases that the Court decides has become too small to enable the Justices to become or remain experts in these bodies of law."[4] A constitutional court of the European type, in contrast, does not have to worry about this risk. It can concentrate all its attention on constitutional issues because the final disposition of ordinary legal questions is in the hands of another institution—a separate supreme court (which, in turn, is internally specialized).

This potential advantage of the European model comes with some costs, however. Tensions may arise between the constitutional court, on the one hand, and the ordinary supreme court, on the other.[5] The tensions are likely to be especially pronounced at the founding moment: whereas the constitutional court represents a new beginning and engages in the attractive discourse of fundamental rights, the ordinary supreme court is somehow linked to the past. With the passage of time, the sharpness of this dichotomy disappears, but the risk of conflicts is still present, for it is not always easy to specify who is competent to decide what. Things are relatively simple when the constitutional court is "pure"—that is, when its only task is to test the validity of legislation.[6] Things get more complicated when the court has jurisdiction over other matters that are connected to ordinary adjudication. When the court hears constitutional complaints, for example, as it does in Germany and Spain, it has to determine the boundary that distinguishes ordinary legal issues from issues that have constitutional implications. However carefully the system has tried to fix the division of labor among the courts in this area, there is always some room for conflicts. As Lech Garlicki, a former judge of the Polish Constitutional Tribunal, puts it: "It would be naïve to suggest that any pattern of coexistence could be completely free of tensions and problems. While the Kelsenian model has proven to be efficient and attractive in Europe, it contains also some built-in deficiencies."[7]

The degree of purity of the constitutional court is an important factor. If the court's only task is to assess the constitutionality of legislation, it will have sufficient time to study and decide the issues in a proper way. If, in contrast, the court also has other functions to attend to, it can get unduly distracted from its task of legislative review. The Italian Constitutional Court, for instance, used to have jurisdiction over crimes committed by government ministers. Such power was exercised once, in the Lockheed corruption case of 1979. This case paralyzed the court for a long while, to the detriment of its major function of constitutional review of legislation. Fortunately, an amendment was passed in 1989 transferring these criminal matters to the ordinary judiciary.[8]

The Spanish and the German constitutional courts are not in an ideal position in this regard. They have to deal with thousands of complaints brought by individuals every year. These courts are normally asked to review on appeal whether the ordinary judges that decided a particular case have duly protected or respected the fundamental right that the appellant invokes. The validity of a piece of legislation is not usually at issue. Since the amount of work that the complaints jurisdiction generates is very large, the heavy docket has to be distributed among smaller panels of judges. Simplified procedures exist to quickly dispose of many applications, but these courts are still swamped by them.[9] To counteract this situation, it seems advisable to reform the system and give constitutional judges discretionary jurisdiction when such petitions are lodged—or at least to grant them more flexibility than they currently enjoy for purposes of deciding which cases to examine.[10] Alternatively, the complaints procedure could be restricted in scope so that only the constitutionality of statutes—not their application to the specific controversy—could be challenged.[11] If the current complaints jurisdiction is not reformed, an important potential advantage that can be derived from the European model cannot be fully realized, and this is unfortunate.

MAXIMIZING PROFESSIONAL DIVERSITY ON THE COURT

A second potential virtue of the European model is tied to the composition of the constitutional court: its members can be selected according to different criteria from that normally used to recruit ordinary judges in the civil-law tradition. In particular, the most prestigious professionals can be chosen, and a wider variety of backgrounds can be represented. A constitutional court in Europe typically includes not only senior lawyers, prosecutors, and judges, but also professors, high public officials, and former politicians. The presence of different voices is to be welcomed, for they can contribute interesting intellectual perspectives to the task of constitutional review.

Lawyers, Prosecutors, and Judges

Members of constitutional courts are selected, first, from among those who have been involved in ordinary adjudication for many years and have attained professional prestige. The presence of this legal elite is critical if the court is to understand the operation of the legal system, of which the constitution is a part.

It is important to note, in this regard, that civil-law countries normally use a "bureaucratic" method to recruit ordinary judges—in contrast to the "professional" method that prevails in common-law countries.[12] The lowest courts are often run by very young judges, who are appointed soon after they graduate from law school. Many of them have never practiced law or have practiced only for a short period of time. Only the highest courts are composed of seasoned jurists. In the context of this "bureaucratic" model of judicial recruitment, it would not be very reasonable to establish a decentralized system of constitutional review of legislation: the delicate decision whether to disregard a statute on constitutional grounds should not be placed in the hands of such young judges who lack the necessary experience and maturity. Only the highest courts should be empowered to make such decisions. The decentralized model is not problematic in common-law countries that follow a "professional" system of judicial selection: if judges are appointed after they have had a relatively long period of successful legal practice, they are sufficiently mature jurists.

Professors

In addition to lawyers, prosecutors, and judges, constitutional courts typically include university professors, especially professors of public law. If, as Alexander Bickel said when justifying judicial review in the American context, judges should have "the leisure, the training, and the insulation to follow the way of the scholar in pursuing the ends of government,"[13] it seems advisable to appoint some professors who have pursued their theoretical inquiries in an academic atmosphere of peace and quiet. For instance, Georges Vedel, the leading professor of public law in France for over forty years, became a member of the French Constitutional Council, as have other prominent academics, such as François Luchaire and Robert Badinter. Similarly, the Constitutional Court of Spain has included Francisco Rubio Llorente, Pedro Cruz Villalón, and Luis López Guerra, three of the most influential professors of constitutional law in the nation, and the Italian Constitutional Court can boast of great academic figures, such as Vezio Crisafulli, Sabino Cassese, Constantino Mortati, Leopoldo Elia, Livio Paladin, Antonio La Pergola, Carlo Mezzanotte, and Gustavo Zagrebelsky. The Federal Constitutional Court of Germany is especially professorial and academic in its composition. As of 2008, the vast majority of judges (thirteen out of sixteen) had written doctoral dissertations at a university, and most of them (nine out of sixteen) had devoted the majority of their time to teaching and research.[14] Among past members of the court, one finds very prominent scholars in the field of constitutional law, such as Gerhard Leibholz, Ernst Benda, Ernst-Wolfgang Böckenförde, and Dieter Grimm.

Sometimes these scholars have done their research in other fields, such as sociology, economics, or history, and are not experts in the law. In France, for example, one current member of the court, Dominique Schnapper, is a sociologist who has no law degree. These experts can offer broader vistas on constitutional problems, thus enriching the internal deliberations of the court.

Governmental Officials

It is not rare for high public officials to be appointed to the constitutional court, especially in France.[15] Their presence is likely to have a positive effect on the court's jurisprudence. Officials who have occupied important positions can explain to their colleagues the needs of government in certain areas, thus injecting a measure of prudence into legal reasoning. On the other hand, they can also encourage the recognition and enforcement of certain limits on the government. Precisely because they have administrative experience, they are well equipped to judge whether the arguments advanced by the government are really compelling. They may feel rather confident that such arguments are weak, whereas other members of the court who lack that expertise might be more reluctant to disagree with the executive branch.

Politicians

Another type of experience that is reflected in the composition of constitutional courts is tied to politics. In Belgium, for example, the law requires that at least half the judges appointed to the court have a minimum of five years of experience as members of either the federal parliament or a regional or communal parliament.[16] Of course, those who are not lawyers are then in need of clerks (*référendaires*) to understand the legal issues they have to confront.

The presence of judges with political background is also strong in France: over half the members of the Constitutional Council appointed between 1959 and 2004 had served in the parliament as politicians, and others had served in its secretariat.[17] The inclusion of such figures is less frequent in Germany, however. Actually, the general trend in Germany is to have a smaller number of constitutional judges with experience in politics, a development that is criticized by some.[18]

The contributions of people with this political past can be useful in various ways. Hans Kelsen suggested that it would be a good idea to have a constitutional court composed of both legal experts and politicians. Since political convictions will inevitably influence the interpretation of the constitution, it would be advisable, he argued, for the court to include some members whose political background was explicit and visible. They would take care of the more pronounced political considerations that may arise in constitutional cases, and the other members of the court would feel liberated from those considerations and could thus focus on the more technical questions.[19]

Another way to understand the contribution of former politicians is this: to the extent that a bill of rights typically speaks in the language of abstract political morality, the presence of political figures can help ensure that the court does not forget that, over and above the applicable legal doctrine, there is always a constitution that has to be reinterpreted in light of new circumstances. These political figures may bring an external and fresh perspective on the body of legal doctrine elaborated by the court in past cases.

At the foundational moment, moreover, a court may benefit from the insights of former politicians who participated in the framing of the constitution. It is interesting to note, for example, that the first president of the Italian Constitutional Court—which was established in 1956—was Enrico De Nicola, who had signed the constitution of 1947 in his capacity as president of the republic after the Second World War.

In addition, politicians can help the court acquire a better sense of what the social reactions to its decisions are likely to be. Even if, as I argue at a later point, the court should not be shy, it needs to have some clues as to what the more general environment is. Also, insofar as the court is asked to review the constitutionality of legislation, an accurate picture of how the legislative process works is sometimes necessary. The presence of former members of parliament, for example, may thus be welcome.[20]

A potential advantage of constitutional courts, in sum, is that they make it possible for legislative review to be exercised by a group of prominent figures whose different backgrounds and areas of expertise are relevant to the task of giving concrete meaning to fundamental principles as they bear on complex problems of an evolving democratic society. Such a collective body is better equipped to deal with *les grands problèmes* that constitutional review entails, as Charles Eisenmann put it.[21]

Consider, for example, the great issues that were raised by the process of German unification after the fall of the Berlin wall.[22] What were the constitutional terms under which West and East Germany would be reunited? What democratic procedure did the federal constitution impose to this effect? A new electoral law, under which the first all-German legislative elections were to be held, required political parties to obtain 5 percent of the votes of the entire unified nation in order to get parliamentary representation. Did this law violate the principle of equality, given its harsher impact on parties from the East than from the West? Legal provisions were also enacted denying restitution of the land that had been expropriated in East Germany during 1945–1949. Such provisions were instrumental to obtaining the Soviet Union's support of German unification. Were they valid, however, given the constitutional protection of private property? And was the new abortion statute of 1992, which tried to find a middle ground between the more restrictive law of the West and the more liberal law of the East, constitutionally acceptable? What about the drastic measures that were introduced to modernize the economic system of East Germany and that made many people jobless? Were these measures in keeping with the constitutional principle that makes Germany a "social state"? Laws were also enacted to exclude particular types of East German officials from public office on political grounds. Were they constitutionally valid? Could espionage agents of the East be prosecuted under the new regime for their earlier activity against the West? With respect to foreign affairs, what were the constitutional limits to the deployment of German armed forces in foreign countries? These are philosophically deep and politically delicate questions. A constitutional court seems better equipped than ordinary judges to deal with them. Peter Quint has observed that the Federal Constitutional Court sought to act as a powerful mediating organ when it confronted those issues, seeking an accommodation of competing interests and, particularly, "mitigating the strength of western views" when they seemed to overbear eastern interests too completely.[23] This kind of intervention is not purely "legal" in the ordinary sense of the word. Of course, German unification was a seismic event—constitutional adjudication does not normally pose such large issues. But it does deal with very important matters nevertheless.

As already noted, the precise mix of professionals that make up the constitutional court varies from country to country. Some courts are more "political," and others are more "professorial" or "judicial." In Central and Eastern Europe, for example, there is a higher representation of professors and senior members of the regular judiciary than former politicians—a lack of trust in politicians was inherited from the authoritarian regime, whereas academics and even judges are held in higher regard.[24] Whatever the specific balance that is struck, the important point is that constitutional tribunals exhibit more internal professional plurality than ordinary courts do.

This potential advantage of the centralized model is facilitated, of course, when constitutional courts are of the "pure" type, for judicial expertise in procedural matters is not necessary then. When statutes are reviewed, the procedure to be followed is very simple, and there is no need for most justices to have adjudicatory expertise.[25] If, instead, the court is not patterned after the pure model, that sort of expertise starts to be necessary. If the court, for example, has jurisdiction to decide appeals of decisions rendered by regular judges, it has to follow more complex procedures and needs to be acquainted with the workings of ordinary adjudication. This requires a certain knowledge that only legal practitioners from the bench and the bar can provide.

One may object that there is no need to establish a special constitutional tribunal in order to attract people of different professional backgrounds to serve as judges. The Supreme Court of the United States, for example, currently includes four former professors: Stephen G. Breyer, Anthony M. Kennedy, Antonin Scalia, and Ruth Bader Ginsburg. It may be replied, however, that lower courts, which share with the U.S. Supreme Court the power of constitutional review, are mainly in the hands of more ordinary lawyers and judges. In general, in a system in which constitutional issues are examined in the course of ordinary litigation, it is harder to attract people who have not practiced law. As Christopher Eisgruber argues, there is an advantage in having an institution like the French Constitutional Council, which has no responsibility for deciding nonconstitutional legal issues or for overseeing the general court system. Since the constitutional problems it is asked to address are not complicated by technical questions of jurisdiction and procedure, it is easier, he contends, to appoint nonlawyers to such a tribunal than to the regular judiciary.[26] The difference between the European and the American models is certainly a qualified one in this regard, but it is relevant nevertheless, especially when the constitutional court is relatively pure, like the French Constitutional Council.

So far, I have referred to professional diversity. There may be a special need, however, for members of the court to belong to different social groups, reflecting the pluralism that exists in the political community. Belgium is an extreme illustration of this need. The Constitutional Court of Belgium is composed of twelve judges, six of whom must belong to the Dutch-language group and six of whom must belong to the French-language group. One of the judges, moreover, must have an adequate knowledge of German. Each linguistic group selects its own president, and the presidency of the court as a whole alternates between these two presidents each year.[27] As Francis Delpérée explains, the idea behind this arrangement is that decisions by the Constitutional Court must be the product of an effort to accommodate the interests of the diverse linguistic groups in Belgian society. An unbalanced court would be an easy prey to criticism and would thus lack the necessary authority.[28]

THE RELATIVE AUTONOMY OF CONSTITUTIONAL DISCOURSE

The composition of the constitutional court is likely to affect the kind of discourse that the court generates. To put it in a rather simplified manner, the professors on the court will tend to be more "philosophical," governmental officials will be more sensitive to policy considerations, former politicians will have insights into what is feasible for the court to do given the existing political climate, and the regular lawyers and judges will bring their expertise in more technical ordinary law. The court will construct a jurisprudence that mediates between these different spheres. Its discourse will be relatively autonomous and different from the more "legalistic" kind of reasoning that one can expect from ordinary judges, especially in civil-law countries, as well as from purely political discourse.

The fact that the constitutional court is relatively detached not only from the political branches but also from the ordinary judiciary helps maintain the relative autonomy of its discourse. The institutional contrast helps highlight the "atypical" character of the court's functions.[29] The Italian Constitutional Court, for example, in its own description of itself, insists that it "interacts with the Italian judiciary, but it is not itself entirely a judicial institution."[30] The physical location of the Italian court, it observes, is a symbolic expression of its special position: it stands in Rome's highest hill, the Colle del Quirinale, opposite the official residence of the president of the republic (appointed, like the court, as impartial guarantor of the constitutional system) and at some distance from the buildings of "political" Rome and "judicial" Rome.

The relative institutional separation of the constitutional court can thus preserve the distinct quality of its discourse vis-à-vis ordinary legal reasoning. Since the most delicate task of interpreting the constitution for purposes of deciding the validity of parliamentary enactments is assigned to the constitutional court exclusively, it is possible to maintain a more formalist legal culture for the rest of the judiciary if such culture is thought to be valuable, as tends to be the case in many civil-law countries.

Now, what does this relative autonomy of constitutional discourse amount to in practice? How does it manifest itself? Though it is difficult to generalize, for each country has its own traditions of legal reasoning, we can say that one of the key features of constitutional courts is that they do not shy away from the more abstract principles of political morality that are included in the bill of rights. The ordinary courts working in the civil-law tradition, in contrast, would feel more uncomfortable with such broad and controversial principles as standards against which the validity of legislation is to be measured.

The general tendency is for constitutional courts to assert that most fundamental rights can be restricted by the government if there are good enough reasons for doing so. The legitimacy and weight of the interests that the government advances must therefore be assessed. The concrete tests and doctrines used by courts for these purposes vary from country to country, but there is a basic requirement of reasonableness that underlies this common enterprise. The Italian Constitutional Court, for example, uses a reasonableness test (*ragionevolezza*): a law must be rationally related to the government's goals and must cohere with other legislative choices made in similar areas. Balancing the different interests at stake (*bilanciamento*) is part of the analysis. The Federal Constitutional Court of Germany has elaborated a tripartite framework to assess the validity of restrictions on fundamental rights. This framework has been quite influential in other countries (Spain, for instance) through the scholarly work of Robert Alexy.[31] According to this test, the court must first ask whether the restrictive measure that the legislature has established is useful for achieving a legitimate aim. If so, the next step is to inquire whether it would be possible for the legislature to achieve the same end (to a sufficient extent, at least) through a less restrictive measure than the one it has chosen. If the answer is no, the court moves to the third stage, which requires balancing: Is the goal sufficiently important to compensate for the cost that the restriction imposes?

Whatever the variations on the precise formulation of the test, the important point is that when a court is charged with enforcing abstract rights, it has to engage in a complex analysis that involves both normative and policy considerations. This type of reasoning is employed frequently in common-law jurisdictions, but ordinary judges in civil-law countries generally are not comfortable with it. It is one thing for ordinary judges to read and apply statutes in a flexible manner so that unreasonable outcomes are avoided. There is always some room for revision of statutes at the edges. It is quite another thing to subject the central legislative choice to higher standards of justice when those standards are as abstract as the fundamental rights guaranteed by the constitution. The matters of principle and policy that constitutional review brings to the table are too distant from the more technical considerations that ordinary judges in the civil-law tradition are usually trained for. Thus the advantage of creating a separate constitutional court composed of a different mix of experts.

Italy offers an interesting example to illustrate the different attitudes of constitutional courts and ordinary judiciaries when addressing fundamental principles. The constitution of 1947 provided that the regular courts would have the power of judicial review of legislation until the new constitutional court was established—which was not to happen until 1956.[32] The experience during this transitional period clearly revealed that ordinary judges were very reluctant to apply the abstract principles of the constitution's bill of rights. The ordinary judiciary soon drew a distinction between constitutional provisions that were sufficiently specific to be legally enforceable (*precettive*) and those that were too abstract and thus considered merely programmatic (*programmatiche*). The more abstract clauses—most of which protected rights—were insufficiently "legal," as it were. Once the Constitutional Court was established in 1956, however, it disqualified this jurisprudential construction. In its very first decision (1/1956), it made clear that the whole constitution was to be taken seriously, including those provisions that had been considered to be merely "programmatic" because of their more abstract character. The court thus restored the unity of the constitution against attempts to reduce it to a more limited set of specific clauses.[33]

Constitutional tribunals are not only more comfortable with abstract principles. They are also less reluctant to resort to unwritten principles. The French Constitutional Council is notable in this regard: apart from the Declaration of the Rights of Man and of the Citizen of 1789 and other social principles enumerated in the preamble to the constitution of 1946, the court has resorted to unwritten standards (general principles) to test the constitutionality of legislation. Ordinary judges would have been too timid to bring about such a deep transformation of the constitution of 1958—which does not have an explicit bill of rights.[34]

Another possible manifestation of the relative autonomy of constitutional discourse concerns the publication of dissenting opinions. Civil-law countries have traditionally rejected this practice. The authority of judicial decisions is thought to be undermined if the public realizes that judges are divided about the interpretation of the law.[35] Also, judicial independence is thought to be better secured against external pressures if judges speak publicly with a single voice, even when they are internally divided.

It bears emphasizing, incidentally, that jurists trained in the civil-law tradition recognize that the law can be understood in different ways. Even the formalist "deductive" style that characterizes French judicial decisions, which is more extreme than the style one finds in other European countries, should not be taken to imply that jurists fail to appreciate the extent to which there is room for interpretive disagreement. French judges present their conclusions in a deductive fashion, but they are perfectly aware that various options present themselves in many cases. As Mitchel Lasser explains, the judges have previously deliberated on these options in very frank terms, as internal documents clearly attest. Still, the decisions appear to the outside world as mechanical and unanimous.[36]

When it comes to constitutional law, however, the case in favor of dissenting opinions becomes stronger. Insofar as the constitution speaks to the most fundamental questions of justice and liberty, some of which are deeply controversial, judges should make public their internal disagreements. The democratic conversation gets enriched in this way. The court can signal to the political branches and the general citizenry that there is room for evolution and reconsideration of the issues in the future. True, in some politically charged cases, a decision of a divided court is more fragile. But then, the very fact that the publication of dissents is authorized helps reinforce the authority of judicial decisions when they really are unanimous. Only when dissents are possible does unanimity mean something in practice in such extreme cases.

In this context, the European model offers an interesting institutional possibility: the constitutional court can be allowed to publish dissenting and concurring opinions even though ordinary judges remain under the traditional prohibition. The dualist structure (constitutional court–ordinary courts) permits the introduction of such a difference.[37] In this way, it is possible to accommodate the belief that there are dialogic advantages to dissenting opinions in constitutional matters within a legal tradition that thinks that such opinions are not desirable for judicial decisions in general.[38] This is only a possibility, though. In many European countries even constitutional courts are prohibited from publishing dissents.[39]

These are some of the ways in which the constitutional discourse can distinguish itself from ordinary legal reasoning in civil-law countries. The contrast, of course, is not a categorical one. The constitution is part of the law, and its interpretation cannot be a completely different activity from ordinary legal interpretation. Consider, for example, the role of precedents. One of the characteristics of courts is that while they go about deciding cases, they generate a body of doctrine that they are expected to follow in the future. As we saw in chapter 3, there is no official doctrine of stare decisis in civil-law countries, but courts are expected to be consistent with past decisions. Such consistency is a critical source of legitimacy and a key component of a sound theory of judicial review. For courts to be and appear objective and impartial, they must be able to show the public that their decisions are in keeping with established doctrines. Constitutional courts too must respect this constraint. Were it not for this constraint, it would be hard for them to answer the criticism that they are "legislatures" merely imposing their will. In particular, when a constitutional court reviews statutes in the abstract, it is easy for critics to portray the court's function as that of a "third legislative chamber." For a court to be able to claim that it is not really part of the legislative branch, it cannot enjoy the same kind of institutional liberty that the parliament is accorded. Given the open-endedness of most constitutional clauses, however, the court needs some constraint on its interpretative choices—otherwise, the contrast between judicial and legislative decisions gets blurred. It is here that consistency with precedents acquires such a key role, as European scholars usually emphasize.[40]

Furthermore, to the extent that the constitutional court relies on regular judges to implement its doctrines when interpreting ordinary legislation, the distance in legal styles cannot be too large. In particular, if the court is procedurally linked to the regular judiciary through some sort of appeal (as in Germany, Portugal, and Spain, for instance), it may be a good idea to require that a percentage of the court's members be drawn from the ordinary judiciary. Their presence will help reduce potential dissonances between different styles of reasoning.[41]

In short, the contrast between constitutional discourse and ordinary legal reasoning is a qualified one. Still, there is a contrast to be maintained, and the institutional decision to create a special constitutional tribunal helps keep the distinction alive.

THE "LEGALIZATION" OF THE CONSTITUTION IN THE UNITED STATES

Some of the examples of the relative autonomy of constitutional discourse that I have provided in the previous section would make no sense, of course, as examples of autonomy in common-law countries like the United States. To begin with, the style of judicial reasoning of common-law courts in the area of ordinary law is different from the more formalistic style of their civil-law counterparts: it is more explicitly and consciously sensitive to policy considerations and abstract principles. In the common-law world, moreover, the practice of issuing dissenting opinions in general cases already exists. If one were to exaggerate a little bit, one could say that special constitutional tribunals have been necessary in continental Europe in order to introduce a new kind of reasoning for constitutional matters—one that departs from classic civil-law reasoning and approaches the common-law style.

Still, a complex and interesting process of "legalization" had to occur in the United States before courts could assume the power of judicial review and exercise it in a relatively active way.[42] In what follows, I argue that things might have been a little different if a constitutional tribunal had been created.

As is often observed, the U.S. Constitution does not explicitly grant judges a general power of legislative review. It does establish that state judges must set aside state legislation that conflicts with federal law. The supremacy clause is very clear in this regard. When it comes to judicial review of federal legislation, however, the text is silent. At first, the role of the judiciary was rather modest. At the end of the eighteenth century, the constitution was read to express the fundamental principles of free government that were already part of a larger political tradition. The written character of the constitution was relatively irrelevant, for such principles were considered to be binding anyway, as principles of natural law. Judges could certainly defend them by refusing to enforce in a particular case a law that was plainly unconstitutional. But they had this power not because they were experts in expounding the law, but because they acted as agents of the people. In the same way that the citizens themselves could refuse to obey a law that was clearly against the principles of free government, judges and other officials could ignore it too. Judicial review was acceptable, but only in this weak form: only the laws that were unconstitutional beyond any reasonable doubt could be set aside by courts when deciding cases.

Gradually, however, the U.S. Constitution was "legalized." The decision in *Marbury v. Madison* was a crucial step in this process. Courts started to treat the constitution as ordinary law. Its written character became a very important property to highlight: the constitution had to be interpreted by judges according to the canons of statutory interpretation. An important consequence resulted from this: judges would have the responsibility not only of setting aside the laws that were clearly unconstitutional but also of fixing the meaning of the constitution in doubtful cases. After all, when ordinary law is not sufficiently clear, it is the judges' role to establish its meaning. The same idea should apply to the U.S. Constitution. Judges would be escaping their responsibility if they refused to give an answer to interpretive constitutional questions in doubtful cases. A statute could now be disregarded, therefore, even if it was not obviously unconstitutional.

For courts in the United States to move beyond the initial stage of weak review (that is, review whose function is limited to getting rid of statutes that are clearly unconstitutional), toward a more active kind of intervention, they had to reduce the distance between the U.S. Constitution as fundamental law and ordinary law. Only when the constitution was legalized could they start to exercise review in a more aggressive manner.

In contrast to the American evolution, constitutional tribunals in Europe can move beyond weak review and yet resist pressures toward legalization. First, their authority to check statutes under the constitution is explicit in the constitution itself.[43] In some countries, it is even impossible to abolish the institution of judicial review through a constitutional amendment.[44] Second, this authority does not rest on the assumption that the constitution is very similar to statutory law. Rather, the fact that a special institution is created to deal with the constitution suggests otherwise. The constitutional court should not feel embarrassed by the fact that the document it is asked to interpret and enforce is so different in important respects from most legislation. In particular, no matter how special a bill of rights appears, there is no doubt that the court has been conferred the power to give concrete meaning to it for purposes of determining the constitutionality of parliamentary enactments.

It would be a mistake, of course, to claim that courts in the United States are not sensitive to the special quality of constitutional principles. They have always realized that the U.S. Constitution is a special text, as John Marshall famously reminded everyone when he wrote in *McCulloch v. Maryland* that "we must never forget that it is a Constitution we are expounding."[45] Still, the U.S. Supreme Court cannot easily abandon a legalistic approach to constitutional issues. It is dangerous for it to insist too much on the proposition that the interpretation of the U.S. Constitution is a very different kind of activity than the interpretation of a statute. The legitimacy of judicial review appears to be linked to the assumption that the U.S. Constitution is part of the law that judges are experts at interpreting and enforcing in concrete disputes. As Richard Posner has written, "Nonconstitutional cases provide protective coloration" for the Supreme Court, for no one doubts that the Supreme Court is "doing law" when it is deciding statutory cases. "Since the style of the Court's constitutional opinions is similar to that of its statutory opinions," Posner explains, "the impression is created that even when deciding constitutional cases the Justices are doing law, and hence that the Supreme Court really is just another court, doing what normal courts do."[46]

Some consequences seem to follow from this. First, restrictive theories of judicial review are more likely to be attractive in the United States. As Burt Neuborne observes, "The lack of a clear positivist constitutional text authorizing judicial review in the United States continues to roil the intellectual waters to this day, enabling generations of legal academics to gain tenure by positing grand theories of constitutional review and giving rise to numerous theories of constitutional interpretation, some of which are profoundly foolish in seeking a formally positivist fig-leaf for the judicial enterprise." He mentions literalism and originalism as examples of theories whose aim is to narrow the scope of judicial review.[47]

Second, the U.S. Supreme Court is more likely to focus its attention on technical legal arguments, which may obscure the underlying moral issues. Jeremy Waldron, for example, thinks that the Supreme Court is not straightforward enough when it expresses the moral reasons for its judgments: "The proportion of argument about theories of interpretation to direct argument about the moral issues is skewed in most judicial opinions in a way that no one who thinks the issues themselves important can possibly regard as satisfactory." This, he believes, is partly due to the fact that the legitimacy of judicial review is so problematic. "Because judges (like the rest of us) are concerned about the legitimacy of a process that permits them to decide these issues, they cling to their authorizing texts and debate their interpretation rather than venturing out to discuss moral reasons directly."[48] Similarly, Christopher Eisgruber notes that there is a tension between the Supreme Court's responsibility for implementing federal law and its responsibility for interpreting the U.S. Constitution: "Technical legal skill is much more relevant to the former than to the latter. Supreme Court Justices have a natural, and destructive, tendency to iron out the complexities in their role by conceiving of constitutional interpretation as a technical legal exercise. That is, after all, what lawyers do best, and people like to exaggerate the importance of the things they do well."[49]

It seems reasonable to predict that, other things being equal, if a constitutional tribunal were introduced in the United States with the explicit function of determining the constitutionality of federal legislation, the tendencies that these scholars have identified would be weaker. The positivist source of that court's legitimacy would be clear. The court would not feel a strong need to have jurisdiction over nonconstitutional cases (Posner); it would probably be less pressed by restrictive theories of interpretation, such as literalism and originalism (Neuborne); it would tend to discuss moral reasons more directly (Waldron); and it would not insist so much on legal technique (Eisgruber). It would not completely detach itself from ordinary legal discourse, of course, but the distance in style would be larger than it currently is. The increased relative autonomy of constitutional discourse would manifest itself in different ways than it does in continental Europe. After all, the common law is different from the civil law—it has generated a different, less formalistic style of judicial reasoning, and it has traditionally permitted the publication of dissenting opinions. Still, a more pronounced contrast of style might emerge between constitutional discourse and ordinary legal discourse in some respects, like those commented upon by the scholars just mentioned. Arguably, "this would improve the conditions for processes of democratic deliberation and debate about constitutional issues," as Christopher Zurn notes, for "there would be less confusion between constitutional issues and the technical legalisms they often come wrapped within in diffuse systems of constitutional review."[50]

CHAPTER SIX

The Structure of the Constitutional Conversation

SO FAR, I HAVE SUGGESTED some reasons why a constitutional court is better equipped than ordinary courts in civil-law countries to interpret the abstract principles of political morality that the constitution expresses. In this chapter I wish to examine the forms of the constitutional conversation. What is the court asked to focus on? Who can have access to it? Who defends the position of the government? What kind of review (concrete or abstract) can the court exercise? As I argue, various features of the European model help enhance the public visibility of constitutional courts, as well as their impact on political debates.

A CONSTITUTIONAL CONVERSATION THAT FOCUSES ON WHAT PARLIAMENT HAS DECIDED

Legislative review is a major task (sometimes the only task) that constitutional courts perform. It is this function that justifies their existence as special institutions. This is in keeping with one of the basic assumptions on which the European model rests: statutes have a special democratic dignity because of their parliamentary source.

In a parliamentary system, the legislative body is deemed to be the most representative political institution since its members are directly elected by the people, whereas the officials who occupy the other branches of government are not, as a general rule. In particular, the prime minister, who is the head of the executive branch, is dependent on the support of the parliament. Most Western European countries follow this pattern, though in some countries there is also a popularly elected president. Except in France, however, the really important figure in the executive branch is the prime minister supported by the parliament, not the president (where this institution exists).[1]

The centrality of parliament is a qualified one, to be sure. First, in mass democracies that are structured around political parties, the prime minister enjoys a more direct democratic legitimacy than the system formally acknowledges. Formally, the prime minister governs because he or she is supported by the majority in the legislative assembly. As a matter of fact, however, the prime minister governs, to a large extent, because he or she "won the elections." When citizens cast their vote in favor of a particular member of parliament (or list of MPs), they have in mind the different candidates for the prime ministership.

Second, most statutes originate in legislative proposals made by the executive. The parliamentary majority will usually support those proposals, with minor changes. The opposition will hardly ever persuade a sufficient number of members of the majority to break party discipline and change their minds. The normal scenario is for the executive to enjoy stable parliamentary support, through a party or coalition of parties that is rather disciplined. This normal scenario is altered only when there is a crisis in the governing coalition or within the majority party. In such circumstances, some solution or other can overcome the impasse: typically, the prime minister can be removed by the parliament. In some countries, the parliament can also be dissolved by the prime minister with a call for new elections.

As Alec Stone Sweet explains, "Compared with presidential systems (like the American), the degree of centralized control in European parliamentary systems is generally quite high. The rise of prime ministerial (or cabinet) government—reinforced by relatively strict party discipline within parliament, and anchored by relatively stable party systems outside it—has come at the expense of the legislature."[2] Parliaments are thus "arena" legislatures rather than "transformative" legislatures: they tend to ratify the policy decisions made elsewhere. The situation, however, varies from country to country in terms of the number of effective veto players that can oblige the executive branch to reconsider its original projects.

Thus, the existence of a powerful second chamber in the parliament can have a moderating effect on governmental programs. In Germany and Italy, for example, the political process is less centralized than in Spain and France, since the senate is more powerful in the former countries than in the latter.[3]

But even if, as a matter of fact, the institutional centrality of the parliament is a rather qualified one in most European countries, the argument can still be made that statutes have a special dignity because of their source. The legislative process is more transparent than the processes through which other legal provisions, such as administrative regulations, are issued. The tension between the governing majority and the parliamentary opposition, which is an important factor to attract public debates, is more visible when legislative measures are discussed in the parliament than when other norms and acts are approved by the executive branch. Statutes enacted through a procedure of this sort deserve special consideration from a democratic perspective.

The European model of judicial review typically reacts to the higher democratic quality of statutes by establishing a special court as the only institution that can pass judgment on their constitutionality. The parliament is thus granted a "jurisdictional privilege": only the constitutional tribunal, not ordinary judges, can make the delicate decision to strike down one of the parliament's normative products. As Gustavo Zagrebelsky, a former president of the Italian Constitutional Court, explains, the current systems in Europe approach the foundational American idea that legislation is not the only source of rights: fundamental rights announced in the constitution preexist ordinary legislation. Still, he argues, the centrality of legislation in the European tradition is preserved to a certain extent. One of its manifestations is the jurisdictional privilege: the legislature is entitled to have its decisions scrutinized by a special court.[4]

European countries differ, however, as to whether this privilege must be extended to the statutes that were enacted *before* the constitution entered into force. As was mentioned in chapter 1, the constitutional courts in some countries have the sole power to check those statutes, whereas in other countries all courts share that responsibility. The democratic case for the privilege seems weaker when applied to the old laws. Legal certainty, however, argues in its favor.[5]

In any case, the fact that the constitutional court focuses on legislation, especially if recently enacted, helps engage the interest of political parties and the general public. Statutes are relatively visible given the parliamentary procedure through which they are passed. Moreover, they tend to express key policy choices, for they usually prevail over other norms in the legal system (except for the constitution). A court that devotes an important part of its time and energy to checking the validity of statutes is thus likely to attract the attention of politicians and the citizenry.

In addition, the fact that the court can strike down laws—and not simply set them aside in a particular case—increases its public visibility. There is a deep sense of drama when someone challenges a law: everybody is aware of the enormous impact that the court's decision can potentially have. In common-law countries, of course, the presence of a strong doctrine of precedent can produce similar results. The U.S. Supreme Court, for instance, attracts lots of public attention given the force of its holdings, which transcend the disposition of the particular dispute. In civil-law countries, in contrast, only a decision by the constitutional court overturning a statute can produce legal consequences of similar import.

The European model has several shortcomings, however. First, the fact that only the constitutional court can judge the validity of parliamentary enactments makes it more difficult for constitutional issues to "percolate" in lower courts until they are finally settled. In the United States, for example, the public receives a plurality of points of view from different lower courts, all of them ruling on matters of constitutional law, until the Supreme Court finally speaks to the issue. The conversation thus develops over a longer period of time. Lawyers can refine and improve their arguments as new occasions to examine the same question present themselves. The discussion remains open until the Supreme Court intervenes. In contrast, the time for debate is shortened under the European model, for only the constitutional court has the authority to pass judgment on statutes. Ordinary judges have only a limited and preliminary role: they can certify questions to the court, thus preparing the argumentative terrain a little bit.[6]

From this perspective, there is a dialogic disadvantage to a priori review, especially if it is the only kind of review the court can engage in (as was the case in France until the 2008 reform). If the court has to speak at a relatively early stage, soon after the statute is enacted, no other judicial voice is heard before the court's decision is handed down. In France, this shortcoming has traditionally been offset to a certain extent by the fact that the Council of State, in its capacity as an advisory body, issues reports on the legislation that the executive initiates.[7] The Council of State has very often voiced reservations about the constitutionality of certain bills, and participants in the debates in the National Assembly and the Senate have taken these reservations into account.[8] The Constitutional Council benefits from this previous discussion, of course. There is no doubt, however, that by permitting ordinary judges to certify questions to the Constitutional Council, the 2008 reform has facilitated the emergence of a richer constitutional conversation in France.

A second potential weakness of the European model is tied to the crisis of parliamentary legislation stemming from the rise of the "administrative state." There is an increasing tendency in many fields for statutes to delegate regulatory powers to executive and administrative bodies. Parliaments tend to legislate in more open-ended terms, for circumstances change very fast and it is increasingly difficult to generate consensus around clear statutory provisions. Important constitutional issues are likely to arise, therefore, at the executive regulatory level. If the legal provisions that the government issues are accorded the "force of statute" (as is normally the case with emergency decrees and so-called delegated legislation), the constitutional court is usually given jurisdiction to determine their validity. But if the government issues administrative regulations that are awarded a lower rank than statutes in the legal hierarchy, the constitutional courts in many countries have no say at all—or only a limited say. Ordinary courts are instead relied upon.[9]

This relates to a final problem: statutes may be unimpeachable from a constitutional standpoint if they are correctly interpreted and applied. Depending on the way statutes are enforced, a fundamental right may or may not be violated, for example. If the court has no jurisdiction to review administrative or judicial decisions, it is then unable to speak to interesting constitutional issues that may arise at the enforcement and adjudicatory levels. As Francisco Rubio Llorente, a former vice president of the Spanish Constitutional Court, contends, the court cannot fully guarantee constitutional values if its only target is legislation.[10] In this regard, those countries that allow individuals to file constitutional complaints (Germany, Spain, Austria) or to appeal judicial decisions on constitutional matters (Portugal) have an advantage over those that do not (France,

Italy, Belgium, Luxembourg).[11] The problem, as previously noted, is that constitutional courts may be overloaded with appeals and complaints of this sort unless they are granted ample liberty to select the cases that are truly important from a constitutional perspective.

Despite these limitations, the basic assumption upon which the European model rests seems plausible, at least given the traditions of parliamentary democracy. The constitutional conversation should be strongly linked to the controversial decisions that the parliament has expressed in the form of statutes. Accordingly, a major task of the court should be legislative review.

STARTING THE CONVERSATION: THE ROLE OF PUBLIC INSTITUTIONS AND PRIVATE INDIVIDUALS AS CHALLENGERS

Now, who has access to the court to attack the validity of statutes? One of the typical characteristics of the European model is that public institutions—usually of a political character—are granted access through the "constitutional challenges" mechanism. Within the group of Western European countries we are examining, only Luxembourg lacks this institutional device. In Central and Eastern Europe, all countries have included it.[12]

There are good reasons to permit public institutions to initiate constitutional litigation. As Hans Kelsen reasoned, the interest in protecting the constitution against the legislature is a public interest, not merely a private one. It seems reasonable, therefore, to give standing to such entities. Sometimes individuals are so lightly harmed in their own immediate interests that they have no incentive to launch a lawsuit—unless devices such as class actions are adopted. If the general rules on standing are rather strict, moreover, it may sometimes be difficult to find an individual that is in the right position to bring an action challenging a law. Public entities may be needed to fill in these gaps.[13] One could say that in the same way that there is a public interest in discovering those who are responsible for criminal activity and taking action against them, there is a similar interest in discovering and challenging unconstitutional statutes. For these purposes, Kelsen suggested creating the office of a special prosecutor whose job would be to initiate the process of legislative review.[14]

We can reinforce this Kelsenian idea from a different angle. We can argue that the political community as a whole should be interested in discussing whether legislation is constitutional. If so, the process of judicial review should be opened not only to those individuals (or groups) who are personally affected in a more immediate manner but to other players as well.

One of the relatively familiar arrangements that we find in many European countries is that the parliamentary opposition is granted the power to challenge legislation in the abstract.[15] Thus, in Austria, France, Germany, Portugal, and Spain, a qualified minority of members of the parliament are entitled to attack statutes before the constitutional court.[16] In France, in particular, these actions by the opposition are central to the system: in practice, it is the opposition that brings abstract actions against parliamentary legislation.[17]

One of the likely consequences of conferring the power of referral to a qualified parliamentary minority is that more media attention is brought to the issues before the court. The political character of the plaintiffs draws the attention of the public. As Christopher Zurn puts it, an explicit signal is sent to the community "that what is at stake is a fundamental matter of constitutional law, and that there are reasonable disagreements about such fundamental matters that nevertheless need to be settled."[18] The visibility of the court is thus increased.

Another consequence that seems to derive from this procedure, according to many observers, is that the parliamentary debate becomes more constitutionalized. The different political groups in the legislative assembly use constitutional language more often and are sensitive to the court's case law. Alec Stone Sweet's comparative study of the French, Italian, Spanish, and German courts provides evidence to support this thesis.[19] In his view, "abstract review politics facilitate judicialization" of the legislative process.[20] The governmental majority is more willing to reconsider a proposal and negotiate with the opposition if the latter can credibly threaten a successful judicial challenge.

Apart from their impact on political negotiations, the availability of such challenges can improve the quality of legislative debates. Arguments concerning the validity of statutes will be made by the majority and the minority, and the fact that the minority can use its power to refer the issue to the court tends to increase the level of responsibility with which those arguments are made. As French scholars often observe, the existence of the court helps ensure that the "axiom of André Laignel" is rejected. In 1982, Laignel addressed himself to the parliamentary minority and said, "Vous avez juridiquement tort parce que vous êtes politiquement minoritaire." (You are legally wrong because you are in the political minority.)[21] When it comes to constitutional questions, of course, the fact that one is in the minority does not mean that one is wrong. Conversely, the existence of the court prevents the opposition from being too frivolous when it raises objections. As Dominique Rousseau explains, referring to the French system, if the parliamentary opposition wants to be serious when it argues that a statute is unconstitutional, it is expected to bring an action to the constitutional court.[22]

If a challenge is filed, the majority and the minority will have a day in court, and the public will see who is right (according to the constitutional court). The minority will claim victory if the court rules that the statute is indeed unconstitutional. It can then argue that the majority should have been more attentive to the objections raised during the parliamentary debate. If, on the contrary, the court upholds the statute, the minority will suffer a defeat. In this regard, one of the advantages of the publication of dissenting opinions is that it gives the public some measure of the intellectual rigor of both the government and the challengers. If the court is unanimous in its decision to strike down a statute, the frivolity of the government will be obvious. Similarly, a court's unanimous decision to uphold the law will be taken as evidence that the plaintiffs were not sufficiently careful with their claims. A divided court, in contrast, makes the corresponding defeats less humiliating.

Moreover, if the parliamentary opposition chooses not to challenge the statute it has voted against and the court later declares it unconstitutional in a procedure triggered by others (by ordinary judges or by private individuals, for example), the opposition will have to share part of the blame: although it did vote against the statute, it will nevertheless be criticized for not having gone to the constitutional court to dispute its constitutionality.

Writing on the political impact of constitutional adjudication, Dieter Grimm, a former justice of the Federal Constitutional Court of Germany, asserts that one of its good consequences is that "political actors are forced to anticipate the opinion of the court in order to avoid a legal defeat. While arguments of political desirability or usefulness usually prevail in the decision making process, they are now balanced by legal arguments."[23] Similarly, Erhard Blankenburg notes that in Germany, "governments as well as oppositions argue with what they suppose to be the interpretation of the Constitutional Court—governments sometimes anxiously, oppositions rather aggressively—both often in innovative ways."[24] Participants in the legislative debates are thus more careful when they define their positions and when they offer their justifications for them. What they decide to do, and what they say by way of justification at the legislative stage, will be subjected to public scrutiny once the constitutional court has spoken. There is reason to believe that this tendency is reinforced when a parliamentary minority has standing to bring actions against the laws passed by the majority.

Of course, for things to work this way, there must be a broad consensus among political actors and the general public that it is perfectly legitimate for the parliamentary opposition to initiate constitutional review. Sometimes such consensus is fragile, however. In Spain, for example, the governmental majority has sometimes resorted to democratic rhetoric to criticize the opposition for bringing a challenge. "The minority wants to get from the court what it has lost in the parliament" is not an uncommon remark aimed at discrediting the opposition. This, of course, is a misguided criticism. If the constitution places limits on ordinary legislation and entrusts the court with the power to interpret and enforce those limits, there is nothing particularly undemocratic about a parliamentary group having access to the court to review a law that raises constitutional doubts. In any case, if the public is critical of these types of actions, the parliamentary minority will tend to avoid them. This seems to be the situation in Portugal, for instance, where this type of procedure is rarely used, despite the fact that it only takes one tenth of the parliamentary deputies to initiate it.[25]

So far I have stressed the potential advantages in allowing public institutions to challenge statutes. Such institutions should not have a monopoly, however. Private individuals (as well as associations and groups) should also be accorded standing. There are two possible ways for individuals to trigger review within the European model. One is indirect: the "constitutional question" procedure that litigants can request ordinary judges to put in motion if they believe that the statute applicable to the particular case violates the constitution. The other is direct: a constitutional complaint (used in Austria, Germany, and Spain) or a constitutional appeal (Portugal) or even an abstract challenge (Belgium and Hungary).

Until recently, France did not give individuals any kind of access to the Constitutional Council. As was already mentioned, the system was amended in July 2008 so that the ordinary judiciary can now certify questions to the court whenever fundamental rights and liberties seem to be transgressed by the applicable law. For these purposes, the relevant supreme court (the Court of Cassation or the Council of State, depending on the type of case) acts as a filter. This change is to be celebrated.[26] Under the earlier system, any agreement reached by the governmental majority and the parliamentary opposition that a particular statute would not be referred to the court meant that the statute was immune from future challenges—an objectionable result.[27]

There is a fairness argument that we should be sensitive to. A person who suffers the effects of a law should be entitled to call the government to account. The government should explain itself—it should put forth good enough reasons to justify its legislative choice given that harm. This fairness argument seems particularly powerful when a fundamental right is alleged to be violated. From an instrumental point of view, moreover, it is sensible to allow individuals and groups to challenge ordinary legislation: if they are harmed by a law, they have an incentive to look for the best arguments to mount an attack. More importantly, their intervention is necessary to compensate for the passivity of political institutions in some cases. It may happen, for example, that the latter do not realize the extent to which a law can negatively affect the rights and interests of certain minorities in society. It may also happen that it is unpopular to challenge particular types of statutes—those that protect national security, for example. For these and other reasons, the political players may fail to go to court. If individuals are not entitled to react in such cases, a possibly unconstitutional statute gets unduly immunized.[28]

Consider, for example, the 2004 French law banning conspicuous religious symbols from public schools.[29] That law, which seems to cover items such as head scarves for Muslim girls, yarmulkes for Jewish boys, turbans for Sikh boys, and large Christian crosses, is supposed to protect the principle of secularity (laïcité). It was enacted after an investigative committee established by the president in 2003—and headed by the ombudsman (Bernard Stasi)—issued a report recommending its passage. The Constitutional Council, however, had no chance to rule on its validity, since neither the majority nor the opposition in parliament filed an abstract challenge and the groups whose religious freedom was affected had no standing to bring an action. After the 2008 reform, fortunately, this law, as well as any other that is questioned by litigants on the grounds that it impinges upon fundamental rights and liberties, will be scrutinized by the Constitutional Council if the ordinary judge handling the case initiates the new "constitutional question" procedure introduced by the 2008 reform.

The experience in other countries suggests that individuals can enrich the court's agenda in desirable ways. As Gustavo Zagrebelsky observes, the "constitutional question" mechanism, through which ordinary judges can refer issues to the Italian Constitutional Court at the request of the individual litigants (as well as on the judges' own initiative), has created an attractive form of participation for cultural groups at the margins of mainstream political parties.[30] Similarly, the complaints procedure in Germany has been very popular and has helped attract the attention of citizens to fundamental rights. In 1983, for example, over one hundred people filed separate complaints against the Federal Census Act of 1983. These petitions resulted in one of the most important cases ever decided by the Federal Constitutional Court.[31] Similarly, the court in Spain struck down an important tax law on the grounds that it discriminated against married couples, at the initiative of a citizen who lodged a constitutional complaint. The political institutions that could have asked the court to review the law had been totally passive.[32]

DEFENDING STATUTES AGAINST CONSTITUTIONAL ATTACKS: THE RIGHT OF THE GOVERNMENTAL MAJORITY TO BE HEARD

Let us now examine the other side of the dispute: Who defends the statutes that are questioned before the constitutional court? One of the potential virtues of the European model is that it facilitates the right of the governmental majority to defend the constitutional legitimacy of the statute it has enacted. Whether it is the parliament or the executive (or both) that has the right to be heard by the court is of secondary importance in a parliamentary regime.[33] What is crucial is that before a decision is finally made regarding the constitutionality of a statute, the court has heard the point of view of those who speak for the governmental majority. Their opinions are needed in order to get a balanced picture of the underlying problem. Their intervention, moreover, will help enhance the public visibility of the dispute. When a statute has been attacked on constitutional grounds, the public is eager to listen to the government's responses to the objections, especially if the parliamentary opposition is the challenger.

The government's intervention would not be easy to channel in civil-law countries if a decentralized system of judicial review were established. In many ordinary cases, the government is not a party to the proceedings. Ordinary courts would have to notify the parliament or the government every time a statute was questioned in a particular case. This would not be impossible, of course. In the United States, for example, courts must notify the U.S. attorney general (or the relevant state attorney general) if the constitutionality of an act of Congress (or a statute of that state) affecting the public interest becomes an issue in litigation involving private parties.[34] As was mentioned earlier, however, it is typical in civil-law countries for the courts of appeals and even the supreme courts to have an extremely heavy docket. The government would thus have to pay attention to too many cases. Centralizing constitutional review in a special court makes things easier: the government knows where it must concentrate its resources to justify its legislative choices.

The fact, moreover, that the court can strike down statutes enhances the quality of the legal arguments made by the government. Since the statute can be eliminated in a single procedure, there is an incentive for the government to turn to its most prestigious lawyers in order to come up with the best possible arguments to defend its position before the constitutional court. In the same way that centralization of judicial review can attract the best legal minds in the country to become members of the court, it can also attract the best lawyers when it comes to defending the claims of the governmental majority.

THE PRESENCE OF ABSTRACT REVIEW

Finally, we should inquire into the kind of review that the court is asked to exercise. As was already explained in chapter 1, constitutional courts typically have jurisdiction to review statutes in the abstract, that is, with no connection to a specific case. We find this feature in all the Western European countries under examination except Luxembourg, where only concrete review is available. Abstract review may be the only kind of review that is established (as in France, before the 2008 reform), or it may be combined with concrete review (as in Austria, Belgium, Germany, Italy, Portugal, Spain, and France after the 2008 reform). With respect to Central-Eastern Europe, all constitutional courts have been given abstract review powers, as was already mentioned.

Usually, abstract review is connected to procedures activated by public institutions, whereas concrete review is attached to procedures triggered by individuals (whether directly or indirectly). But the question of standing is different from the question whether review is abstract or concrete. Thus, individuals are allowed in some countries to file abstract challenges if they are personally affected by the pertinent law (as in Belgium) or, regardless of whether they are so affected, through an *actio popularis* (as in Hungary).[35]

There are some advantages, one can claim, to a system that includes abstract review. First, it makes it possible for the court to check statutes even when it is difficult to generate a specific case or controversy. Sometimes, when a case finally comes up to the court, it is too late: the statute has already produced most of its effects in an irreversible manner. Abstract review thus expands the scope of the court's intervention—and therefore its relevance in constitutional debates.[36]

Second, this type of review may enhance the court's impartiality. Different judges will decide constitutional issues differently, of course, depending on their moral and political conceptions. Abstract review, however, tends to place them away from the immediate interests of specific litigants—since abstract review is not attached to a particular case. In this sense, it provides a "veil of ignorance," to use the Rawlsian expression.[37] The risk of partiality is especially serious in those civil-law countries in which the doctrine of horizontal precedent has not been strongly developed.

Abstract review, however, is often criticized on several grounds. It is objected, for example, that relevant information about the practical impact of the statute at stake needs to be gathered before the court speaks. There is some merit to this criticism, but we should not exaggerate it. Abstract review does not mean that no knowledge about the world is considered. After all, the legislature discusses and enacts its statutes "in the abstract" too, and there is no doubt that it can rely on an important body of empirical information to make decisions.[38] A constitutional court that examines a statute in the abstract can avail itself of a similar body of data.

Sometimes, moreover, nothing important is learned from the application of a statute in specific cases. Consider, for example, the question whether a criminal statute has a chilling effect on speech because it is too broad, or whether it is sufficiently precise to give fair warning to citizens about the conduct that is being prohibited, or whether it has been approved through the right constitutional procedures, or whether the matter regulated by it belongs to the sphere of competences of the governmental entity that has enacted it. Concrete review is not superior to abstract review in these sorts of cases in terms of the relevance of the information that can be obtained after enforcing the statute. That information can actually distract the courts. It is tempting to accept a criminal statute as valid, for example, when the person bringing the objection has committed what clearly counts as a horrible crime. That courts deciding concrete cases are often prepared to acquit on the basis of such constitutional grounds is to be applauded. But there is no doubt that things are easier when the problem is addressed in the abstract and at an early stage. In a procedure of a priori review, in which all these issues can be decided before the statute is promulgated, the constitutional court enjoys a privileged position in matters of this kind. Its being blind to the concrete cases is liberating.

It is true, however, that the rich variety of situations that arise in social life may have to be taken into account when a statute that covers them is to be measured against constitutional norms. A statute that criminalizes the consumption of illegal drugs, for example, may look constitutionally fine in the abstract, but its enforcement against those who use peyote in their religious ceremonies becomes troublesome. Similarly, a statute that criminalizes public nudity in front of children may be constitutionally acceptable as a general rule, but it runs into problems if it is to be applied to certain forms of artistic expression in the streets. Many examples can be given of statutes that need to be qualified when they are applied in specific situations. To the extent that this is so, it must be admitted that abstract review is epistemically inferior to more flexible concrete review. A court deciding in the abstract cannot anticipate the rich variety of cases a given statute will cover.

Another criticism that is often raised against abstract review is that the vivid circumstances of a specific case involving real people may be necessary to ensure that courts are properly sensitive to constitutional values. Judges may be more eager to recognize the fundamental rights of the accused, for example, when confronted with real-life situations. This is not a very powerful objection, however. There is some reason to doubt that courts will become more sensitive to rights through the concrete cases they decide. As Alec Stone Sweet and Martin Shapiro argue, for example, it is doubtful that the Supreme Court of the United States was moved to recognize the right of indigent criminal defendants to be provided with a lawyer when it learned about the situation of a particular defendant in *Gideon v. Wainwright*.[39] Rather, the Supreme Court chose that case precisely because it was already willing to announce the right.[40]

True, some cases are really extraordinary in terms of the dramatic circumstances in which individuals find themselves. Judges will be moved. It is not clear, however, that this is the ideal setting to interpret and elaborate constitutional principles. It may be difficult for the court to distance itself from those extraordinary cases and adopt a more systematic and nuanced view of the principles and interests at play. Certain aspects of a case may have an exaggerated impact on judges. Thus, speaking of the procedural protections that the U.S. Supreme Court granted welfare beneficiaries in *Goldberg v. Kelly*,[41] Owen Fiss insists that judges should not be carried away by their spontaneous and passionate reactions to the dramatic circumstances of a case. "Because it lays down a rule for a nation and invokes the authority of the Constitution, the Court necessarily must concern itself with the fate of millions of people, all of whom touch the welfare system in a myriad of ways: some on welfare, some wanting welfare, some being denied welfare, some dispensing welfare, some creating and administering welfare, some paying for it." Accordingly, Fiss argues, "the Court's perspective must be systematic, not anecdotal: The Court should focus not on the plight of four or five or even twenty families but should consider the welfare system as a whole—a complex network embracing millions of people and a host of bureaucratic and political institutions."[42]

Insofar as constitutional issues often require a systematic analysis of complex institutions and practices, it is not a bad idea to distance courts from specific and fragmentary stories when they have to determine the constitutionality of legislation.

Finally, abstract review can be criticized from another angle: the public is more likely to be interested in constitutional debates when there is a concrete, real case that sparks the controversy than when abstract questions are being considered. Concrete review is preferable from this perspective. In this regard, Alexis de Tocqueville's observation that judicial review in the United States tends to escape public notice is probably wrong as a description of current practices. He said that "when a judge contests a law in an obscure debate on some particular case, the importance of his attack is concealed from public notice." This is in contrast to what would have occurred, he wrote, if "the judge had been empowered to contest the law on the ground of theoretical generalities," which is what happens when a statute is challenged in the abstract.[43] On the contrary, the public will be more alert and engaged in the constitutional discussion if real-life stories illustrate the issues under examination. Judged from this standpoint, there is no doubt that abstract review has its limitations. It seems advisable, however, to use abstract review in connection with issues that deeply affect the private lives of individuals. The constitutional debates on abortion and euthanasia, for example, are already so complex, and give rise to such passionate reactions, that it may be better to discuss them in the abstract, without having to focus on the private drama of particular individuals.[44]

CHAPTER SEVEN

Overcoming Judicial Timidity

A CONSTITUTIONAL COURT, I contended in the previous chapter, performs its functions in a zone of high public visibility. I now want to claim that, despite this visibility, the court cannot be timid, in two senses. First, the court cannot shy away from constitutional issues; it has to confront them. Second, it is not easy for the court to be extremely deferential toward the legislature. A significant percentage of the laws that are challenged must be found to be totally or partially unconstitutional. Though many different factors can push judges in one direction or the other when it comes to how aggressively they exercise legislative review, some structural components of the European model operate as vectors of activism.

There are good reasons to celebrate this. A system of constitutional review is established to create a forum of principle where fundamental values are taken seriously. It would be unfortunate if the institutions in charge of review were so passive that their contribution to the protection of rights, and to ongoing public debates, were of marginal importance. We may want to subject those institutions to democratic checks (as I discuss in chapters 8 and 9), but we should encourage them to exercise their powers with some bite. The risk of timidity exists, however. Reviewing the validity of legislation means confronting the political branches, and this is always a delicate matter. The danger of passivism is especially serious in civil-law countries, which have inherited from the past a relatively narrow conception of the role of the judiciary. To the extent that constitutional courts exhibit some features that press them in an activist direction, we have a further argument to defend the centralized model in Europe: those vectors of activism will help counteract the natural inertia in favor of passivism.

THE CONSTITUTIONAL COURT IS REQUIRED TO SPEAK

Let us begin with the question of avoidance. There are interesting differences in this regard between the decentralized and the centralized systems of judicial review. Although these differences are a matter of degree, they are significant nevertheless.[1]

A first difference is this: in a decentralized system like that of the United States, it is possible to allow the supreme court to have discretionary jurisdiction to decide a controversy concerning the validity of a statute. Even if the court declines to take the case, the statute has already been checked by lower courts. In contrast, a constitutional court cannot decline to scrutinize a law that is brought to its attention. Since it is the only organ in the system responsible for review, it would make no practical sense to give it the power to decline to exercise review. The statute would escape constitutional scrutiny if the court refused to take the case.[2]

Of course, some procedural requirements have to be met for the constitutional court to be obliged to speak. But these requirements tend to be quite clear and rigid and do not give much flexibility to the court. So, for example, if sixty senators are entitled to challenge a statute, the court cannot decline to take their case. (This is in sharp contrast to the U.S. Supreme Court's more ample room to maneuver when deciding whether political actors have standing to bring suit.)[3] With respect to questions certified by ordinary judges, the requirements may be more complex, governing when the question can be raised, its relevance for the disposition of the case, the sufficiency of the reasons that the judge invokes, and so on. There is here more room for flexibility, which the constitutional court can sometimes use to reject a question that it prefers to avoid for substantive reasons. But the court must work its way through these doctrinal rules. It is not legally free to reject the application.[4]

A second difference between the decentralized and the centralized models concerns the possibility of avoiding constitutional issues through ordinary legal means. In a decentralized system like that of the United

States, it is possible for courts (including the U.S. Supreme Court) to avoid constitutional issues through statutory interpretation. As the Supreme Court has held, "Where a statute is susceptible of two constructions, by one of which grave and doubtful constitutional questions arise and by the other of which such questions can be avoided, [a court's] duty is to adopt the latter."[5] When courts do that, they do not fully answer the question as to what the constitution requires in connection with a particular issue. They see a potential constitutional problem on the horizon but prefer not to confront it. As Frederick Schauer says, they bring the constitution "in a whisper, rather than with a shout."[6] When they resort to the avoidance canon, courts leave undecided the question whether a future statute that clearly expresses the meaning that has been left to one side would be constitutional. Indeed, there have been instances in which the U.S. Supreme Court has finally upheld as consistent with the Constitution a normative content that it had initially avoided, given the doubts it raised.[7]

If the U.S. Supreme Court can employ this strategy of avoidance, it is because, as an ordinary court, it can decide what meaning to ascribe to a statute as an ordinary legal matter. Because it has this authority, it can try to find a construction of the statute that will make it unnecessary to deal with a constitutional problem. Moreover, because the court is both the supreme interpreter of federal legislation and the supreme interpreter of the federal constitution, the authority of its statutory readings vis-à-vis lower courts is always the same, whether or not the foundation of those readings lies in the constitution.[8]

Constitutional courts, in contrast, find it difficult to avoid constitutional issues by resorting to ordinary legal arguments. When a public institution brings an abstract challenge against a statute, for example, or a judge certifies a question, the court is expected to ascertain whether the pertinent statute complies with the constitution. It cannot evade its responsibility through an appeal to ordinary legal grounds, since the latter pertain to the jurisdiction of ordinary courts. Even when individuals file complaints, the court cannot easily decline to talk about the constitution, since the only reasons that it can invoke to justify its decision to quash the judgment of an ordinary court are reasons that derive from the constitution (in particular, the infringement of fundamental rights). This, by the way, sometimes leads to an "overconstitutionalization" of legal problems.[9]

It is certainly common practice among constitutional courts to try to preserve the validity of laws through a saving construction when such construction is possible. Thus, the court may hold that the examined law is constitutional to the extent that it is interpreted in a certain way or to the extent that it is not interpreted in a certain way. Alternatively, the court can use a negative formula: it can assert that the law is unconstitutional if interpreted in a certain way or unless it is interpreted in a certain way.[10]

It is crucial to note, however, that when a constitutional court renders such an "interpretive decision," which identifies the conditions under which a legislative provision can remain in the system, the court does not avoid the constitutional question at all. The court deals with the question fully and gives an answer. The court reads the constitution in a particular way, gives concrete meaning to it, and then decides how the statute must be interpreted in order for it to be in harmony with the constitution. In doing this, the court avoids striking down the statute, but it does not avoid examining and answering the constitutional question itself.

An example will be useful to illustrate this point. In its decision 74/1987, the Spanish Constitutional Court had to review a provision of the criminal-procedure code that grants detained individuals the right to be assisted by a translator if they are foreigners who do not understand or speak Castilian (that is, Spanish). A constitutional challenge was brought by the Basque government against this provision on the grounds that it did not apply to Spanish citizens who are unable to understand or speak Castilian. Although Castilian is the official language in Spain and citizens have a duty to learn it, other languages (Catalan, Euskera, and Galician) are also official in particular regions. It is not impossible, though it is certainly rare, for a Spanish citizen to have difficulty understanding or speaking Castilian. The court held that it would be against fundamental rights of due process and equality to deny arrested individuals who are Spanish citizens the right to have a translator in those circumstances. It then concluded that the statutory provision "is not unconstitutional if it is interpreted in the sense that it does not exclude Spanish citizens from the right to be assisted by a translator if they do not understand or speak Castilian." It is obvious that the court did not keep away from the constitutional issue. On the contrary, it fully addressed it. It held that the constitution requires the legislature to grant Spanish citizens who are unable to understand or speak Castilian the right to be assisted by a translator. It then sought a remedy: it imposed a particular reading or reconstruction of the statute.

Constitutional courts frequently hand down these sorts of "interpretive decisions," which, I hope I have shown, we cannot regard as examples of avoidance.

A third difference between the decentralized and the centralized models of judicial review concerns the ability of courts to engage in case-by-case minimalism. Since judges in a decentralized system are normally deciding specific controversies, they can circumscribe their holdings concerning the validity of a statute to the particular circumstances of the various cases. Constitutional courts can follow a similar strategy when ordinary judges certify questions or individuals file complaints, but they cannot do so when statutes are attacked by means of abstract challenges. Since there is no particular case that abstract challenges emerge from, or are linked to, constitutional courts cannot limit the extent of the attack.[11]

So, other things being equal, a constitutional tribunal within the European model finds it harder than courts in a decentralized system to engage in strategies of avoidance. This, I have argued before, is a desirable feature that helps counteract a certain natural tendency for courts to shy away from politically delicate matters, a tendency that is especially pronounced in civil-law countries.

SOME RISKS: POLITICALLY CHARGED CASES AND RADICALLY NOVEL LEGISLATION

There are risks, of course, under the European system. Writing in the American context, Alexander Bickel wrote extensively about the need for courts to cultivate what he called "passive virtues."[12] The U.S. Supreme Court, in particular, should have the power to "decide not to decide" controversial questions when the context is not ripe for it. When political passions run high, Bickel argued, it is better for the court to abstain from entering the dispute. To retain its moral capital, it should speak in the name of the constitution when the political climate is mature for it. To a certain extent, the European model has an "anti-Bickelian" bias, for it makes it more difficult for a constitutional court to remain silent. In particular, when political institutions or players (such as the parliamentary opposition) file abstract challenges, the court cannot easily decline to rule on their claims.

In general, though, this is not an undesirable feature of the European model. If we aim for a system that encourages public debates about the constitution, we should welcome a court that renders its judgments when the public is still interested in the parliamentary discussion that a statute has generated. Something would be lost if the court spoke too late.

It is true, however, that the political environment is sometimes so charged that it is too dangerous for the court to speak at a very early stage. As Bruce Ackerman has pointed out, with reference to the constitutional courts that were established in Central and Eastern Europe after the fall of communism, it is risky for a young court to have to deal with the political hot potatoes constantly tossed to it by governmental officials.[13] Even more mature courts should have at their disposal some flexible means to protect themselves. To this effect, various strategies are available within the centralized model. The court may sometimes choose to "sit on the case" awhile as the political situation improves.[14] Alternatively, the court may seek to invalidate a statute on narrow grounds, leaving undecided the more controversial issues.[15] Another possibility is for the court to uphold a statute for the time being, making it clear that this is not the end of the story, that the statute may have to be qualified in its application to particular cases that may be brought to the court's attention in further procedures, or that it may have to be reviewed again in the future in light of new objections, more evidence as to its impact in real life, or new social circumstances.

A different sort of concern about the European model is this: review at an early stage, it may be contended, is likely to be too aggressive when radically novel legislation is examined. Given the all-too-human tendency to resist radical changes, people may be critical of a statute just because it is new. The novelty of the statute may be easily translated into unconstitutionality. Later, as the statute is absorbed by the legal and political community, the early objections may lose part of their force. In that case, the court should have means to abstain from ruling too soon. Early review, it can be argued, is a bad idea, in the same way that prior restraints on free speech are not advisable (for at an early moment there is a tendency to exaggerate the possible harms that a given speech may produce in the future).

This is certainly a potential disadvantage. Interestingly, some European countries allow the parliament to easily override the constitutional court when it engages in a priori review. There may be a connection here: if, indeed, early review tends to be too aggressive with respect to radically novel legislation, the parliament should have the opportunity to immediately insist on the constitutionality of that legislation if the court has expressed objections.[16] On the other hand, one could argue, it is not such a bad idea to prevent an extremely innovative statute from being easily absorbed by the legal system if, indeed, the statute is clearly questionable from a constitutional point of view. If a political community is to be loyal to certain fundamental values it has historically committed itself to, as interpreted through a body of judicial precedents, a radical change should be seen for what it is: a radical change. The court should make the public aware that the new law profoundly departs from the prevailing interpretation of the relevant constitutional principles. A more sustained debate should take place in the political sphere before such a deep transformation can be accepted by the court. In France, for example, some decisions of the Constitutional Council in a priori review procedures have triggered a process of constitutional amendment: the court's judgment on the right of asylum (of August 12–13, 1993) was overridden by a constitutional amendment of November 25, 1993, and its decision on gender parity in the electoral lists (January 14, 1999) was overturned through the constitutional amendment of July 8, 1999.

OVERCOMING JUDICIAL PASSIVISM

So far, I have claimed that it is difficult for a constitutional court to avoid constitutional issues: the court is forced to speak—sometimes quite soon. Now, when it speaks, how deferential is it likely to be toward the legislature? In what follows, I want to argue that a constitutional court cannot be extremely deferential: its very existence as a special institution in charge of legislative review would be inconsistent with a highly passive performance. A significant percentage of the laws that are challenged must thus be found to be unconstitutional.

Let me be clear at the outset, however, that the "ratio of unconstitutionality"—that is, the percentage of laws struck down by a court (of the total number of laws that are challenged)—is only a very indirect and imperfect way to measure the level of judicial activism. To begin with, some laws are much more important than others. A court would not be activist if it never imposed constitutional constraints on the governmental majority with respect to key issues, even if it struck down lots of legal provisions of marginal importance. In addition, it may very well happen that a parliamentary majority abstains from enacting particular laws out of fear that the courts will overturn them. A strong judiciary may cause this sort of "chilling effect" on the legislature. So the ratio of unconstitutionality tells us something about activism, but we should not overestimate its informative value.

It is also important to emphasize that judicial activism is linked to many factors. The performance of courts depends on the political system that is in place. According to Alec Stone Sweet, for example, the more "veto points" the legislative process contains (in the form of bicameralism and executive veto), the more moderate the legislative changes are likely to be. Consequently, the disagreements between the legislature and the judiciary in the constitutional field will be less significant. When the political process is highly concentrated, in contrast, the clashes will be more intense—until new judges are appointed by the new political majority.[17] Another factor can weaken this tendency, however: courts may feel more secure against majoritarian retaliations when the political power is fragmented (as in the United States, for example) than when it is greatly concentrated. Thus, courts in Scandinavia have always exercised legislative review with lots of caution, since political power in that region is highly concentrated: the political system is unitary (not federal); the parliament consists of one chamber; political parties are strong; and there is a tight cohesion between the parliamentary majority and the executive.[18]

The historical context is also an important factor in how aggressively courts scrutinize ordinary legislation. Judicial activism in postwar Europe, for example, has to be understood against the background of the moral disaster of Nazism and fascism. It is a commonplace of European constitutional discourse that those totalitarian experiences have shown the need to curb the powers of legislative assemblies.[19] It is not surprising that, with a few exceptions, the first thing we find in the constitutions adopted after the Second World War is a catalog of rights—the regulation of the structure of the state comes afterward.[20] This textual priority is a symbolic expression of a deep collective commitment in favor of rights. The very first article of the German Basic Law, for instance, solemnly declares that "human dignity shall be inviolable" and refers to "inviolable and inalienable human rights" as the basis of every community. Constitutional courts are part of this European postwar consensus.[21]

Another factor to consider in explaining the level of activism is the strength of public opinion. If a court is intensely supported by the public, it will be more eager to overturn legislation that it finds at odds with the constitution. Should the political branches be tempted to evade an unfavorable decision by the court, several groups in society would express their outrage and press those branches toward compliance. The more visible the court's decisions are, the easier it will be for the public to monitor the degree to which the legislature duly respects and implements them. As Georg Vanberg has shown, using the German experience as an illustration, a court can choose to be more aggressive if its decisions are more publicly transparent—provided, of course, that it enjoys sufficient public support.[22]

The performance of courts in the field of constitutional review, therefore, cannot be understood in isolation from the political system they are ultimately a part of, the historical context in which they operate, the role of public opinion, and a host of other factors. This does not mean, however, that it does not much matter whether a country chooses to set up a special constitutional court instead of relying on ordinary judges to exercise legislative review. Other things being equal, a constitutional court is more likely to be activist, as I discuss in what follows.

A COURT WITH A SPECIFIC MISSION

Constitutional courts, as we know, have been established with the specific mission to check the legislature. I argued in chapter 5 that the establishment of these courts suggests that there is something "special" about constitutional interpretation, something that makes it impossible to reduce it to ordinary legal discourse. At the same time, however, their presence is also an indication that the political community regards it as sufficiently likely that statutes will be found to be inconsistent with the constitution. The unconstitutionality of a statute becomes a relatively "normal" event. A powerful legislature may indeed overstep its constitutional limits often enough to make it worthwhile to set up a body with the specific mandate to provide the necessary checks.[23]

Now, a constitutional court is not likely to earn its own space in the institutional system if it regularly upholds the statutes that are challenged before it. What would be the point of establishing a court whose main function is to determine the validity of legislation if it turned out that such a court rarely struck down statutes? In contrast, in a decentralized system of constitutional review, courts do not feel the same pressure—though other factors, of course, can also direct them toward activism. Since their space in the system as ordinary judges is absolutely protected, they have more flexibility to decide how actively they want to exercise their constitutional function, which is somehow "additional" to their basic function as ordinary enforcers of the law.[24] True, in some decentralized systems there is an explicit clause in the constitution that clearly grants ordinary judges the power of legislative review.[25] Still, the fact that this is not the only function they are expected to perform makes it easier for them not to carry it out in a robust manner: they are not there primarily to check parliamentary enactments, but to resolve ordinary legal disputes. Constitutional courts, in contrast, are not only explicitly authorized to exercise legislative review, they are created for this very purpose.

Constitutional framers seem to have been aware of this contrast. During the deliberations to enact the Italian constitution of 1947, for example, those who rejected judicial activism were against the establishment of a constitutional court. They preferred to rely on ordinary judges instead. They predicted, quite rightly, that the latter would be very reluctant to find laws unconstitutional, whereas the former would be more eager to do so.[26] Indeed, the Italian Constitutional Court's very first decision (1/1956) struck down the law at issue—on the grounds that it violated freedom of speech. That was a clear indication that the court was eager to exercise its powers in an assertive manner. Finding a statute unconstitutional was not going to be a rare event.

The Italian system, however, relied so heavily on ordinary judges as initiators of the process of constitutional review that there was a risk that the court would play a marginal role if those judges underutilized the mechanism placed at their disposal. To counteract this danger, a law was enacted in 1948 requiring judges to raise questions to the court whenever one of the parties claimed that the applicable statute was unconstitutional and the claim was not obviously ill-founded (*manifestamente infondata*).[27] Any doubt about the validity of the statute had to be resolved by referring the issue to the court. In practice, the Italian Constitutional Court has received a large number of questions from ordinary judges, which has helped generate a rich constitutional jurisprudence through the years.

Portugal is another interesting example to illustrate this drive toward activism that animates the centralized model. Ordinary courts in Portugal have traditionally been authorized to exercise legislative review—the constitutions of 1911 and 1933 explicitly granted them this power. They scarcely exercised it in practice, however, until a constitutional court was established in 1982. This new institution was created to maximize the protection of the constitution against the legislature. A wide variety of procedures were designed to ensure an intense control of parliamentary enactments. The Portuguese have clearly succeeded in this connection, since the court exercises review with bite: about 50 percent of its decisions have found laws to be unconstitutional.[28] What is interesting to observe is that lower-court judges are also more aggressive now. Why? Because they are under the supervision of the Constitutional Court, which can quash their decisions in the field of legislative review. The institution that sits at the top for these matters is no longer the Supreme Court of Justice, whose basic function was (and still is) the interpretation of ordinary law, but a special body that is specialized in checking the validity of legislation. The Portuguese Constitutional Court is an activist engine that drives lower-court judges away from their traditional timidity. Not surprisingly, any proposal in Portugal to eliminate the Constitutional Court and rely on ordinary judges exclusively (under the guidance of the Supreme Court of Justice) is considered to be a regression in constitutional terms: it would mean going back to the kind of situation that existed under the constitutions of 1911 and 1933, when judicial review was absent in practice.[29]

These different experiences suggest that if one held the view that only those statutes that are "obviously unconstitutional" should be overturned by courts, it would be wrong to advocate the creation of a constitutional tribunal. It would be better to rely on ordinary judges for these purposes, under the superintendence of a traditional supreme court. Those judges would perform their ordinary function of deciding concrete cases according to the law. In the rare event that the applicable statute were found to be clearly unconstitutional, it would be disregarded. Even if this happened very rarely, nobody would question the institutional relevance of those courts. Moreover, it would seem advisable to rely on ordinary judges, who do not specialize in constitutional law, to apply the "clear mistake" rule.

If a statute is so obviously unconstitutional, one would imagine that any judge would be able to notice it.

From this perspective, it makes sense that Denmark, Sweden, and Finland have decided not to establish constitutional tribunals. In these countries, only a very deferential conception of judicial review is thought legitimate. To a large extent, this is because the political system is highly concentrated, as was previously indicated. In these Nordic countries, a unicameral legislature is strongly linked to the government through a disciplined party system. Courts have been very cautious. It was not until 1999 that the Danish Supreme Court rejected a politically important statute as unconstitutional. In Sweden and Finland, the constitutions explicitly announce the clear-mistake rule: only when a statute is unconstitutional beyond any reasonable doubt may a court set it aside for purposes of deciding a case.[30] If these countries want to maintain such a deferential rule, it would be pragmatically inconsistent to erect a constitutional court.

Parenthetically, it is interesting to note that James Thayer, writing in the American context, gave the following argument to justify his thesis that courts in the United States should strike down statutes only when they are clearly unconstitutional: "The judiciary may well reflect that if they had been regarded by the people as the chief protection against legislative violation of the constitution, they would not have been allowed merely [an] incidental and postponed control. They would have been let in, as it was sometimes endeavored in the conventions to let them in, to a revision of the laws before they began to operate. As the opportunity of the judges to check and correct unconstitutional Acts is so limited, it may help us to understand why the extent of their control, when they do have the opportunity, should also be narrow."[31]

This argument may not be very convincing, for although courts in the American system exercise judicial review in an incidental manner, it does not follow that they should be very deferential toward the legislature when they have the opportunity to exercise review. In any case, Thayer's argument in favor of extreme deference would not apply to a constitutional court, for the latter has indeed been specifically set up as "the chief protection" against legislative violations of the constitution. If statutes can be attacked in the abstract, before any case is brought to the ordinary judiciary, Thayer's thesis in favor of extreme deference does not apply. A constitutional court, we can thus say, not only exhibits an "anti-Bickelian" bias, in the sense that it is difficult for the court to implement the avoidance rule, as we saw earlier, but it also has an "anti-Thayerian" bias: it is difficult for such a court to follow the clear-mistake rule that Thayer tried to introduce in the United States.

This does not mean, however, that constitutional courts have to be activist on all fronts of their jurisprudence. They can instead prefer certain fields to others. In federal polities, for instance, statutes can be reviewed on grounds of both federalism and individual rights. A constitutional court may choose to be very deferential when examining legislation in light of individual rights, say, but to be more activist on the federalism front. Its institutional space will still be safe. In contrast, in unitary countries, the constitutional court has no role to play in the area of federalism. It is then more difficult for the court to be very deferential in human-rights issues, since the constitutional clauses protecting rights are likely to be the central provisions that will be invoked to challenge statutes.

The court can also change the target of its activism from one period to another. For example, during the first decades of its existence, the Italian Constitutional Court directed its activism against laws that preceded the adoption of the 1947 constitution, most of which were of Fascist origin. Since the new parliament, out of political inertia, had not repealed them, the court had to intervene. As Carlo Mezzanotte puts it, the court found a "gold mine" in the invalidation (or radical reconstruction) of Fascist legislation for purposes of building its own legitimacy within the new political system. By vindicating the constitution against the previous regime, the court kept alive the memory of the unity against fascism.[32] It was later, once the court had acquired enough moral capital through this backward-looking jurisprudence, that it started to confront the policy choices of the modern (republican) legislature. It acted more cautiously in this field, though it could still be relatively assertive, for the constitutional consensus in Italian society had grown stronger through the years.[33]

So constitutional courts need not exercise aggressive review in all legislative domains: they may prefer to be very deferential in some areas and less so in others. What is important to emphasize is that they have to be relatively daring in a significant part of their jurisprudence if they want to earn a space in the system.

VECTORS OF ACTIVISM

I have so far argued that constitutional courts in general are pressed toward some degree of activism given their special mission. Other features of courts, however, can reinforce this tendency or, on the contrary, weaken it.

Their degree of purity, for example, can matter. A court will have a harder time justifying a jurisprudence of extreme deference if its only task is to review legislation than if it has some other things to do as well. The French Constitutional Council, for instance, which is rather pure, is quite activist: around half its decisions have found the challenged provisions to be totally or partially unconstitutional.[34] As already noted, the Portuguese Constitutional Court, whose major task is legislative review, has a similar record. The German court, in contrast, seems to be less activist in this field. According to Thomas Gawron and Ralf Rogowski, "Every third [legislative] act controlled by the Court is declared wholly or partly unconstitutional."[35] This fits with Erhard Blankenburg's observation that "in general, the Court has been supportive of the parliamentary majorities of the day rather than of the opposition[,] and its decisions have provided judicial legitimacy to the arguments of the legislators and not to those of diverse opposition groups."[36] In part, this may be due to the existence of the complaints jurisdiction, which gives the German court an important role as the ultimate appellate court in the area of fundamental rights. The more attention it devotes to supervising judicial decisions of lower courts, the more deferential it can choose to be toward the political branches when it examines the laws that have been enacted. The Spanish Constitutional Court's tendency toward passivism vis-à-vis the legislature is even more pronounced.[37]

The specific professional background of the members of the constitutional court can also play a role in this regard. With reference to France, for example, Georges Vedel contended that the presence of former politicians allowed the constitutional court to review legislation in a relatively activist way. If only regular judges had been appointed, he explained, they would have stuck to their traditional deference toward written legislation and the court would have been less assertive.[38] This may also be true of other countries that belong to the civil-law tradition.[39]

Finally, judicial activism can also be a function of the flexibility of the remedies that a court can shape after it finds a statute unconstitutional.

If the court can find ways to soften the consequences of a declaration of invalidity, it is likely to be bolder in its constitutional interpretations. In this regard, some of the Kelsenian techniques to protect legal certainty (which were briefly mentioned in chapter 3) can also be understood as instruments to facilitate judicial activism. Thus, if the invalidation of a law can be held to have no retroactive effects, and if the effects of the decision can be delayed so that the parliament has enough time to modify the statute (or if an old statute may be applied again to fill in the legal gap), then the court can be confident that declaring a statute unconstitutional will not cause much harm.[40] Similarly, if, as Hans Kelsen suggested at some point, a deadline is established after which enacted laws are immune from constitutional attack, the potential retroactive effects of the court's decisions will be more moderate, since the challenged laws will have been operating only for a brief period of time. Even more drastically, if constitutional review is a priori, the court will be very comfortable with the consequences of invalidation: those statutes will not have changed the legal status quo. In short, the softer the consequences of a declaration of unconstitutionality, the more eager the court will be to subject legislation to a relatively strict scrutiny under the constitution.

CONCLUSION

As a result of various factors, I have argued, constitutional courts are forced to address the issues that statutes pose, and they cannot be very deferential toward the legislature. There is no compelling reason to criticize this. If we want a forum in which constitutional principles are addressed, interpreted, and enforced against legislative decisions that erode those principles, courts should not be shy. The introduction of vectors of activism is particularly necessary within the civil-law tradition given the historical timidity of ordinary judges.

With this, we have set the stage for the final issue in this part of the book: How do we square a relatively robust form of judicial review with democratic principles? Is it acceptable to have this sort of review in a political community that is based on democratic ideals? In the context of this discussion, are there any advantages to the centralized model that most European countries follow? I address the issue at a general level in the next chapter and then proceed in chapter 9 to explore the potential advantages of constitutional courts in this respect.

CHAPTER EIGHT

The Democratic Objection to Constitutional Review

THE CHARGE IS WELL KNOWN: from a democratic point of view, it is contended, it is not legitimate for courts to invalidate statutes that a popularly elected assembly has enacted. What can be said in response to this democratic objection, which is usually referred to as the "counter-majoritarian difficulty"?[1]

THE TENSION BETWEEN JUDICIAL REVIEW AND DEMOCRACY: THE MAJORITARIAN PREMISE

Even if we are ultimately in favor of judicial review, we should acknowl-edge that there is an important connection between the democratic prin-ciple and the enactment of a statute by the majority of a popularly elected parliament. Democracy is conceptually tied to the existence of a procedure that gives citizens an equal opportunity to participate with their voice and their vote in the discussion and approval of collective decisions. In modern circumstances, democracy has to be organized around a representative scheme given the advantages of the division of labor. But the underlying aspiration is to honor the equal status of citizens when it comes to decid-ing what laws to enact in the name of the political community. As Jeremy Waldron has stressed, majority rule has an intrinsic value to the extent that it counts all the votes equally, it does not prefer a particular outcome over another, and it does not privilege the views of those who are in favor of maintaining an existing law against the views of those who think it better to change the law. Majority rule treats citizens equally and is neutral among the different positions or choices that are being considered.[2]

True, there are sometimes good reasons to depart from simple majority rule. Certain kinds of decisions should be more difficult to make than others. It is reasonable, for example, for a constitution to be biased against war or against suspending fundamental rights in a state of emergency. A parliamentary supermajority may be required to authorize the government to bring the nation into one of these situations.[3] A constitution may also provide that only a supermajority can permit the country to join a supranational organization that imposes significant restrictions on its members and from which it is not easy to withdraw in the future.[4] These and other exceptions to simple majority rule seem justified.

When a court strikes down a statute enacted through a majoritarian parliamentary procedure, a democratic loss is generated. The fact that the law is disqualified by an institution that is relatively detached from the electoral process entails a cost from a democratic point of view. The question arises, then, how to compensate for this cost. What can be said in favor of judicial review, in order to offset this democratic deficit?

Before we proceed, we need to face some arguments that deny, or can potentially deny, the tension between judicial review and democracy.

FUNDAMENTAL RIGHTS AS PART OF DEMOCRACY

A first set of arguments try to dissolve the tension through a "substantive" conception of democracy. For example, Luigi Ferrajoli, an influential Italian scholar, believes that democracy has to be understood and justified according to a theory that makes fundamental rights part of the very definition of democracy. The democratic ideal, he argues, provides us with no reason to challenge judicial review of legislation, for when judges strike down laws that violate fundamental rights, they are actually protecting democracy.[5] Similarly, Aharon Barak, a former president of the Supreme Court of Israel, contends that "democracy has its own internal morality based on the dignity and equality of all human beings." Democracy, he asserts, "cannot exist without the protection of individual human rights—rights so essential that they must be insulated from the power of the majority." Judicial review may not be strictly necessary in all countries, he argues, but it is generally to be preferred in order to protect democracy itself.[6]

In the American context, Ronald Dworkin has also claimed that there is no democratic deficit when courts overturn laws on the grounds that they do not satisfy certain preconditions that the political process must respect before it is entitled to any moral value. These "democratic conditions," as he calls them, are necessary to guarantee individuals their moral membership in the political community. The community must give each person a part in any collective decision, a stake in it, and independence from it. That is, each person must have an opportunity to make a difference in the collective decisions; each person's interests must be taken into account with equal concern; and each person must be left free to take personal responsibility for deciding what kind of life he or she values.[7]

This demanding conception of democracy that Ferrajoli, Barak, Dworkin, and many others endorse is perfectly acceptable. There is no need to quarrel with the proposition that a genuine democracy can exist only if certain fundamental rights are respected. Even Jürgen Habermas, who seems to espouse a more procedural interpretation of democracy, insists that fundamental rights are strongly intertwined with it, so "the constitutional court should keep watch over just that system of rights that makes citizens' private and public autonomy equally possible."[8] The real question is this: Are the political processes in the countries we are talking about—when we talk about judicial review—decent enough from a democratic perspective, or on the contrary, are they too flawed?

Dworkin's view is that they are decent enough. In particular, he claims that the political system in the United States passes the threshold of legitimacy. He writes: "In a decent working democracy, like the United States, the democratic conditions set out in the Constitution are sufficiently met in practice so that there is no unfairness in allowing national and local legislatures the powers they have under standing arrangements. On the contrary, democracy would be extinguished by any general constitutional change that gave an oligarchy of unelected experts power to overrule and replace any legislative decision they thought unwise or unjust. Even if the experts always improved the legislation they rejected—always stipulated fairer income taxes than the legislature had enacted, for example—there would be a loss in self-government which the merits of their decisions could not extinguish."[9]

It is different, however, Dworkin argues, "when the question is plausibly raised whether some rule or regulation or policy itself undercuts or weakens the democratic character of the community, and the constitutional arrangement assigns *that* question to a court."[10] He gives the example of a law that makes it a crime for someone to burn his own American flag as an act of protest—a law that restricts freedom of speech.

The reason Dworkin offers to support his thesis is this: if the court gets it right and strikes down a statute like that (a statute that presumably undercuts or weakens the democratic conditions), a democratic gain is obtained; the court has preserved the democratic conditions that such a law undermined. It is true, he acknowledges, that if the court gets it wrong, there is a cost. "Certainly it impairs democracy when an authoritative court makes the wrong decision about what the democratic conditions require—but no more than it does when a majoritarian legislature makes a wrong constitutional decision that is allowed to stand. The possibility of error is symmetrical."[11] This leads him to conclude that the majoritarian premise on which the democratic objection is based is "confused."

This argument is not persuasive, however. Either the political system is not working well enough for us to say that it satisfies the democratic conditions to a sufficient extent, or it is. If it is not, there is certainly no cost when unelected experts or courts strike down statutes enacted by the popular assembly and replace them with better ones. If, on the contrary, the political system is in good order and does respect those democratic conditions, there will be a cost when unelected experts or courts strike down the laws that derive from it. The cost will register whether or not courts get things right. More specifically, if courts get it right when they invalidate a law on the grounds that it undermines the democratic conditions, they will generate a democratic gain that will outweigh the democratic cost. But the cost will be present.

Suppose, to use Dworkin's example, that the legislature enacts a law that prohibits burning the American flag as an act of protest. If Dworkin is consistent with his initial assumption that the American process works sufficiently well, he must accept that the democratic conditions of the political process that has created that law are sufficiently met. Let us call P_1 that political procedure. If a court overturns a law that has been generated by P_1, there is a democratic cost in that judicial decision, just as there would be a democratic cost, according to Dworkin, if a body of experts struck down tax laws generated by P_1, even if the experts replaced those laws with better ones.

It is true that there is a difference between the two cases. If the law against flag burning undermines the democratic conditions, whereas the tax law—however unwise—does not, there will be a gain of a democratic sort if the court invalidates the former, whereas there will be no gain of that sort if it invalidates the latter. What the court does in the first case is react against the political procedure that emerges *after* the enactment of the flag-burning law. This new procedure (P_2) is defective in light of the democratic conditions, for freedom of speech is unduly restricted. By invalidating the statute, the court restores the previous procedure (P_1). Because P_2 does not satisfy the democratic conditions whereas P_1 did, there is a democratic gain when the court restores P_1. But there is still a cost. After all, the flag-burning law was enacted by P_1, a procedure that was unimpeachable from a democratic perspective.

It would be tempting to believe that it does not much matter whether there is a democratic loss. If, in the end, there is a democratic gain that offsets any possible loss, why should we care whether there really is such a loss? But we should care. If there is a democratic loss, we need to believe that courts will produce the democratic benefit that can override it. And this belief depends on the expectation that, when it comes to the democratic conditions, the judiciary will get things right more often than the majoritarian legislature. And we need, of course, an instrumental argument to support this expectation. If we have serious doubts about the plausibility of that instrumental argument, we will have a reason to reject constitutional review by courts in order to avoid the democratic loss. In contrast, if we think, as Dworkin does, that no democratic cost is at stake, there is no similar pressure to make sure that there is an instrumental advantage to judicial review. Under Dworkin's theory, even if we doubt the plausibility of the instrumental argument, we can still hold to judicial review; since there is no democratic loss to take into account, there is no democratic reason to prefer the majoritarian political process over courts.

THE CONSTITUTION AS THE WILL OF THE PEOPLE

There is another way one could deny the tension between judicial review and democracy. One could argue that statutes have a weaker democratic pedigree than the constitution. Both Alexander Hamilton in *The Federalist* No. 78 and Chief Justice John Marshall in *Marbury v. Madison* emphasized the popular character of the constitution. Whereas the constitution embodies the will of the people, they claimed, statutes enacted by the legislature are merely the expression of the will of their representatives.

This dualism in the theory of democracy has been defended by modern scholars in different countries. Bruce Ackerman, for example, argues that there is no democratic objection to judicial review: when courts strike down a statute, they preserve the principles that rest on the considered judgments of the people, as expressed in those extraordinary moments of democratic deliberation that he calls "constitutional moments," against their erosion by the will of ordinary politicians in times of normal politics.[12] Jed Rubenfeld similarly views the constitution and its amendments as the best expression of democratic will through time: the people truly govern themselves when they lay down enduring political commitments. The constitution, which embodies such commitments, does not really constrain democracy—it is democracy.[13]

In a similar vein, but speaking within the French constitutional tradition, Dominique Rousseau and Michel Fromont take the constitution to be a more genuine expression of democratic will than ordinary legislation. By invalidating a statute in the name of the constitution, a court tries to preserve a norm that is directly connected to the deep convictions of citizens about their rights, against the contrary decisions of politicians.[14] Every time the French Constitutional Council subjects a statute to scrutiny, for example, it acts as a mirror that allows the people to look at themselves and to realize that they are indeed the sovereign, entitled to fundamental rights, whereas their representatives are not, even if they speak in the name of the people.[15] Another version of this idea is offered by Philippe Blachèr when he suggests that the court preserves the will of the perpetual people, which is composed of a chain of generations.[16] Whatever the rationale for this dualism, the French Constitutional Council seems to have a similar theory in mind. It declared in a famous decision that "la loi votée . . . n'exprime la volonté générale que dans le respect de la Constitution."[17] That is, the law enacted by a vote in parliament does not express the general will unless it respects the constitution. This holding entails the rejection of the traditional understanding that prevailed in France during the nineteenth century and part of the twentieth century, which conceived of ordinary legislation as the unconstrained expression of the general will. The constitution is now regarded as incorporating a more profound general will of the people, a will that ordinary legislation must respect.

The extent to which the democratic system is structured along these dualist lines depends on the particular characteristics of each country. If, indeed, the constitution is the expression of a higher form of democratic politics than an ordinary statute enacted by the parliament, there is certainly a democratic gain if a court strikes down a statute that is unconstitutional. The problem is that in many cases, controversy inevitably arises as to how the constitutional text is to be interpreted. Abstraction is a source of interpretive indeterminacy, as the scholars and judges who defend the dualist theory are fully aware. The court can get things right when it tries to interpret the will of the people that the constitution embodies, but it can also get them wrong.

The question, then, is whether we can completely disregard the judgment of the majority of a popularly elected parliament when it comes to interpreting the constitution. It seems implausible to do so. Something of democratic value is at stake when the judgment of a parliamentary majority is disqualified by a court. The fact that the document that is being enforced as higher law is more strongly linked to the people than the ordinary statute does not alter this conclusion. It is a court that is interpreting the document, and the court is less connected to the people than the popularly elected parliament is. If an unelected king were allowed to nullify the laws passed by a democratically elected assembly, it would not be sufficient to point to the popular source of the constitution that the king was interpreting, in order to answer the democratic objection to his having that power.

THE DEMOCRATIC VIRTUES OF THE JUDICIAL PROCESS

A third strategy to undermine the majoritarian premise that inspires the democratic objection to constitutional review appeals to the intrinsic virtues of the judicial process. Lawrence Sager, for example, accepts that democracy means that people can participate as equals in the process of deliberation about rights, but he believes that democracy has two faces or modalities. One is the "electoral" modality: people participate as equals by being equally entitled to vote for political representatives. The other mode of participation is "deliberative": it consists in having one's interests and rights seriously considered by those in authority. As he describes it,

"Any member of the community is entitled, on this account, to have each deliberator assess her claims on its merits, notwithstanding the number of votes that stand behind her, notwithstanding how many dollars she is able to deploy on her behalf, and notwithstanding what influence she has in the community."[18]

Sager argues that although legislatures are the preferred venues for the electoral modality of democratic participation, courts are better forums for the deliberative modality. "When a constitutional protagonist turns to the courts," Sager writes, "she can be anyone; she can represent a minority of one or be a member of a group that is widely ridiculed or deplored." Much of what is good in constitutional law, he observes, has been brought about by the claims of such groups. "What matters is the strength of her argument in the eyes of judges, and, failing her success, she is entitled to an explanation of why her claim was found wanting."[19]

Sager's interesting argument invites us to enrich our understanding of the intrinsic virtues that the political and judicial processes can each offer in terms of democratic values. It reinforces, for example, a point I made earlier, namely, that it was objectionable that there was no way in France (until the 2008 reform) for individuals to go to the courts and argue the unconstitutionality of a statute that affected them. Under that arrangement, whether someone was entitled to go to court and complain about a majoritarian piece of legislation depended on the number of votes that supported him or her: sixty deputies or sixty senators were needed. From a democratic point of view, Sager would argue, this was an undesirable restriction.

Sager's insight points to the need to take into account the two forms of democratic participation that he distinguishes. But it is important to balance them in the right way when institutions are designed. The deliberative modality cannot simply replace the electoral one. Democracy, of course, is not only a matter of making one's voice heard and having one's opinions seriously taken into account by others. It is also a question of participating in the decision-making process itself. Courts may be better than legislatures at carefully listening to the arguments that a citizen makes. But when it comes to deciding what to do, once the debate is over, courts have a democratic disadvantage when compared with legislatures. Citizens participate indirectly in the legislative process, for they periodically elect their representatives and can make them accountable, whereas courts are protected against popular pressures and are not accountable through regular elections.

Sager acknowledges all of this: "No society without a robust place for popular politics [by which he refers to the electoral form of democratic participation] can be counted as democratic or just."[20] Accordingly, he thinks that the domain of constitutional justice (the matters that the constitution addresses in order to constrain the legislature) needs to be limited: it should not "unduly congest the field over which democratic choice can be made."[21] Still, at some point, Sager seems to give too much weight to the deliberative modality of participation. Suppose, he says, that Great Britain and the United States were identical in their conformity with the fundamental requirements of justice. If the only difference were that judicial review of legislation existed in the United States but not in Great Britain, would we conclude that Great Britain was a more democratic political community than the United States? His answer is no: Great Britain would not be more democratic than the United States. Actually, he thinks that the United States would get some extra points: "A democratic state is if anything enriched *in coin of democracy itself* by the inclusion of a constitutionally responsible judiciary within its portfolio of governing institutions."[22]

This conclusion is exaggerated, I think. It is one thing to emphasize the democratic virtues of a judicial process in terms of deliberation. It is quite another to believe that those virtues are weighty enough to offset the democratic loss that judicial review entails from an electoral point of view. Suppose that an unelected queen in a small community had the power to issue legislation, but only after having carefully heard the opinions of all citizens and after having responded to their arguments in written form. Sager would no doubt think that any democratic gain in terms of deliberative participation would not be sufficient to compensate for the fact that it is the queen who ultimately enacts the laws, instead of members of a popularly elected assembly. This extreme example suggests that the electoral dimension of equal participation has a special force within the world of democratic virtues. The virtues of the deliberative form of participation are important, as Sager rightly insists, but they are insufficient to extinguish that special force.

RESPONDING TO THE DEMOCRATIC OBJECTION

What can we say, then, to "respond" to the democratic objection if, indeed, we are to accept that there is a tension between judicial review and democracy? The first thing to say, it seems to me, is that the instrumental arguments to support judicial review should trump other considerations connected to the intrinsic virtues of the democratic process. In previous chapters, I have contended that we have reasons to believe that a constitutional judiciary can help the political community take fundamental rights seriously and in a principled manner. If that line of defense is plausible, we should be prepared to pay the price that judicial review entails in terms of intrinsic democratic values. Getting the right result in matters of substantive justice should be our priority—whether or not the principles at stake are to be viewed as part of the definition of democracy. As John Rawls put it, referring to the constitutional restrictions that limit the space for the right of political participation, "The relevant point is that to justify these restrictions one must maintain that from the perspective of the representative citizen in the constitutional convention the less extensive freedom of participation is sufficiently outweighed by the greater security and extent of the other liberties."[23] Jeremy Waldron, who is a strong critic of judicial review, accepts the idea that instrumental arguments that point to substantive justice have a special weight and should override contrary arguments that appeal to the intrinsic merits of procedures.[24]

Representative democracy, for example, may be thought to be less democratic from an intrinsic point of view than direct democracy, but we have reasons of an instrumental kind to prefer the former to the latter: overall, representative democracy tends to generate better outcomes. Thoughtful and careful deliberation is necessary in order to make the right decisions on a regular basis. Since in modern circumstances it would be impossible for all citizens to devote their time to discussing public issues, it is reasonable to introduce a division of labor between citizens and their representatives.[25] A similar move can be made regarding constitutional review: if there is an instrumental advantage to it, in connection with certain issues, we should not be reluctant to establish it, despite the democratic costs that the judicial invalidation of a statute entails.

Second, we should note that the role of constitutional judges is inevitably limited, even when they exercise their functions in a rather activist manner, for their job is specialized: they generally deal with fundamental rights as side constraints on governmental policies. They are not in the business of making the central policy decisions in many areas of social life. There is thus ample room for democratic decision making with respect to a great number of issues that are both substantively important and very high on the public's agenda, as Frederick Schauer has pointed out in the American context.[26]

Third, we need to minimize the democratic problem that judicial review poses, to the extent possible—that is, to the extent that the instrumental considerations that justify the institution permit. Here we face a tension between two aspirations. On the one hand, we want constitutional judges to be sufficiently protected against majoritarian pressures. Judicial independence is an important condition that makes it possible for courts to make their contribution. On the other hand, the values that we want constitutional judges to interpret and elaborate are those that are part of the political consensus that the constitution embodies. It is values that have this democratic pedigree that are to be safeguarded. A link must therefore be established between constitutional judges and the democratic branches. As Owen Fiss suggests, the idea is not to make courts a democratic institution like a parliament, but rather to make them part of a larger whole that is democratic.[27]

There are two fundamental ways in which this link can be established. One is through the appointment process: judges who are in charge of constitutional review can be selected by the democratic branches. The other depends on the avenues that the political institutions are authorized to use to respond to judicial interpretations that they disagree with. The political reactions to the court can be articulated in various ways. "Soft" responses can be expressed at the legislative level. It may be possible, for example, for the parliament to pass a new statute that conflicts with the established judicial doctrine in order to generate a second round of debate that will give the court the opportunity to reconsider its earlier holdings. It seems reasonable, however, to require the passage of a certain period of time. As a general rule, the legislature should not reenact a statute immediately after it has been invalidated by the court.[28] "Strong" responses can be articulated through constitutional amendments. It should not be too easy, however, for the political process to resort to this kind of response. If there is an instrumental argument in favor of judicial review, the court's decisions should be shielded against easy political override. The process of constitutional amendment should be relatively onerous (requiring a parliamentary supermajority or successive votes or a referendum or a special convention, for example).[29]

Of course, to the extent that courts are checked by the political branches in these various ways (*ex ante,* through judicial appointments; *ex post,* through legislative and constitutional responses), courts do not have an unlimited capacity to go against majoritarian currents. As Barry Friedman has argued, a systematic study of the conditions under which judges carry out their task reveals that the space for a countermajoritarian performance is rather limited.[30] Still, there is some space for it. The U.S. Supreme Court's responsiveness to public opinion, for example, "is not to immediate popular preference so much as to a body of opinion that endures over time."[31] We should therefore design the system so that courts do a good job when they exercise constitutional review in that relatively limited space and so that the democratic checks on their performance are properly articulated.

With all this background in mind, let us now turn to the European model. Are there any potential advantages in having constitutional courts when it comes to subjecting judicial review of legislation to the necessary democratic checks?

CHAPTER NINE

Democratic Checks on Courts

FOR EUROPEAN COUNTRIES of the civil-law tradition, I want to claim, there are indeed some advantages to constitutional courts in terms of democratic checks.

APPOINTING CONSTITUTIONAL JUDGES

Consider, first, the appointment process. European countries have generally felt the need to place legislative review in the hands of judges who are chosen through a procedure in which the democratic branches have an important say. As Pedro Cruz Villalón explains, the historical emergence of constitutional review was possible only because the bodies in charge acquired an intense democratic legitimacy.[1]

The problem, however, is that most European countries prefer a nonpolitical method to recruit the ordinary judiciary. Even though the executive or the legislature sometimes takes part in the selection processes, more independent bodies of several kinds, largely staffed by senior judges, have been created to limit their discretion. The tendency in many nations is to better protect judicial independence through new arrangements that try to reduce the influence exerted by the political branches.[2] It is revealing, for example, that the European Charter on the Statute for Judges, which was adopted in 1998 within the framework of the Council of Europe, sets out a general principle against the political selection

98

of judges: "In respect of every decision affecting the selection, recruitment, appointment, career progress or termination of office of a judge, the statute envisages the intervention of an authority independent of the executive and legislative powers."[3] Moreover, "the statute excludes any candidate being ruled out by reason only of their sex, or ethnic or social origin, *or by reason of their philosophical and political opinions* or religious convictions."[4] Although this document has no binding force, it captures the nonpolitical model of judicial selection that civil-law countries in Europe tend to follow.

The creation of a separate constitutional tribunal, of course, helps satisfy both needs: it is possible to have a more democratic procedure for appointing constitutional judges and to preserve the more bureaucratic or professional system for the rest of judges. This contrast is very typical in Europe.[5]

True, the appointment process that applies to constitutional judges does not generate as intense a public discussion as one finds in the United States when Supreme Court vacancies have to be filled. Indeed, there is sometimes criticism in Europe for the excessive secrecy of the political bargains that lead to the choice of constitutional judges.[6] Still, the process for selecting constitutional judges registers the inputs of the democratic institutions in a way that is generally not true of the method used to pick ordinary judges in European civil-law countries.

The dualist structure, moreover, makes it possible for the appointing authorities to evaluate the judicial candidates differently, depending on the diverse fields of the law they are to be chosen for. The kinds of questions those authorities may want to ask when selecting judges for the constitutional court differ from those that are relevant to picking judges for the supreme court's chamber that is specialized in tax law, say. These distinctions are not possible in the United States, where the U.S. Supreme Court is both a constitutional tribunal and the highest court in charge of federal ordinary law. According to Richard Posner, "The more that constitutional law dominates the Court's docket, the more that appointments to the Court focus on the candidate's likely position in constitutional cases rather than on competence in business law and other statutory fields."[7]

There is a further argument to be mentioned in favor of constitutional courts, an argument that applies to those nations that have started a democratic era after suffering an authoritarian regime. This was the situation in Italy and Germany after the Second World War, for example, and in Spain after Franco's death in 1975. If the regular courts have not been sufficiently purged of judges who were attached to the values of the past regime, it makes no sense for the new constitution to bestow upon them the power to review legislation enacted by the new democratic parliament. It is better to establish a constitutional court, whose members can be drawn from a group of jurists who pass the necessary liberal and democratic tests. With some qualifications, this is also part of the reason Central-Eastern European countries tended to favor constitutional courts after the collapse of the Communist regimes.[8]

In sum, the dualist structure that characterizes the centralized model of judicial review can be used to enhance the democratic legitimacy of constitutional judges while maintaining the more traditional (bureaucratic or professional) system for the selection of ordinary judges—a system that many countries in Europe wish to retain.[9]

LIMITING THE TERMS OF CONSTITUTIONAL JUDGES

Similarly, the dualist structure of the European model makes it possible to treat the members of the constitutional court differently from regular judges when it comes to tenure: limited tenure can be established for the former, whereas tenure for life or until a prescribed retirement age can be accorded to the latter. We find this distinction in many European countries, such as France, Germany, Italy, Portugal, and Spain.[10]

The idea behind this arrangement is that no wide gap should emerge between the court's constitutional jurisprudence, on the one hand, and the basic moral beliefs of the people and their political representatives, on the other. Limited tenure seems better than life tenure to prevent this from happening. It is not problematic to give ordinary judges tenure for life (or until retirement age), since their statutory interpretations can be easily overridden by ordinary legislative means. Constitutional judges, in contrast, cannot be so easily checked, since burdensome procedures must be followed to amend the constitution. As Gustavo Zagrebelsky argues, life tenure for constitutional judges has the disadvantage that it cannot guarantee in a satisfactory manner "the constant adequacy of the Court to the changes in the cultural conditions of the country."[11]

Interestingly, an increasing number of scholars in the United States are of the view that life tenure for federal judges is a bad idea, for democratic reasons.[12] Ronald Dworkin, for example, has written: "We must not condemn judicial review as undemocratic whenever we disagree with the decisions the Court makes. I am worried, however, about an ideological administration appointing young ideological justices whose tenure on the Court will last for generations, long after the nation has steered itself back to the middle as, so far, it always has." For this reason, he recommends amending the U.S. Constitution "to institute a term limit for Supreme Court justices, a maximum of fifteen years' tenure, perhaps."[13]

One is entitled to have some misgivings about limited tenure, however. Judicial independence may suffer, even if constitutional judges cannot be reappointed for a second term. (In France, Germany, Italy, Portugal, and Spain, for example, the members of the constitutional court cannot be reappointed.[14] This is in contrast to the situation in Central-Eastern Europe, where the prevailing pattern is that judges can be appointed for a second term.[15]) The prohibition against reappointment is probably insufficient, for judges may be worried about their future jobs. Charles Eisenmann, writing in 1928, criticized limited tenure on these grounds. What is truly important, he reasoned, is not how the judges of the constitutional court are selected but whether they have anything to fear or to expect from the political authorities once they are appointed. The best guarantee of judicial independence, he claimed, is life tenure.[16] Similarly, referring to constitutional courts in Europe, Christopher Eisgruber points out that "judges who serve a single, non-renewable term have no reason to worry about retaining their jobs as judges, but they do have to worry about what they will do next. They might simply retire after serving on the court, but they might want high-paying jobs in the private sector, or they might want to run for political office, or they might covet another political appointment—as, say, attorney general or ambassador to Italy."[17] Indeed, it is not rare for former judges of constitutional courts to be appointed by the political branches to very interesting positions. As Alessandro Pizzorusso suggests, commenting on the Italian experience, "It is questionable whether non-reeligibility for nomination is really sufficient to ensure the judges' independence. If we consider that some of them, at the end of their term of office, have been nominated or elected to important political offices, some doubt on the matter seems justified."[18]

It would be inconsistent to deny that there is a risk to judicial independence here while insisting on the importance of the fact that the terms of judges who serve on the constitutional court are not renewable. If the political branches could affect judicial independence by using the carrot of renewing judicial terms, why should we believe that they cannot affect independence by using the carrot of attractive posts after the terms have expired? Actually, getting a new job after stepping down from the court may be more interesting than being appointed again. After some years of sitting on the court, one may get tired!

One way to counteract this risk to judicial independence is to prohibit the publication of dissenting opinions. The secrecy of the votes would shield judges against undue external pressures.[19] As John Ferejohn and Pasquale Pasquino have argued, the diverse judges on the constitutional court will try to moderate their views and reach an accommodation if they know that they are prohibited from filing dissents for the public to read. The court will tend to be "internally deliberative" instead of "externally deliberative."[20] This practice may protect the court against political retaliation.

It is a pity, however, that we must resort to this solution in order to safeguard judicial independence. As I argued in chapter 5, there are dialogical advantages in allowing the publication of dissenting opinions. Dissents are especially necessary in the European model. Whereas in a decentralized system of the American type, lower courts have offered their constitutional points of view before a case finally reaches the supreme court, within the European model, the constitutional court is the only court to speak. No other judicial voices are heard (or only very soft voices are heard to the extent that ordinary judges can ask the constitutional court to review a statute they have some doubts about). There is a dialogic disadvantage in the European model in this regard, as was already noted. To offset, to a certain extent, this absence of plurality, it is necessary to permit the public expression of the internal plurality that exists within the constitutional court. Such transparency, moreover, helps attract the attention of the media and the general public.[21] The publication of dissents should therefore be welcome. But in that case, limited terms are not advisable.

Another disadvantage of limited terms is that if the composition of the constitutional court changes very often, the justices are prone to be less sensitive to the future consequences of their rulings, for they may believe that the future court will not feel strongly bound by what they now hold. This is not advisable in terms of generating a consistent juris-prudence. As Adrian Vermeule has explained in the American context, the durability of the general and prospective rules that a court sets out is of major importance in enhancing the likelihood that those rules will have the right content. Durability has a veil-of-ignorance effect. Because the court will have to stick to the consequences of its present ruling in future cases, and since it is not easy to predict who will be affected by it, the court has an incentive to be careful. If, in contrast, the court knows that the doctrines it announces today will be easily ignored by future judges, that incentive is weaker.[22]

For all these reasons, one may doubt that limited tenure is the best institutional choice, even for members of a constitutional tribunal. Tenure until retirement age may be a better option. Some European countries that have constitutional courts (Austria, Belgium, and Luxemburg, for instance) follow this system.[23] The potential gap between the court and popular sentiment can still be reduced, for there is a significant difference between life tenure, on the one hand, and occupying judicial office until a fixed retirement age (seventy years, say), on the other. Under the latter arrangement, judges do not get extremely old or out of touch with the general environment. If a supermajority of the parliament, moreover, is required for the selection of constitutional judges (or for most of them), it is unlikely that an important divorce will emerge in the future between the court's jurisprudence and the basic beliefs of the popular branches: the supermajority requirement tends to guarantee that the judges who are appointed to the court do not belong to the ideological extremes but are instead rather centrist. We find this arrangement in Belgium, Germany, Italy, Portugal, and Spain, for instance.[24]

In any case, whether or not limited tenure for constitutional judges is ultimately a good idea, the important point is that the dualist structure that characterizes the European model makes it possible to introduce flexibility in the system when dealing with these matters. Specific rules may be designed for constitutional judges, different from those that apply to ordinary judges, to enhance the democratic legitimacy of the consti-tutional court.

RESPONDING TO THE COURT: CONSTITUTIONAL AMENDMENTS

Finally, when it comes to the political responses to judicial interpreta-tions of the constitution, there is another reason for civil-law countries to prefer constitutional courts. Such democratic checks can be activated in the right way only if the political branches get a clear picture of what the courts are saying. If legislative review were decentralized, ordinary judges would reach different conclusions and it would take some time before the supreme courts could settle the interpretive disagreements. The various supreme courts, moreover, might lay down contradictory doctrines. The centralized system seems to be a better option: the government and the legislature do not have to pay attention to what ordinary judges do. When it comes to the constitutional dialogue over parliamentary enactments, the interlocutor is the constitutional court exclusively.

It is important to note, in this regard, that in some countries, only when political checks of the right sort have been set up has judicial review of legislation finally been accepted as a legitimate arrangement. France is a good example. In the nineteenth century, Alexis de Tocqueville ex-plained that the reason the French could not accept judicial review under the constitution of 1830 was that it was not possible to amend the constitu-tion. "If in France the tribunals were authorized to disobey the laws on the ground of their being opposed to the constitution, the constituent power would in fact be placed in their hands, since they alone would have the right of interpreting a constitution of which no authority could change the terms." In contrast, he wrote, "in America, where the nation can al-ways reduce its magistrates to obedience by changing the Constitution, no danger of this kind is to be feared."[25]

Similarly, Hans Kelsen insisted on the amendability of modern con-stitutions. He argued that the constitution is not immutable natural law. As any legal norm, it is created at a particular moment and can be modi-fied at any time following certain political procedures. Actually, Kelsen drew an extreme conclusion from this basic idea when he argued that all instances of unconstitutionality are in the end formal: even if a statute is unconstitutional because its content is incompatible with the substantive standards that the constitution embodies, the statute has merely a formal defect in that it has not been enacted through the right procedures. The norm that the statute expresses would have been valid if it had been approved as a provision of constitutional rank through the procedure that is used to amend the constitution.[26]

One of Kelsen's French students, Charles Eisenmann, similarly insisted that unless the constitution was detached from immutable natural law, there was no hope for judicial review to be introduced in France. The bill of rights, in particular, had to be made part of the constitution and thus susceptible to future modification like any other constitutional clause.[27]

It is precisely the possibility of amending the constitution of 1958 that is often mentioned by French scholars as a crucial ingredient of the democratic legitimacy of judicial review.[28] Thus, Louis Favoreu argued that the constitutional court does not frustrate the will of the people when it checks statutes: it merely indicates whether the ordinary legislative track or the constitutional track must be followed to enact a particular norm. The court acts as a "switchman" (*aiguilleur*) that directs the normative train to one track or another.[29] Georges Vedel enriched this metaphor by comparing a constitutional amendment to the old institution of *lit de justice*. In the ancien régime, the sovereign king could appear before a court (parlement) to overturn any judicial ruling. Vedel argued that "the obstacle the law encounters in the constitution can be removed by the sovereign people or their representatives if they take recourse to the supreme mode of expression: constitutional revision. If judges do not govern, it is because, at any moment, the sovereign, on the condition of appearing in full majesty, can, in a sort of *lit de justice,* overturn their rulings."[30]

According to some scholars, especially those of a more "positivist" bent, the French Constitutional Council obtained full democratic legitimacy in November 1993, when the constitution was amended to override the court's judgment on the right of asylum.[31] This was the first time that an amendment had been enacted to respond to the court. It happened again in July 1999, when the constitution was modified to overturn a judgment striking down a law that imposed gender parity in the electoral lists.

The French Constitutional Council has made clear, moreover, that it has no power to review the validity of constitutional amendments, even if the constitution declares (in article 89) that the republican form of government is unalterable and that the integrity of the territory must be respected.[32] After the constitution was amended in 1999 to make it possible for the legislature to impose quotas to ensure gender parity in political institutions, for example, a new statute on this matter was challenged by a group of senators. The court rejected their complaint, reasoning that it is perfectly possible for the *pouvoir constituant* to introduce new rules in the constitution in order to derogate from the principles that the court had invoked in earlier decisions.[33]

That the constitution can be changed by the political branches is indeed of key importance in increasing the democratic acceptability of judicial review of legislation. In some countries, however, courts have something to say about the validity of constitutional amendments. Sometimes their intervention is mainly "procedural." In Austria and Spain, for instance, all parts of the constitution can be changed, but there are two different amendment procedures.[34] A general procedure has been established for ordinary modifications, whereas a more onerous one is required for those amendments that entail a total revision of the constitution or that affect certain sections or basic principles that are considered to be of fundamental importance. Although a parliamentary supermajority is normally sufficient to change the constitution, a popular referendum is necessary to approve a total revision or an amendment that affects certain aspects of the constitution. This means that the court can strike down an amendment that has been enacted through the ordinary procedure when the more onerous one is required. Thus, on October 11, 2001, the Austrian Constitutional Court declared for the first time the invalidity of a constitutional reform, on the grounds that it amounted to a total revision of the constitution and should therefore have been approved by the people themselves in a referendum.[35]

In other countries, however, the court's intervention is more "substantive," for the constitution explicitly places certain principles beyond the reach of the amendment power, or it is interpreted by judges and scholars to do so. In Germany, for instance, article 79.3 of the Basic Law explicitly gives absolute protection to the principles enshrined in article 1 (human dignity) and in article 20 (democratic principles, the rule of law, and the right to resistance), as well as certain federal principles (the division of the federation into Länder and their participation in legislation). The Federal Constitutional Court of Germany has asserted its authority to review constitutional amendments in light of these intangible principles.[36] Similarly, in Italy the court has claimed its power to declare the invalidity of constitutional amendments that offend certain basic principles.[37] Apart from the republican form of government, which the constitution explicitly entrenches against any future reform (article 139), the court has referred to certain implicit "supreme values" that the constitution is based on. Scholars usually mention the democratic principle, inviolable rights, and the rigidity of the constitution itself as part of this untouchable essence that the court must shield against revisions.[38] The Portuguese Constitution, in turn, includes a long list of principles that the amending power must respect, such as national independence and the unity of the state, the republican form of government, the separation of church and state, citizen rights, rights of workers, political rights, judicial independence, constitutional review, and local and regional autonomy (article 288). The Portuguese Constitutional Court (as well as lower courts) is clearly entitled to review amendments in light of the constraints that this provision enumerates.[39] Even in the United States, it bears mentioning, some scholars have argued that there are substantive limits to constitutional amendments, even if they are not explicit.[40]

It would seem that the democratic links between the political branches and constitutional judges are weaker if certain principles are entrenched against amendment. Still, there is room for dialogical interactions, for when courts have to interpret the unalterable principles, they can be sensitive to the constitutional changes brought about by the political actors. Since its enactment in 1949, for example, the German Basic Law has been revised many times (fifty-two amendments have been introduced so far). The court, however, has never declared any of them to be contrary to the unalterable principles. To a large extent, this is because the political branches have been careful not to deviate from the court's rulings. But there have been interpretive disagreements in some cases: with respect to abortion, for example, and concerning the conflict between religious liberty and the protection of animals.[41] Similarly, the jurisprudence of the Italian Constitutional Court has been qualified through amendments— in connection with gender parity, for example, and with respect to constitutional guarantees of the rights of criminal defendants.[42] So, even if there are substantive limits to constitutional amendments, there seems to be interpretive room for the political branches to respond to the court's case law.

PART THREE CONSTITUTIONAL COURTS UNDER PRESSURE

CHAPTER TEN

Decentralizing Tendencies in the System

IN THE PREVIOUS CHAPTERS, I have presented a cluster of arguments to support the case in favor of creating and maintaining a centralized model of judicial review in European civil-law countries. Some forces, both internal and external to the domestic legal systems, however, are pushing the model toward a more decentralized arrangement. Internally, the pressure comes from the principle that ordinary judges should interpret statutes in conformity with the constitution. Externally, the pressure derives from supranational developments. Ordinary judges, working under the guidance of the European Court of Justice, are entitled to review national legislation to guarantee that the laws of the European Union are respected. In some countries, moreover, ordinary judges can also invoke the European Convention on Human Rights, as interpreted by the European Court of Human Rights, to set aside domestic legislation.

These developments must be taken seriously, since they may harm some of the values that inspire the centralized model. To what extent are these values in danger, and what should be done to better serve them? Are there any corrections to be introduced? In this chapter I take up the internal aspect of the problem, and chapters 11 and 12 are devoted to the external dimension.

READING STATUTES IN LIGHT OF THE CONSTITUTION

It is commonly observed by European scholars that the establishment of a constitutional tribunal that is relatively detached from the ordinary judiciary does not mean that the latter can be indifferent to constitutional principles when deciding specific controversies. Even if regular courts are not authorized to disregard parliamentary enactments on their own, they should still act as guardians of the constitution. In particular, they should seek interpretive ways to make statutes cohere with the constitution. Thus, before certifying a question to the constitutional court (where this mechanism exists), ordinary judges are expected to look for an interpretation of the applicable law that will save its validity.[1] Constitutional courts have actually encouraged judges to do so, sometimes pushing them in a strongly "antiformalist" direction.[2]

It bears emphasizing that courts do not avoid a constitutional issue when they ascribe a particular meaning to a statute in order to make it comport with the constitution. On the contrary, they fully deal with it. They declare that the constitution guarantees a particular principle, and they hold that the statute must be read in a certain way in order to fully respect that principle. They avoid the conclusion that the statute is unconstitutional (and, therefore, they avoid asking the constitutional court to invalidate it), but they do not avoid the underlying interpretive controversy about the constitution.

Now, if ordinary judges must interpret legislative provisions in harmony with the constitution and only the constitutional court can set them aside, it is necessary to distinguish between those statutory readings that count as genuine "interpretations," on the one hand, and those readings that are no longer interpretations in that they entail a "correction" or "amendment" of the statutory provision under consideration, on the other. Obviously, if the division of labor that underlies the centralized model is to be respected, an ordinary judge cannot be allowed to make a legal provision say what nobody could reasonably read it to say. That would be equivalent to setting aside the statute in its original form and replacing it with a new one. The judge, in other words, would be "repairing" the statute to remove its constitutional defects. In a centralized system, only the constitutional court is entitled to do that. It is one thing to interpret a law in a way that ensures its conformity with the constitution. It is quite another to repair the law at the remedial stage, once the statute has been found to be unconstitutional. Ordinary judges can do the former but not the latter.[3]

Now, how serious is the risk that ordinary judges will engage in these kinds of statutory readjustments? Traditionally, the risk has been negligible. As was noted in chapter 7, judges in the civil-law tradition have historically been quite timorous when dealing with constitutional issues. As the constitution takes root in the legal culture, however, judges are more likely to take it into account in an assertive manner. They may be tempted to distort statutes under an interpretive guise in order to make the statutes cohere with what they think the constitution requires. Gustavo Zagrebelsky, for example, refers to the Italian experience in the 1970s, when some left-wing judges started to use the constitutional principle of equality in very activist ways, under the inspiration of the jurisprudential movement called *uso alternativo del diritto*. The Italian Constitutional Court had to intervene to protect legislation against potentially disruptive judicial developments.[4] Conservative judges, of course, could also erode statutes they disagreed with through "interpretation." As Zagrebelsky explains, the constitutional court's function nowadays is not only to check legislation but also to protect it against an excess of activism on the part of some ordinary judges. The court has become both the *censore* and the *difensore* of the legislature.[5]

As we will see, it is not always easy to determine whether a particular reading of a statute counts as a fair interpretation of it. The distinction between readings that are "possible" and those that are "too strained" is a matter of degree. But the distinction needs to be maintained, however difficult it may be to draw the line in the grey area. Otherwise, the European system of constitutional review collapses, and the values that are associated with it are put at risk.[6]

Consider legal certainty. As a general rule, there is a lot of controversy about the specific meaning to be ascribed to many constitutional clauses. Ordinary judges will have different views about this, and their disagreements over the meaning of the constitution will color their different readings of the legislative provision to be applied. If judges do not confine themselves to the statutory interpretations that are possible, but instead transcend those interpretations in order to correct what they think are the statute's constitutional defects, legal certainty is harmed. It is one thing for an ordinary judge to choose an interpretation of a statute that makes it cohere with the constitution when that interpretation is possible. It is quite another for a judge to correct the statute on constitutional grounds through an interpretation that is no longer possible in that it departs from what the statute rather clearly says and was meant to say. A forced reading that corrects a law may be justified in those rare cases in which there is no reasonable controversy as to the meaning of the constitution. It is then reasonable for individuals and citizens to predict that a given law will be read in a rather strained way in order to guarantee its consistency with the constitution. After all, courts have always revised statutes through corrective interpretations in order to avoid what everybody would agree are absurd outcomes. If there is controversy, however, judges should not distort the meaning of statutes.

Imagine, for example, that a criminal statute on abortion establishes in a rather clear way the list of situations in which abortion is permitted. It is obvious that different judges, relying on different theories about the constitutional provisions that protect life, dignity, privacy, liberty, and equality, can go in very different and unpredictable directions if they start to "correct" the statute on constitutional grounds through very farfetched interpretations—whether restrictive or expansive—that deviate from what appears to be its rather clear meaning. To preserve legal certainty, they should instead ask the constitutional court to express its judgment if they conclude that the statute offends constitutional principles.

The democratic values that inspire the centralized model press in the same direction. If a statute can fairly be read to mean different things, it makes sense for an ordinary judge to presume that the parliament did not mean to breach the constitution. It is therefore reasonable for the judge to choose an interpretation of the statute that ensures compliance with that higher law. When the statute cannot be so read, however, the system of public deliberation requires that the ordinary judge not depart from the meaning that most naturally flows from it. The parliament spoke through that law. The public debate that took place, both inside and outside the parliament, focused on the norm that was fairly ascribable to the enacted text. The statute was defended and criticized on the assumption that it meant, in accordance with conventional rules of language and ordinary legal interpretation, what was reasonable to understand it to mean. What is more, the governmental majority was probably convinced that the statute, so interpreted, was perfectly constitutional—that no correction was needed.

Within the centralized model, the governmental majority is entitled to have the statute reviewed in that special forum that has been created for these matters: the constitutional court. This body has a different composition than ordinary courts and is more strongly linked to the democratic branches. This is the institution that has the relevant expertise and legitimacy to give concrete meaning to the abstract principles that the constitution embodies. If an ordinary judge corrects the statute through a rather strained interpretation and does not send it to the constitutional court for review, the judge alters the division of labor that the system is based on. The ordinary judge, moreover, deprives the governmental majority of the opportunity to make its case. The government may want to convince the court that the questioned law needs no correction, that it is perfectly constitutional as it naturally reads. The ordinary judge also deprives the community as a whole of the more vibrant debate that a decision by the constitutional court can generate. Because of its higher public visibility, more attention is paid to the decisions of the constitutional court than to those rendered by ordinary judges. Finally, the capacity of the political branches to respond to judicial interpretations of the constitution in a coherent manner is diminished when they have to deal with the contradictory readings that may come from different ordinary courts instead of focusing on the constitutional court exclusively. For all these reasons, the European system cannot celebrate the idea of ordinary judges correcting statutes through strained readings.

The relevance of the distinction between interpretation and correction or amendment has also been appreciated in the United Kingdom since the enactment of the Human Rights Act 1998, which incorporates the European Convention on Human Rights into the domestic legal system. One of the interesting features of this law is that it establishes two techniques for courts to use when they review statutes for their conformity with the human rights that are enumerated in the act. First, all courts are required to interpret statutes (as well as other legal provisions) so that they are in harmony with human rights, "so far as it is possible to do so" (section 3). The second technique comes into play when it is not possible to interpret a statute so that it comports with human rights. The highest courts (not all the courts) are then authorized to issue a "declaration of incompatibility" against the statute. The effect of such a declaration is not to invalidate the statute or to set it aside for purposes of deciding the case. The court merely expresses its judgment that the statute should be amended, and a serious public debate is then expected to take place. The majority in the British parliament must decide whether to modify the law, given the court's judgment. (A fast legislative procedure can actually be initiated to enact the necessary amendments.)

Now, it is clear that the difference between these two techniques established by the Human Rights Act (interpretation in conformity and declaration of incompatibility) presupposes that it is feasible in most cases, though it may be difficult in others, to draw a line between interpretations of a statute that are possible and those that are not. A declaration of incompatibility is to be issued when the meaning of the legislative provision is clear enough and the relevant court thinks that it offends a particular human right. The most important dialogue between courts and the British parliament is expected to take place through the incompatibility mechanism. If judges resorted to fancy readings of statutes in order to avoid making a declaration of incompatibility, they would unduly frustrate the public debate that such a declaration is supposed to trigger.[7]

The centralized model of constitutional review relies on a similar distinction between statutory interpretations that are possible and those that are not. In the United Kingdom, what is at stake is whether a declaration of incompatibility (which has no binding legal effect) needs to be issued. In the centralized model, in contrast, what is at stake is whether the constitutional court, instead of ordinary courts, should speak. But the distinction that is doing the work is the same: the distinction between interpretations that are possible and those that are too strained to be acceptable. Moreover, in both systems there is a dialogic rationale in favor of this basic contrast. Judges in the United Kingdom should not prevent the political debate that a declaration of incompatibility is supposed to generate, and ordinary judges in the centralized model should not preclude the more vibrant debate that a decision by the constitutional court would attract given its higher public visibility.

PRESSURES TOWARD AN EXPANSIVE CONCEPTION OF INTERPRETATION

The problem, of course, is that it is hard to identify the conditions that the reading of a statute must satisfy for it to count as an interpretation that is possible rather than a contrived reading that amounts to an amendment. The contrast, as I said, is a matter of degree. There is no clear line that sharply separates interpretation from correction, but a continuum between the two extremes. Some European constitutional scholars have tried to furnish criteria to identify a relatively clear line, but their conclusions are rather vague.[8] The reading of the statute, they say, must be one that the text permits. That is fine, but the question is how to decide whether the text permits a particular interpretation. A literal interpretation is not always the only possible interpretation. Implicit exceptions, for example, can be read into a statute, and analogical extensions of its scope are sometimes allowed. (In the civil-law tradition, this is called "teleological" interpretation.)[9]

There is an institutional factor, moreover, that may push ordinary judges toward a rather generous view of what counts as a possible interpretation of a law: the length of time it takes the constitutional court to answer the questions put to it. The court needs time to respond, and during this time the parties to the original lawsuit have to wait. The longer the court takes to hand down its opinions, the more likely it is that ordinary judges will refuse to send statutes to the court and will instead resolve the underlying constitutional problems themselves through rather imaginative statutory readings.

The length of the delay varies greatly from country to country and from case to case. It can take a few months in Luxembourg, up to one year in Austria and Belgium, between one and two years in Italy, longer in Germany, and even longer in Spain (sometimes up to ten years!). It should be mentioned, in this connection, that the European Court of Human Rights condemned Germany in 1997 for a violation of article 6 of the European Convention on Human Rights, which guarantees the right to a fair and speedy trial, because the German Constitutional Court had taken seven years and four months in one case, and five years and three months in another case, to decide a constitutional question raised by an ordinary judge.[10] Quite apart from these extreme cases, judges in general may be tempted to engage in very flexible interpretations of statutory provisions in order to avoid staying the proceedings of the cases they are handling. To the extent that they do so, of course, the logic of the centralized system is undermined.

So what should be done? Three ideas come to mind. First, reforms should be introduced in countries such as Spain and, to a lesser extent,

Germany, where constitutional courts take too long to address the issues posed by ordinary judges. The root of the problem is that these courts have been given too many responsibilities beyond legislative review. It makes no sense to establish a special court whose main task is to test legislation for its conformity with the constitution and then assign so many other functions to it that it can no longer perform in an efficient manner what was initially regarded as its major task. A constitutional court need not be "pure," but it should be designed so that it can act as an efficient counterweight to the legislature. It should be able to render its judgments rather promptly whenever parliamentary enactments are challenged by ordinary courts (or by other institutions).

Second, provided the situation is not pathological, ordinary judges should be patient. They should understand that the system as a whole benefits enormously if they stay the proceedings and petition the constitutional court to review a statute. It is true that the parties to the lawsuit have to wait, but everybody gets the benefit of a ruling by the constitutional court, which will settle the issue with binding effects on all judges.

Third, an internal correction may have to be introduced in the centralized model with respect to those relatively rare cases in which, given the court's precedents, there is no doubt as to the meaning of the constitution. Let me explain this proposal in some detail.

READJUSTING THE CENTRALIZED MODEL: A MODEST CHANGE

European countries may have to reconsider in part the division of labor that characterizes the centralized model of constitutional review. The fundamental distinction between interpreting and setting aside legislative provisions should be enriched and qualified with a second distinction: Concerning a particular problem, has the constitutional court sufficiently fixed the meaning of the relevant constitutional clauses? The answer to this question is of key importance.

If the court has not yet had occasion to interpret the constitution with respect to a particular problem, or if the court's case law is not sufficiently clear, it is risky for an ordinary judge to depart from the relatively clear meaning of the applicable statute in order to make it comply with what he or she thinks the constitution requires. The ordinary judge is in that case working with his or her own interpretation of the constitution, and the judge may be wrong (or, more precisely, the constitutional court, which is the central and final authority on these matters, may disagree with the judge). The ordinary judge may be pushing the statute in a "constitutional direction" that is not actually the right constitutional direction. It may be the case, for example, that the plain meaning of the statute is perfectly constitutional and that there is no reason to deviate from it.

If, in contrast, the constitutional court has offered sufficient guidance about the meaning of the constitution with respect to a particular issue, the ordinary judge should be allowed to offer a rather strained reading of the pertinent statute, or even to formally set it aside, if this is the only way to preserve constitutional values. What matters is that the judge's interpretation of the constitution be clearly sound in light of the constitutional court's body of precedents.

This is not currently possible in most European countries, even in extreme cases. Suppose that the constitutional court invalidates a particular law and that some time later, an ordinary judge has to decide a case in which another law that has exactly the same content—or a very similar one—applies. There is no doubt that if the constitutional court invalidated the first legal provision, it would also find unconstitutional the second one. And yet, under the current model, the ordinary judge is usually not allowed to disregard the second law on his or her own authority. The judge must instead ask the constitutional court to review it, even if there is no reasonable doubt as to the answer.[11]

This is not very efficient. It would be better if ordinary judges were permitted to set aside legislation on their own authority in such cases—when the precedents established by the constitutional court are sufficiently clear. Litigants should not have to bear the cost of waiting for the constitutional court to decide a question the answer to which is obvious to almost everybody given the existing precedents. There is an enormous proliferation of legislation nowadays, and it is not uncommon for two statutory provisions to be very similar. In federal (or quasi-federal) systems, for example, it is possible for a statutory provision enacted by one of the states or regions to be identical or very similar to that of another state or region. In such instances, the centralized model is too rigid in that it does not allow ordinary judges to complement the work of the constitutional court.

Would legal certainty suffer if this minor change in a decentralizing direction were introduced? Not much. Legal certainty would be in danger if ordinary judges could refuse to apply statutes when the constitutional court has not offered enough guidance. But when such guidance has been given, judges would strongly converge. Note that the system I am proposing would still be different from the American model, where the power of judicial review can be exercised by all courts, even when the U.S. Supreme Court has not yet spoken in a specific way about the issue that a particular statute poses. In the United States, the "hard cases" are first handled by lower courts. Such cases percolate throughout the judicial system until the time is ripe for the U.S. Supreme Court to settle the controversy. Under my proposal, in contrast, ordinary judges in the European model would be authorized to disregard statutes only when the cases were relatively "easy" given the constitutional court's precedents. If no such precedents existed, judges would have to certify a question to the constitutional court. The system would therefore remain centralized for the hard cases, the types of cases that require the attention of an institution like the constitutional court, given its composition and specialization.

It must be acknowledged that the distinction between easy cases and hard cases is not an easy one to draw, for whether the case law of the court has sufficiently fixed the interpretation of the relevant constitutional clauses is a matter of degree. Still, it would be more efficient to use this distinction as part of the foundation for the division of labor between the ordinary judiciary and the constitutional court than to rely exclusively on the distinction that is currently doing all the work—a contrast between readings of a statute that are possible and those that are too strained. Both distinctions are a matter of degree, and they can interact in the following way: the clearer the case law of the constitutional court, the more strained the statutory interpretations that ordinary courts should be authorized to engage in. If the case law is sufficiently clear, I submit, ordinary courts could even be permitted to formally disregard the pertinent statutes.[12]

A final point needs to be made. Suppose that the parliament enacts a law that clearly contradicts the court's interpretation of the constitution in order to express disagreement with the court. In chapter 8 I argued that there must be mechanisms for the democratic branches to respond to constitutional judges. In particular, I endorsed the idea that, after a reasonable period of time has elapsed, the parliament may enact a new law that is identical or very similar to the one that had been overturned by the court.

Now, to ensure that the new statute is properly brought to the constitutional court, instead of being directly set aside by an ordinary judge, the following technique could be used: the parliament could include in the new statute a *jurisdictional clause* to the effect that only the constitutional court is entitled to review the statute. As a result, an ordinary judge deciding a case would have no authority to disregard the statute, no matter how clearly it ran counter to the court's established doctrine. A judge would have to petition the court to review it, and a second round of discussion would develop there, giving the government the opportunity to present its constitutional arguments to justify the new law.

The enactment of a jurisdictional clause of this sort would, of course, express the legislative majority's awareness that, given the court's precedents, the law has some constitutional problems. A signal would be sent to the political community that further constitutional debate is necessary. This technique would be similar in spirit to the "notwithstanding clause" of the Canadian Charter of Rights and Freedoms, which allows the legislature to protect a statute against the effects of judicial review (for a renewable period of up to five years).[13] The difference would be this: whereas in Canada the statute is protected against any type of judicial review, under my proposal, in contrast, it would be shielded only against review by *ordinary judges,* for the constitutional court would still be authorized to invalidate it. If this mechanism were introduced, it would be possible to accommodate the parliament's interest in having a second round of debate at the constitutional court in exceptional cases, even if the system became more decentralized along the lines I have suggested.

Apart from the arguments I have here adduced, there is another important reason to introduce this marginal correction to the centralized model: this proposal would make the system more similar to the system of judicial review that has been established to enforce the law of the European Union, as we will see in the next chapter.

CHAPTER ELEVEN

The Impact of the European Court of Justice

IF CONSTITUTIONAL COURTS worked in a domestic legal vacuum, the only source of potential erosion to worry about would be the interpretive powers that ordinary judges can exercise if they are not contained in the right way, as we explored in the previous chapter. But the international forces that have given birth to the European Union and to the Council of Europe have complicated the picture. These organizations may affect in serious ways the centralized Kelsenian system of judicial review that exists at the domestic level. (In this discussion, I often refer to the centralized model as "Kelsenian" rather than "European" to avoid confusion with the judicial system that has been articulated at the European supranational level.)

Constitutional tribunals now encounter two powerful courts, the European Court of Justice (ECJ) in Luxembourg (in the context of the European Union) and the European Court of Human Rights (ECHR) in Strasbourg (in the context of the Council of Europe). The jurisprudence of these two courts empowers ordinary judges in ways that undermine, or could potentially undermine, the centrality of constitutional tribunals when it comes to reviewing national legislation. In this chapter I focus on E.U. law and the ECJ, and the next chapter is devoted to the ECHR. The aim of these two chapters is rather modest. I cannot address all the constitutional issues that the existence of these two European courts has raised. My aim is simply to offer some thoughts on how well or how poorly the Kelsenian model fits with the judicial arrangements that have been established in the supranational sphere and what should be done to guarantee a better fit.

THE LEGAL ARCHITECTURE OF THE EUROPEAN UNION

To frame our discussion, I need to say a few words about the legal architecture of the European Union. This organization, which currently includes twenty-seven members, is based on three so-called pillars, the most important of which is the first, which includes the European Community and the European Atomic Energy Community (Euratom). The second pillar, which deals with common foreign and security policy, and the third, which is devoted to police and judicial cooperation in criminal matters, are of a more intergovernmental character. For purposes of our discussion here, we can focus on the problems that arise in the context of the European Community.[1]

The Treaty of Rome, the foundational treaty of 1957 that created the European Community (which was originally called the European Economic Community), established a complex distribution of legislative powers between the Community institutions and the national authorities. The European Community can regulate only certain matters that are enumerated in the treaty; the rest remain in the hands of the member states. Several institutions were created to exercise the competences assigned to the Community. When it comes to lawmaking, the European Commission, the Council of Ministers, and the European Parliament are the most relevant entities. Depending on the subject matter, the Community can issue regulations, which are equivalent to ordinary legislation, or directives, which are framework statutes that bind member states as to certain results but leave to states the choice of the methods of achieving those results. The law of the European Community (E.C. law) thus comprises both the foundational treaties (primary law) and the legal provisions enacted by the Community institutions (secondary law).

The interpretation and application of E.C. law in ordinary legal disputes is basically left to the courts of the different member states. These courts work under the guidance of a central court that sits in Luxembourg: the ECJ.[2] This court is composed of twenty-seven judges (one per member state) and eight advocates general. The latter are responsible for presenting, with complete impartiality and independence, an "opinion" in the cases assigned to them. Depending on the type of case to be decided, the court may sit as a full court (though it has long ceased to do so), in a grand chamber of thirteen judges, or in chambers of three or five judges.

The ECJ's jurisdiction covers different types of cases. The court, for example, can hear complaints that a particular state has failed to fulfill its obligations. It can also review the validity of decisions and laws enacted by the Community institutions or the legality of an institution's failure to act. Actions for damages against the Community for noncontractual liability are also part of its jurisdiction. Its most important function, however, is to guarantee that E.C. law is interpreted and applied in a uniform manner in all member states. For these purposes, the court has been conferred the authority to answer questions sent by national judges concerning E.C. law. This procedure is called "preliminary reference."[3] Whenever a national court deciding a case has doubts about the proper interpretation of E.C. acts, it can raise a preliminary reference to the ECJ for clarification. Similarly, if the national court has doubts about the validity of any of those acts, it can certify a question to the ECJ.[4]

This mechanism is widely regarded to be of key importance to the proper operation of the system—it is "the jewel in the Crown."[5] It is so central, actually, that the E.C. treaty provides that when a national court is deciding a case as the court of last resort, it is no longer free to ask the ECJ but is actually *required* to do so whenever a question concerning the interpretation or validity of E.C. law arises.

Through this procedure, the ECJ has had the opportunity to announce basic principles. It took an important first step in 1964, for example, when it proclaimed that E.C. law (both primary and secondary law) must prevail over national legislation in case of conflict. This is the so-called principle of primacy. Even a statute passed by the democratic national parliament, therefore, has to yield to the higher authority of E.C. law.[6]

From a political point of view, this step was relatively easy for the ECJ to take. As Joseph Weiler has explained, most E.C. laws at that time were enacted through a procedure that required the unanimous consent of the national governments sitting on the council. The primacy of E.C. law was not hard for the governments of the member states to swallow if they retained a veto over the content of that law. When unanimity was later abandoned in favor of supermajority rules in an increasing number of areas, however, the principle of primacy started to show its bite: a member state that voted against a piece of E.C. law nevertheless had to accept its higher status over national legislation.[7]

For a long while, however, the ECJ did not say how the primacy of E.C. law had to be enforced at the domestic level. But everything changed in 1978, when it handed down its historic judgment in the *Simmenthal* case.

THE REVOLUTION THAT *SIMMENTHAL* BROUGHT ABOUT

Before 1978, different solutions seemed to be available to the member states for reacting against national laws that allegedly offended E.C. law. The Italian Constitutional Court crafted a doctrine that was very faithful to the Kelsenian spirit animating the centralized model. It held that a national statute that contradicts E.C. law is not only directly contrary to E.C. law but also indirectly contrary to article 11 of the Italian Constitution, which links the Italian republic to international organizations. This holding reinforced the primacy of E.C. law in Italy. The most important consequence, however, was that it preserved the monopoly of the Italian Constitutional Court within the Italian system. If an ordinary judge concluded that a national statute violated E.C. law, the judge had to raise the question to the Italian Constitutional Court. The judge could not set the statute aside on his or her own authority.

This was a very coherent move given the assumptions upon which the centralized model rests. If, as we have seen in earlier chapters, there are good reasons for Italy and many other European countries to have created a centralized system of judicial review of legislation when the higher norm to be safeguarded is the national constitution, those reasons would also seem to be sufficiently powerful to justify a similar centralization when the set of higher norms to be guaranteed is E.C. law.

The ECJ, however, rejected this Kelsenian solution developed by the Italians. In the *Simmenthal* case,[8] the ECJ laid the foundations for a decentralized system of judicial review. It asserted that a national court that is called upon to apply provisions of Community law "is under a duty to give full effect to those provisions, if necessary refusing of its own motion to apply any conflicting provision of national legislation." Therefore, "*it is not necessary for the court to request or await the prior setting aside of such provision by legislative or other constitutional means.*"⁹ That is, all national judges in charge of specific disputes are empowered, on their own authority, to disregard any domestic statute that contradicts E.C. law. They need not stay the proceedings and wait for the formal invalidation of that statute by the national constitutional court.

Obviously, this deeply transforms the role of ordinary judges in Europe: they are now authorized to review, by themselves, the validity of parliamentary enactments under higher norms. Constitutional courts have lost the monopoly they used to have. They still retain their monopoly over the determination of the validity of statutes under the national constitution, but they have lost their general monopoly over statutes. Ordinary courts too can now check them under E.C. law. The holding in *Simmenthal* seems a crime of high treason against the Kelsenian order of things! Ironically, here we have a European supranational court that has "Americanized" the practice of judicial review of legislation in the diverse member states of the European Union.

This revolution was not quickly accepted in all jurisdictions. It has taken some time for the doctrine to take domestic root.¹⁰ The different countries in Europe, moreover, have translated the *Simmenthal* doctrine into national constitutional terms in different ways.¹¹ The doctrine is now quite settled, however, and we should inquire into its justification and explore the extent to which it fits with, or departs from, the rationales that support the Kelsenian system.

WHY *SIMMENTHAL*?

There are basically two substantive arguments that the ECJ relied on to justify its holding in *Simmenthal*.¹² The first appeals to efficiency. The ECJ reasoned that the effective enforcement of E.C. law would be impaired if the ordinary courts in charge of handling specific disputes were not authorized to immediately set aside national statutes that contravene E.C. law. If courts had to stay the proceedings and ask the national constitutional court to intervene, there would be a delay in the resolution of cases. This delay would amount to an impediment to the full effectiveness of E.C. law, even if "only temporary" in nature. The application of E.C. law, the court held, should be "direct and immediate."¹³

This may sound like a convincing argument, but the countries that have established constitutional courts should not be impressed by it. The centralized model of judicial review is based on the assumption that this delay is a price worth paying—provided, of course, that the delay is not unreasonably long. As was argued in the previous chapters, the issue raised by the statute can be definitively settled by the constitutional court from the very beginning; there is no need to wait for the case to get decided by the highest courts after various appeals. A single decision by the constitutional court striking down the statute, moreover, has the power to bind all judges immediately. These advantages of centralization seem perfectly applicable when domestic legislation is to be reviewed for its conformity with E.C. law.[14]

There is a second and more powerful argument to justify the holding in *Simmenthal,* however. The major task of the ECJ, as we know, is to answer national judges' questions regarding the proper interpretation of E.C. law. What would be the point of requiring those judges to raise a question to their national constitutional court whenever they deemed a particular statute to be inconsistent with E.C. law? If the case law of the ECJ is not sufficiently clear for judges to ascertain whether the applicable statute is valid, it is the ECJ that must clarify things—not the national constitutional court.[15] If the latter were entitled to intervene, moreover, it would probably decide the issues concerning E.C. law without first consulting the ECJ. (As a matter of fact, constitutional courts have been very reluctant to send preliminary references to Luxembourg. Only recently have some of them done so, in a few cases.)[16]

So the *Simmenthal* decision was strategically wise. If national constitutional courts had been permitted to centralize (for domestic purposes) the function of reviewing national legislation under E.C. law, they would have gone their own ways. They would have done the checking themselves, without first asking the ECJ. This would have been disruptive of the E.C. legal order. The ECJ is the supreme interpreter, but it needs to be petitioned by national judges in order to speak its supreme judgment. (Folklore has it that the judges in Luxembourg opened several bottles of champagne when they received their first case in 1954.) Since the ECJ had reason to believe that ordinary judges would be more eager than constitutional courts to use the preliminary-reference mechanism, a centralized system, like the one that Italy had set up before the *Simmenthal* decision, had to be rejected.

Now, what are the costs of the decentralized arrangement that the

ECJ imposed? How are the values that inform the Kelsenian model affected?

LEGAL CERTAINTY UNDER *SIMMENTHAL*

Let us start with legal certainty. The first thing to note is that, in general, E.C. law is quite different from national constitutions. A constitution is a very special text that often expresses broad and morally charged principles, the interpretation of which is deeply controversial. The conflict between a statute and the constitution is often the conflict between a detailed legal provision and a rather abstract and fundamental principle. In contrast, E.C. law is basically made up of "ordinary legislation" that is expressed in rather specific terms. The conflict between a national statute and E.C. law is often a clash between two pieces of ordinary legislation. To the extent that this is so, controversies over whether national statutes comply with E.C. law will not be as deep and extended as constitutional controversies. A decentralized system in the field of E.C. law is thus more tolerable.

This contrast cannot be taken too far, however. Some parts of E.C. law do resemble constitutional norms. The market freedoms that are protected by E.C. law, for example, can be restricted by member states in the name of a compelling public interest. Judges must apply the principle of proportionality and decide whether the restriction is ultimately justified.[17] Fundamental rights are also protected under E.C. law—both as foundational "general principles" and as part of secondary legislation. Member states are bound by such rights when they act in an area governed by E.C. law.[18] Domestic judges, of course, are likely to disagree among themselves when they have to check national legislation for consistency with E.C. law in such cases.

Fortunately, however, there is an important mechanism that ensures uniformity: the preliminary-reference procedure. As has already been noted, national judges can directly consult the ECJ whenever they need guidance. What's more, the national courts whose decisions are not subject to appeal are *required*, as we know, to send a preliminary question to the ECJ if an interpretive problem arises under E.C. law.[19] The ECJ's intervention is of great import, since its rulings are widely believed to be legally binding. The answers that it provides in the form of preliminary rulings are to be followed not only by the judges who raised the pertinent questions but also by all other judges in all member states. The ECJ has clearly claimed this authority, and the majority of scholars have accepted it.[20]

Parenthetically, it is interesting to observe that although there is reluctance in civil-law countries to officially accept the binding character of the doctrines established by the respective domestic supreme courts, there is no such reservation when it comes to the ECJ. Why this difference? In part, the reason is—ironically enough—that the ECJ has no jurisdiction to quash the decisions of national courts that depart from its rulings. Precisely because of this feature of the current judicial architecture, it has become imperative for the legal community to internalize the idea that the ECJ's precedents must be followed and to strongly criticize those judges who fail to do so. As was explained in chapter 3, countries within the civil-law tradition have not felt a strong need to emphasize the role of precedents set by the highest courts, in so far as the latter can impose their views by regularly overturning the decisions of lower courts. This is in contrast to the situation in the common law, we noted, where the doctrine of precedent is a cultural stabilizer that compensates for the fact that it is hard to bring cases to the supreme court. In the context of the European Community, the situation is really extreme: the supreme interpreter of E.C. law—the ECJ—has no power whatsoever to overrule the decisions rendered by national courts. The need to inculcate the culture of precedent in lawyers and judges is therefore absolutely vital.

Actually, the role of precedents in making the system operational is of increasing importance. The ECJ has introduced an exception to the duty of national courts of last resort to raise a preliminary question: they need not ask for a preliminary ruling when there is no reasonable doubt about the meaning of the relevant E.C. legal provision. This is the so-called *acte clair* doctrine (clear-act doctrine). The absence of doubt is usually linked to the existence of precedents. If the question that is being examined by the national court is identical to a question already decided by the ECJ, there is no need to consult the ECJ. Even when the question is different, there is no need to send a reference if the answer can be derived from ECJ precedents.[21]

Because the ECJ is more and more overloaded with preliminary questions, it is necessary to insist on the responsibility of national courts to apply the existing case law themselves. The ECJ should focus on those preliminary references that pose new problems and rely on the capacity of national courts to read the existing precedents on their own and apply the rules that have been clearly established.[22]

Notice that this way of understanding the preliminary-reference procedure is similar to the system that I proposed in chapter 10 as an internal correction to the Kelsenian model of constitutional review of legislation at the domestic level. I suggested that ordinary judges should be allowed to set aside legislation on their own authority provided that they interpret the national constitution in light of the precedents furnished by the constitutional court that have sufficiently clarified the underlying issue. A similar arrangement is in place in the European Community under the clear-act doctrine.

In general, the ECJ is quite careful when it makes its rulings. True, its reasoning is too "cryptic" and "Cartesian," as Joseph Weiler has observed critically.[23] The more detailed opinions of the advocates general may compensate for this argumentative deficit to a certain extent, but it would be better if the ECJ were more explicit about the underlying reasons that support its holdings.[24] For purposes of securing legal certainty, however, what matters is the extent to which the court generates a consistent body of rules. In this regard, its overall performance seems to be acceptable.[25]

For all these reasons, legal certainty is not at grave risk, even though all national judges are empowered under *Simmenthal* to check the conformity of domestic legislation with E.C. law.

AN INTERNAL CORRECTION TO THE *SIMMENTHAL* DOCTRINE

There is room for improvement, however. First, constitutional courts should be allowed to intervene to review national legislation when the ECJ delegates the resolution of important legal issues to the national judiciary. Let me explain.

In some areas of E.C. law, the ECJ thinks it advisable not to frame very detailed answers to the preliminary questions that domestic courts raise. This is especially true when fundamental rights are at stake. As Daniel Sarmiento has explained, the ECJ seems to move to a different beat when it handles legal questions of a constitutional nature, such as fundamental rights. It abandons its general position as a sort of supreme federal court and opens itself to interpretive pluralism.[26] This is understandable: it makes sense for the ECJ to delegate certain matters to the interpretive and fact-finding powers of the national judiciary. In the *Bauer Verlag* case,[27] for example, an Austrian court had to determine whether a national statute prohibiting businesses from offering consumers free . gifts linked to the sale of goods or the supply of services was consistent with E.C. law. In that particular lawsuit, a German publisher would have been prohibited, under that statute, from selling a weekly magazine in Austria that offered readers the chance to take part in games for prizes. The ECJ was consulted by the Austrian court on several points. The ECJ reasoned that the national statute restricted both freedom of movement of goods and the fundamental right to freedom of expression. It also held that to justify this restriction, the state could legitimately invoke its interest in maintaining press diversity. Diversity could indeed be in danger if small publishers were unable to offer prizes like those offered by the largest companies. However, it was for the Austrian court, the ECJ held, to decide whether the restriction was necessary in order to achieve this goal. "It is for the national court to determine whether these conditions are satisfied on the basis of the study of the Austrian press market," the ECJ said.[28]

It is perfectly legitimate, in cases of this sort, for the ECJ to prefer not to give a detailed answer. The national courts may indeed be in a better position to decide certain issues. But if this is the case, I submit, constitutional courts should be allowed to intervene. Recall that the *Simmenthal* doctrine is based on the assumption that ordinary courts at the national level will get enough guidance from the ECJ. But if the ECJ declines to give enough guidance because it feels that the national judiciary is in a better position to determine certain points of law, then the constitutional court should be allowed to step in and unify the domestic legal answer. In the *Bauer Verlag* case, for instance, the Austrian Constitutional Court should have been authorized to review the statute under E.C. law. It would thus have given a unified answer to the several important questions that the ECJ had transferred to the national judiciary. To the extent that the *Simmenthal* doctrine seems to exclude this type of intervention by the constitutional court in a case like this, the doctrine should be reconsidered.

Second, the *Simmenthal* power of ordinary judges to disregard national legislation that contravenes E.C. law should not be taken to exclude the possibility of establishing *additional* systems of legislative review. The advocate general, Gerhard Reischl, was explicit about this in his opinion in *Simmenthal*. He argued that even if ordinary courts were given the power to immediately disregard legislation on their own authority, there would be no need to eliminate the procedures of constitutional review that the Italian legal system had devised to formally cancel legislation that breaches E.C. law. Proposals along these lines have been made by various scholars, and some constitutional courts have been sensitive to them.[29]

SIMMENTHAL AND DEMOCRATIC VALUES

What about the other values that the Kelsenian model seeks to serve? In previous chapters I argued that the model allows the governmental majority to offer its justification of the legislative measures it has enacted. I claimed, in addition, that the model better satisfies the need for courts in charge of review to be sufficiently linked to the democratic processes. How well are these democratic values preserved under the *Simmenthal* arrangement?

The Right of the Governmental Majority to Be Heard

Under *Simmenthal,* the ordinary court handling a particular lawsuit is empowered to set aside the statute even if, in most cases, the government is not a party to the case and will not be notified of the proceedings. Is this fair?

As a general rule, the answer is yes. The government has the opportunity to defend its point of view—not before the ordinary court, but before the ECJ. Suppose that a statute raises an issue of E.C. law and that there is no ECJ case law that sufficiently resolves the matter. The national judge then asks the ECJ for a preliminary ruling. (Recall that when the case gets to the highest court, this petition is compulsory.) The ECJ then notifies the E.C. institutions and the governments of all the member states, who can submit their views.[30] Since the decision to be rendered by the ECJ will give concrete meaning to the relevant provisions of E.C. law, all the member states are interested in influencing the outcome and are consequently allowed to express their points of view.[31] In this way, the governmental majority whose statute is being examined by the ECJ has the chance to argue in its defense: it can give the reasons it thinks that E.C. law is not being breached. The other states can support the government's argument or object to it. If they have enacted similar legislation, they have an incentive to participate and insist that the measure under examination is not at odds with E.C. law.

Sometimes, however, the ECJ is not addressed by the national judge. If, for example, the ECJ has laid down precedents that sufficiently clarify the underlying issue raised by the national statute, the domestic judge will normally refuse to certify a preliminary question. In this situation, the governmental majority that supports the statute will not be heard by the ECJ. Is this unfair? Not really. The government had an opportunity to express its point of view in the past, when the ECJ established the relevant precedent (or set of precedents). At that time, the governments of all the member states were asked to express and justify their interpretive positions regarding E.C. law. That was the key moment when those governments had the chance to contribute to the process through which E.C. law is construed.

Imagine now that the following situation arises. The governmental majority is perfectly aware that a new statute it has enacted is inconsistent with E.C. law as interpreted by the precedents established by the ECJ. The majority insists, however, that the ECJ's interpretation is wrong. How could the system allow the government to make its case? Maybe a jurisdictional clause similar to the one that I suggested in chapter 10 could be included in the controversial statute. The clause would explicitly require the national court deciding a case to send a preliminary reference to the ECJ if the court concluded, given the ECJ's precedents, that the statute violated E.C. law. Of course, the ECJ could still give a quick answer to the national court through a reasoned order that makes reference to the past precedents.[32] The ECJ, however, might give some weight to the disagreement that the national parliament was expressing through that clause and might be more willing to hold a full hearing in which the E.C. institutions and the governments of all member states would be allowed to express their positions. This institutional device would seem particularly acceptable in cases where the applicable jurisprudence of the ECJ is deeply controversial, as may be the case when certain fundamental rights are involved, for example.

Finally, what happens when the existing case law is insufficient to decide an issue, the national court certifies a question to the ECJ, and the ECJ's answer is very open-ended because the ECJ believes that the national judiciary is better equipped to deal with particular aspects of the underlying legal problem? I have earlier argued that in this type of case, the constitutional court should be authorized to step in on grounds of legal certainty. The right of the governmental majority to be heard presses in the same direction: if the ECJ has given discretion to the national judiciary to decide whether the statute violates E.C. law, the constitutional court should intervene so that the government can express its arguments in support of the statute.

The Links between Courts and the Democratic Branches
Let us now turn to the necessary links between courts in charge of legislative review and the democratic branches. How does the *Simmenthal* arrangement affect these links? To answer this question, we need to distinguish between two types of situations, as we did before.

Suppose, first, that the ECJ has offered a rather detailed elaboration of the meaning of E.C. law. In such cases, we must focus on the ECJ and consider the appointment of ECJ judges and their terms of office, as well as the ways in which the political branches can respond to its jurisprudence.

As to the appointment and tenure of ECJ judges, there is not a systematic deficit on this score, in comparison with constitutional courts. The political branches participate in the judicial selection process: ECJ judges are appointed by common accord of the governments of the member states. And the judges do not sit for life: they hold their offices for a limited period of six years (though the term can be renewed).[33] If there is a loss from a democratic point of view, it is because there is not a European public opinion comparable to the national public opinion that operates at the domestic level. The decisions to appoint the judges of the ECJ may be less visible than the decisions to appoint the members of a national constitutional court.

On the other hand, as I argued in chapter 9, democratic links should not be designed in ways that can harm judicial independence. The process of interpreting E.C. law must be sensitive to the points of view of the democratic branches, but it must also include a supranational dimension. The ECJ must aim for an interpretation of E.C. law that protects the general interests of the Community, and this is possible only if the ECJ enjoys a sufficient degree of independence from the national democratic branches. In this regard, the fact that judges are appointed by common agreement, and not simply by each national government, is an important feature. In contrast, the fact that they can be reappointed after the six-year term has expired is detrimental to their independence. (The prohibition against filing dissenting opinions diminishes the risks, though, since the court speaks with one voice and the national governments cannot easily monitor the individual performance of the judges.)

With respect to the capacity of the political branches to respond to the ECJ, things are not too bad either. I argued in previous chapters that it is desirable for judicial decisions regarding the constitution to attract debate and be subjected to public scrutiny and political checks. The intuition behind the Kelsenian model is that, given the legal and political conditions in many European countries, this goal is facilitated by centralization, as well as by the fact that the decisions rendered by constitutional courts have general effects (when the courts check legislation). In the context of the European Community, this goal is sufficiently satisfied. When the ECJ answers a preliminary reference, it does not decide a particular case. It answers a general question, and its answer is binding on all. The question and the answer may be more or less specific, but the ECJ makes a ruling that has *erga omnes* effects similar to those that result from a decision by a constitutional court striking down a statute. Actually, the impact of the ruling by the ECJ is even wider: the ECJ does not hold that a particular statute passed by a particular parliament violates E.C. law; it instead holds that a particular normative content violates E.C. law, and any statute that has that content, whichever country enacts it, is automatically judged to breach E.C. law. Even statutes that have a different content but are similar for purposes of the ECJ's holding are also to be regarded as contravening E.C. law. As a result, it is quite clear that the public and the political branches must focus their attention on the ECJ.

Of course, the extent to which the ECJ is actually checked by the political branches and by public opinion does not depend on the architecture of courts exclusively. It also depends on the features of the political system. There is an open debate about the seriousness of the democratic deficit of the E.C. political process. It is not easy to build a supranational organization that is as democratic as member states are. There is probably ample room for improvements on this level. But at least the judicial architecture does not make it difficult for member states to activate the relevant supranational democratic checks—to the extent that they exist. A well-known example of a political response to the ECJ is the positive-action provision that was inserted by the 1997 Treaty of Amsterdam into article 141 of the E.C. treaty. The political branches reacted in this way against the ECJ's controversial decision in the *Kalanke* case, which established a very restrictive jurisprudence on the legality of affirmative action programs for women.[34]

So when the ECJ establishes in a rather specific manner the interpretation to be followed by national courts, there is no strong reason to criticize the current system on democratic grounds.

In contrast, when the ECJ does not establish specific rulings but grants discretion to the national judiciary, we have good reason to criticize the current arrangement under *Simmenthal*. If, given *Simmenthal*, the constitutional court is not authorized to speak as to the validity of the national statute and ordinary courts instead must address the issue on their own authority, some of the democratic principles that support the centralized model are negatively affected. As we know, in many European countries, the selection process for ordinary judges is not as democratic as the selection process for members of the constitutional court. Moreover, the capacity of the democratic branches to respond to the judicial interpretation of E.C. law is made more difficult in a decentralized system, for different courts may disagree and as a result no clear message will be sent to the democratic branches until the supreme courts gradually establish the relevant case law. If, in contrast, the constitutional court were the entity responsible for reviewing the statute, the conversation with the political institutions would be easier.

NATIONAL CONSTITUTIONAL CHECKS ON THE EUROPEAN COURT OF JUSTICE

A final point on the advantages of constitutional courts in the context of the European Union is in order. A recurring theme in the debates about the construction of Europe is the issue of primacy: Is E.C. law, or are national constitutions, the supreme law of the land? May national judges disregard E.C. law if it violates a basic principle or rule embodied in the national constitution? In particular, may national judges refuse to apply a piece of E.C. legislation on the ground that it conflicts with fundamental rights as protected by the national constitution—even if the ECJ upholds that legislation as consistent with fundamental rights at the European level?

This is an interesting and complex issue that has attracted the attention of many scholars. It is beyond my present purposes to examine this question.[35] But there is a marginal point worth making here: when such extraordinary cases arise, it seems reasonable to resort to the constitutional court to channel the dialogue (and the tension) between the national judiciary and the ECJ.[36] The constitutional court can concentrate all the potential "disobedience" to the latter. This system has several advantages. First, it provides clarity. It would be more chaotic if all the different ordinary courts could decide themselves whether to accept the enforceability of E.C. law depending on whether they thought that the ECJ human-rights case law was good enough. It is better for the constitutional court to be in charge of this delicate matter. The position of the national judiciary should be expressed in a clear way. The constitutional court should be the entity that talks to Luxembourg in the name of ultimate principles rooted in the national constitution. Second, if a constitutional court made public its own reservations about the acceptability of the ECJ's jurisprudence in the area of rights, it would send a strong warning to Luxembourg. As Dieter Grimm explains in the context of the German Constitutional Court, a preliminary reference raised by the German court to the ECJ could be used to signal the existence of a potential conflict that needs to be worked out. The warning would be stronger if it came from the constitutional court than if it emerged from lower ordinary courts.[37] Finally, the constitutional court is more likely to be prudent in these potential fights. Precisely because its decisions have a greater impact than those of ordinary judges deciding concrete cases, the constitutional court is encouraged to think twice before it holds that E.C. law conflicts with fundamental rights protected by the national constitution.

CONCLUSION

In this chapter I evaluated the extent to which the Kelsenian model of constitutional review at the domestic level is undermined by, or is in tension with, the decentralized system that the ECJ established in *Simmenthal*. As we have seen, certain features of the E.C. legal order make the potential tension between the two systems a relatively tolerable one. However, to the extent that the ECJ is sometimes very open-ended in its rulings because it prefers to grant discretion to the national judiciary, the *Simmenthal* regime may end up being too disruptive of the foundational values of the Kelsenian model. In those cases, a stronger presence of constitutional courts is to be welcomed.

In general, we should find ways to ensure that the logic of the system of judicial review of legislation under E.C. law is not too different from the logic of the domestic system of constitutional review patterned after the Kelsenian model. If the difference is too large, the two systems may not be able to coexist smoothly. Their combination may become explosive at some point. It is necessary to introduce some adjustments in order to make them less distant from each other. In chapter 10 I suggested a marginal correction to the Kelsenian model, in a decentralizing direction, that would enlarge the role of ordinary judges in the area of constitutional review. This correction puts the domestic system of constitutional review closer to the institutional arrangement that stems from *Simmenthal*. But, as I have suggested in this chapter, some adjustments should also be introduced in the other direction: the *Simmenthal* system needs to be refined so that it does not depart too radically from the Kelsenian intuition in favor of centralization.

CHAPTER TWELVE

The Impact of the European Court of Human Rights

IN THIS FINAL CHAPTER we should now turn to another important organization, the Council of Europe, a principal mission of which is to protect human rights. The European Convention on Human Rights, which the Council of Europe adopted in 1950, must be observed by national legislation. As I will argue, however, there is no reason to depart from the centralizing logic of the Kelsenian model in this context. To justify my claims, I will emphasize some of the differences between E.C. law and the European Convention on Human Rights.

THE EUROPEAN CONVENTION ON HUMAN RIGHTS AND THE ENFORCEMENT MACHINERY IN STRASBOURG

One of the most notable achievements of the Council of Europe (which is currently composed of forty-seven states) is the European Convention for the Protection of Human Rights and Fundamental Freedoms of 1950, normally known as the European Convention on Human Rights. This international treaty was an important step for the collective enforcement in Europe of some of the rights set out in the 1948 Universal Declaration of Human Rights. In addition to the convention, the states can choose to ratify several protocols that expand the list of protected liberties.[1]

The convention created a mechanism for the enforcement of the obligations entered into by the contracting states:[2] the European Court of

Human Rights (ECHR) was established in Strasbourg in 1959 with the authority to hear complaints against states for violations of the convention. A commission was created to determine the admissibility of complaints, but it was abolished in 1998.[3] The Committee of Ministers, which is composed of the ministers of foreign affairs of the member states of the Council of Europe (or their representatives), supervises the execution of the court's judgments.

The Strasbourg system has evolved during the years as several protocols have been ratified to change its structure and procedures. An important improvement to highlight in this evolution has been the recognition of the right of individual applicants to bring cases directly to the court. Complaints against contracting states can be filed by another state that is a party to the convention (article 33) or by "any person, non-governmental organisation or group of individuals claiming to be the victim of a violation" of human rights (article 34). In practice, it is rare for states to bring complaints. Private individuals are generally the plaintiffs.

One of the problems of the Strasbourg system, unfortunately, is that the ECHR is overwhelmed by an excessive number of cases. Even though the workload is distributed among different panels of judges, the court is unable to cope with the situation in a satisfactory manner.[4] In 1999 (after the abolition of the commission), around 22,600 cases were referred to the court. In 2005, the figure went up to 45,500.[5] Several reforms have been proposed to solve the caseload problem. Protocol 14, which was adopted in 2004 and has not yet entered into force (Russia has yet to ratify it), will introduce some institutional and procedural changes that will allow the court to deal more expeditiously both with complaints that are clearly inadmissible and with those that can be easily resolved on the basis of well-established law. But more radical changes are being considered given the seriousness of the problem: 97,300 applications were pending as of December 31, 2008![6]

THE DOMESTIC STATUS OF THE EUROPEAN CONVENTION ON HUMAN RIGHTS

Now, how should the states that follow the Kelsenian system of constitutional review organize themselves domestically when it comes to the application of the European Convention on Human Rights?

A first fundamental point to bear in mind is that the ECHR has held that the contracting states have discretion as to the domestic legal status of the convention. In particular, it is up to each state to decide what national courts should do when confronted with a statute that conflicts with the convention. Judicial review of legislation is not imposed.

In the United Kingdom, for example, the convention was not part of the legal system until the enactment of the Human Rights Act 1998. National judges, therefore, could not test legislation against convention rights. The ECHR, however, held that this was not objectionable.[7] Even with the enactment of the Human Rights Act 1998, courts in the United Kingdom cannot set aside statutes as being contrary to any of the convention rights. They can seek an interpretation that harmonizes the statute with the convention, but if the conflict cannot be resolved through interpretation, the only thing that some of the highest courts can do is issue a declaration of incompatibility, which the political branches are expected to take seriously; the statute is not set aside, and it remains applicable in the particular case. This arrangement is fully acceptable as far as the Strasbourg doctrine is concerned, for the ECHR has never required the establishment of a domestic system of judicial review of legislation under the convention. (This is an important difference from the arrangement one finds in the European Community. As we saw in the last chapter, the ECJ's *Simmenthal* doctrine has obliged states to establish a decentralized system of judicial review of national law under E.C. law.)

The only exception that the ECHR seems to have introduced is this: if it holds that a particular law of the defendant state breaches the convention, the courts in that state should refuse to apply it in future controversies.[8] Apart from this exceptional case, however, the ECHR respects the existing internal arrangements. In some countries, the convention has been accorded the same force as a statute; it enjoys a higher rank in others. If the latter option is chosen, it is also up to each state to decide which courts should review national legislation in light of convention rights. In some jurisdictions, all courts have been conferred the power of legislative review, whereas in others only the constitutional court has been given such power.[9]

Interestingly, in some countries the judiciary enjoys a greater authority to check legislation when convention rights are invoked than when the national constitution is at stake. In the Netherlands, for instance, the constitution explicitly forbids judges to refuse to apply legislation on constitutional grounds, but it requires them to disregard such legislation if it is not in accord with international treaties.[10] Similarly, ordinary judges in France have traditionally played no role, as we know, when it comes to constitutional review. After the 2008 reform, they can now initiate a process to have the Constitutional Council review a particular statute. If they find that statute inconsistent with international treaties, however, they have the power to set it aside on their own authority.[11] As French scholars explain, there is a centralized system of judicial review of *constitutionnalité,* and a decentralized system of judicial review of *conventionnalité.* The same distinction applies in Belgium.

The case of Spain is interesting in this regard. Article 10.2 of the constitution provides that the domestic bill of rights will be interpreted in light of the human-rights treaties that Spain has ratified, including the European Convention on Human Rights.[12] In addition, the convention prevails over contrary legislation. Like its French counterpart, the Spanish Constitutional Court has declared that it is not in charge of checking national laws under international instruments—this task is left to ordinary judges. It seems to follow, therefore, that ordinary judges can refuse to apply a statute on the grounds that it infringes upon a convention right, without having to petition the constitutional court.[13]

In practice, though, this ability of ordinary courts to review laws under the convention has not given rise to a high level of judicial activism in these countries. To a large extent, this is not surprising: ordinary courts in civil-law jurisdictions are reluctant to check legislation under abstract principles, like those that figure in the European Convention on Human Rights. Still, to the extent that judicial review of parliamentary enactments under the convention is technically possible in some countries that have established constitutional tribunals, a potential tension is introduced in the system. This tension, I submit, should be avoided. A decentralized system of judicial review of national laws under the European Convention on Human Rights is not a good idea. The value of legal certainty, as well as other considerations of a more democratic character, all press in favor of preserving the centralized model. What sense does it make to grant the constitutional court exclusive authority to check legislation under the *national* bill of rights if we then empower all ordinary courts to scrutinize legislation under the *European* bill of rights?

LEGAL CERTAINTY

Legal certainty will be seriously affected if a decentralized system is established. Different courts in a given state will reach opposite conclusions as to whether a particular statute violates a right guaranteed in the convention (or the relevant protocols). In contrast to what happens in the context of the European Community, we cannot rely here on certain features of the system to reduce judicial divergence to tolerable levels.

First, the European Convention on Human Rights is not "ordinary legislation" in the way that most E.C. law is. The convention enshrines a body of fundamental principles, the interpretation of which is often deeply controversial. Actually, the main source of interpretive controversies at the domestic level is the bill of rights of the national constitution. The convention, of course, is nothing but a bill of rights. The likelihood is very high, therefore, that different ordinary courts will reach different conclusions about the compatibility of a particular statute with the convention.

Second, the ECHR in Strasbourg cannot be consulted by national judges in case of doubt as to the proper interpretation of the convention. There is no preliminary-reference procedure like the one used in the judicial system of the European Community.[14]

Third, the ECHR's jurisprudence cannot introduce a sufficient level of certainty. The court constantly resorts to case-by-case balancing. Its reasoning follows the *pro et contra* method, which acknowledges the values and countervalues that can be invoked to attack and defend a national measure.[15] This balancing exercise does not yield a categorical rule. The court's judgment is instead very sensitive to the particular circumstances of the case. In many areas, it is difficult to derive a relatively categorical rule to the effect that a certain kind of national law should be deemed to be invalid, as an infringement of a human right, quite apart from the various circumstances the law may be applied to.

In the field of freedom of speech, for example, the ECHR tends to formulate very general principles for the interpretation of this right, as well as a list of factors and considerations that are relevant in evaluating the extent to which speech is being restricted, and the court applies this general scheme in a way that is highly sensitive to the particular circumstances of the different cases. The court pays lots of attention, for example, to the relative gravity of the civil or criminal sanctions that have been imposed on speakers. The principle of proportionality leads the court to be more or less ready to find a violation of freedom of speech depending on the seriousness of the sanctions imposed by the national authorities in a particular case.[16]

This does not mean that the Strasbourg doctrines have no bite. Because the court's decisions do have bite, I argue later in the chapter that there should be some room for national institutions to express their reservations. But the spirit with which the ECHR builds its jurisprudence is casuistic in many fields.

There is thus a contrast between the ECJ and the ECHR, which can be partially explained on functional grounds. The ECJ is aware that one of its principal missions is to ensure the uniform interpretation and application of E.C. law. It is the institution in charge of fixing the meaning of a body of law that flows from a quasi-federal legal system. It has an institutional incentive, therefore, to establish relatively clear and categorical holdings for national courts to follow. The ECHR, in contrast, is not a supreme court working within a quasi-federal legal regime. Rather, it is an international court that provides, from the outside, an additional layer of protection for fundamental rights. Uniformity in the interpretation of human rights is not the most important justification for its existence.

As was mentioned in chapter 11, the ECJ also tends to be less clear and categorical when fundamental rights are involved. I suggested that, in those cases, a stronger presence of national constitutional courts should be welcomed. But what tends to be an exception to the general rule in the context of E.C. law becomes the general rule in the context of the European Convention on Human Rights. Whereas E.C. law is basically ordinary law that only sometimes incorporates fundamental rights, the convention is nothing but a bill of rights.

For these various reasons, a decentralized model of judicial review of legislation under the convention would be inimical to legal certainty. It is much better for the constitutional court to retain its classic monopoly. (We will not be surprised to learn, by the way, that Hans Kelsen was also in favor of concentrating in the constitutional court the task of reviewing statutes under international treaties.[17])

I thus propose that if an ordinary court concludes that a national statute applicable to a given case is at odds with the convention, the court should certify the issue to the constitutional court. The latter should then take into account the case law of the ECHR and clarify, for domestic purposes, whether that statute breaches the convention. If the constitutional court holds that the statute is valid, ordinary courts will have to enforce it. The ECHR may ultimately have the opportunity to decide a case in which that statute has been applied and may disagree with the constitutional court's holding. But, for the time being, the constitutional court will have unified the answer to the problem that the statute poses under the convention, for domestic purposes.[18]

The centralization I am advocating is possible, of course, only if the convention is taken to be part of the set of standards whose protection is in the hands of the constitutional court. This is the situation in Austria, for example, where the convention was incorporated into the constitution in 1964.[19] Some voices have been raised in France and Belgium in favor of a similar sort of arrangement. They fear that otherwise, the constitutional court will lose much of its authority in the area of fundamental rights.[20] In Spain, the incorporation of the convention into the constitution for these purposes would be facilitated by article 10.2 of the constitution, which links the Spanish bill of rights to the relevant international treaties.

Interestingly, even in Portugal the system of judicial review of legislation under the convention is partially centralized. Judicial review of statutes under international treaties is patterned after the system that applies when the constitution is at stake. Lower courts in Portugal have an initial responsibility in these matters, but the intervention of the constitutional court is required in the end. If a lower court concludes that a given statute must be disregarded because it is incompatible with an international treaty, its decision must be examined by the constitutional court. More specifically, the law obliges the public prosecutors' office to lodge an appeal in such cases to ask the constitutional court to speak to the matter.[21]

The centrality of constitutional courts should be preserved so as not to jeopardize legal certainty.[22] In some special cases, however, it seems reasonable to qualify that centrality. As was already noted, the ECHR has held that when it finds that a particular legal provision enacted by a contracting state offends the convention, all the courts in that state (not only the constitutional court) must set it aside in subsequent cases. This is perfectly sensible. But we could go a little further than this and allow ordinary courts to disregard a statute that is relatively similar to another one that has already been found wanting by the ECHR—even if issued by a different state. What is important in such special cases is that the case law of the ECHR is sufficiently clear that a particular kind of law is invalid.

A similar requirement of jurisprudential clarity should operate when judges read national statutes in rather strained ways in order to make them comport with the convention.[23] Here we encounter the same institutional division of labor that we considered in chapter 10, a division that relies on the distinction between "interpretation" and "correction" of statutes. The thesis that I suggested there is applicable here: ordinary judges may engage in rather strained interpretations of statutes (and may even formally disregard them) only if the ECHR's precedents are sufficiently clear. When, in contrast, the legitimacy of the national law under the existing case law is more controversial, ordinary courts should ask the constitutional court to intervene and express its position.

DEMOCRATIC VALUES

The democratic considerations that we explored in earlier chapters in connection with the Kelsenian model of constitutional review press in the same centralizing direction: the question whether a parliamentary enactment respects a fundamental right protected under the European Convention on Human Rights should be decided, at the domestic level, by the constitutional court. In this way, the governmental majority can articulate its arguments in support of the statute, and the necessary links between courts and the democratic branches are preserved.

The Right of the Governmental Majority to Be Heard

If the national parliament has enacted a statute that arguably violates the convention, the special forum for constitutional matters at the domestic level should be opened. Ordinary judges deciding cases should refer the issue to the constitutional court, thereby giving the governmental majority a chance to defend its legislative choice. Even if the ECHR has generated relevant case law, there is usually room for interpretation given the casuistic character of its case law in most fields. The governmental majority should be granted the right to express its view on the matter and defend the statute against the claim that it violates the convention.

It is important to realize, moreover, that when the ECHR examines a complaint against a state, the parties to the case are normally the victims of the alleged violation and the state that is responsible for it. The other contracting states are not parties to the case. They may ask the president of the court to invite them to participate, but they are not called upon as of right.[24] In practice, they rarely intervene. The fact that the ECHR does not generally lay down categorical rules in its decisions, but instead applies the pertinent principles to the specific circumstances of the case in a rather flexible and casuistic manner, probably makes it less necessary for the governments of all the contracting states to participate and express their points of view. They know that if they are sued in the future, they will have the chance to explain themselves and to argue that the particular circumstances of the cases are different. (All of this is in contrast to what normally happens in the context of the European Community when a preliminary-reference procedure is initiated, as we saw in the previous chapter.)

In the context of the European Convention on Human Rights, therefore, it is not possible to argue that the governmental majority already had the opportunity to participate in the European judicial procedure that yielded the relevant jurisprudential rule. In practice, this kind of intervention is very rare. Therefore, for the governmental majority to have a first chance (maybe the only chance) to make its case in support of a particular parliamentary enactment, the constitutional court must be asked to intervene.

The Links between Courts and the Democratic Branches

We can reach similar conclusions if we now focus on the other democratic considerations. To the extent that Strasbourg case law usually gives broad discretion to the national judiciary, the constitutional court should be the domestic body in charge of providing the jurisprudential details when the validity of a national statute is at issue. In this way, the delicate decision to strike down a piece of legislation is placed in the hands of an institution that has stronger democratic credentials than ordinary courts. Also, the political branches can pay attention to what the constitutional court does when it uses its discretion to interpret and implement ECHR case law. They can then react to the constitutional court's decisions using some of the techniques discussed in chapter 9 (such as reenactment of statutes or constitutional amendments). The internal dialogue between the judiciary and the democratic branches, within the area of discretion that the

ECHR grants to the contracting states, should be channeled through the constitutional court.

What about the links between the ECHR itself and the democratic procedures? Concerning, first, the method for selecting the Strasbourg judges, the system is acceptable in terms of the degree of participation of the political branches. Judges on the ECHR (whose number is equal to that of contracting states) are selected by the Parliamentary Assembly of the Council of Europe, which is composed of political representatives appointed by the national parliaments. This assembly votes on a short list of three judicial candidates put forward by each government.[25] The term of office of the judges of the ECHR, moreover, is limited to six years,[26] though judges may be reelected, which is not an ideal arrangement in terms of their institutional independence. (If protocol 14 finally enters into force, judges will enjoy a nonrenewable term of nine years, which is much better.)

Concerning the capacity of the democratic branches to respond to the ECHR and generate a dialogue on the interpretation of human rights, things get more complicated. It is very difficult for the contracting states to respond collectively to the decisions of the ECHR. Whereas in the context of the European Community, it is very hard, but not impossible, to amend the treaties (and it is relatively easy to modify secondary legislation), it is impossible, in practice, to amend the European Convention on Human Rights, which requires the unanimous consent of the contracting states (there are forty-seven of them as of this writing). It is therefore crucial that mechanisms that can serve as a dialogic constraint on the ECHR be available at the domestic level.

The convention establishes two mechanisms that a contracting state can employ to make a national law prevail over ECHR case law, but neither mechanism is useful for channeling the kind of dialogue we are considering here. Article 15 of the convention allows states to derogate from certain rights "in time of war or other public emergency threatening the life of the nation." When the national authorities resort to such derogation, however, they are not disagreeing with the ECHR, at least not necessarily. They are simply suspending the operation of a right during the emergency. Similarly, it is possible under article 57 of the convention for a state to make a reservation to the effect that a particular national law should be maintained, notwithstanding the convention. But this technique can be used only when the convention is signed or ratified. It is not available later, for example, when the ECHR issues a ruling that a particular country disagrees with. (In the end, of course, it is always possible for a state to denounce the treaty and get out of the Strasbourg system of protection of rights. But this is too drastic a measure.)

Constitutional courts become important at this juncture as forums where a dialogic check on the ECHR can be initiated at the national level when there are doubts whether a parliamentary enactment conforms with Strasbourg doctrine. National legislative assemblies must comply with the convention, of course, and must take ECHR case law seriously. But they are entitled to disagree with the ECHR or to think that some qualifications to a decision are appropriate. The governmental majority that supports a statute at odds with the extant doctrine of the ECHR should be allowed to make its case to the constitutional court. Maybe the court will accept the arguments put forth by the government and uphold the statute. It may feel that a controversial ECHR decision should indeed be reconsidered or qualified. If the constitutional court, instead of ordinary courts, passes judgment on the statute in that sort of situation, the quality of the national interactions with the ECHR is thereby enhanced. If a case finally gets to Strasbourg, the ECHR will have to examine the position and the reasoning of the constitutional court. The ECHR will not receive a contradictory collection of views coming from different courts in that state, but a more clearly articulated position by a single court. When parliamentary laws are being reviewed, constitutional tribunals should play a key role in channeling and facilitating the European conversation in such a large organization as the Council of Europe.

Constitutional tribunals, moreover, are as structurally devoted to the protection of fundamental rights against the legislature as the ECHR is. Certain institutional factors push them toward a certain level of activism, as I suggested in chapter 7. They are not as "timid" as ordinary courts in many civil-law countries are when it comes to scrutinizing parliamentary enactments against higher standards of justice. Accordingly, a decision by a constitutional court to sustain a statute against the charge that it breaches convention rights has special meaning. The decision comes not from a court that regularly applies statutes in a passive manner, but from an institution that is seriously devoted to legislative review.

National checks of this kind would not be appropriate, of course, if the ECHR confined itself to protecting the most basic and uncontroversial rights that make a society decent and democratic. A role of this sort may have been the original understanding (among some countries, at least) of the function of the ECHR given the historical background of the Nazi experience against which the Strasbourg system was established.[27] We should not want states to escape the strictures of the Strasbourg system in clear cases of human-rights violations. As a supranational institution, the ECHR is in a better position than national courts to react against what are commonly regarded as grave violations of basic rights, especially those perpetrated by executive and administrative bodies and officials. But this minimal function is no longer the only mission that defines the ECHR, which is now interpreting the convention in a more activist way. The court renders judgments on controversial issues that are currently discussed in mature democracies. The "margin of appreciation" it accords states in determining the extent to which a restriction of a fundamental right is or is not necessary in a democratic society has been narrowed in many areas.[28] The court is still deferential with respect to issues that are profoundly controversial throughout Europe, such as abortion,[29] euthanasia,[30] the adoption of children by homosexual couples,[31] and the ban on in vitro fertilization in case of unilateral withdrawal of consent.[32] But the court has been less deferential when addressing other issues that are also debatable and that have generated no consensus among the contracting states.

The ECHR, for example, has espoused a very broad conception of the sphere of privacy of public figures. Thus, in *Von Hannover v. Germany*,[33] the court held that Germany had violated the right of privacy of Princess Caroline of Monaco. The German ordinary courts had granted the princess an injunction prohibiting the press from publishing certain photographs that showed her at particular moments of her private life, but refused to grant an injunction in connection with other photos. The German Constitutional Court concluded that some of the photos in the latter group were covered by the princess's right to privacy but that others were not—those that showed the princess at a market or on horseback or riding a bicycle, for example. These were not taken in a secluded place, but in a public one, and their publication was therefore protected speech. The ECHR disagreed. It found that the "spatial isolation" criterion articulated by the German Constitutional Court was wrong and ruled that "the decisive factor in balancing the protection of private life against freedom of expression should lie in the contribution that the published photos and articles make to a debate of general interest."[34] It concluded that those photos were covered by the right to privacy.

The holding of the ECHR may well be right, but there is no doubt that there is room for reasonable disagreement about this issue. The same is true, to give another example, of *Hirst v. United Kingdom (No. 2)*,[35] a case in which the court held that denying the right to vote to convicted prisoners, while they serve their sentence, is a breach of article 3 of protocol 1. I confess to being strongly sympathetic to the court's position in favor of prisoners' voting rights. Still, there is room for reasonable disagreement. As the dissenting judges in that case noted, "There is little consensus [in Europe] about whether or not prisoners should have the right to vote. In fact, the majority of member States know such restrictions, although some have blanket and some limited restrictions." And they concluded: "Taking into account the sensitive political character of this issue, the diversity of the legal systems within the Contracting States and the lack of a sufficiently clear basis for such a right in Article 3 of Protocol No. 1, we are not able to accept that it is for the Court to impose on national legal systems an obligation either to abolish disenfranchisement for prisoners or to allow it only to a very limited extent."[36]

In so far as the ECHR does not perform a minimal function but is instead at the vanguard of human-rights discourse in an increasing number of cases, the establishment of a system of checks and balances between the national institutions and the ECHR becomes important. The democratic nations that are parties to the European Convention on Human Rights should be able to voice their reasoned disagreements in controversial cases. The national parliaments are important settings where this disagreement can be expressed, and constitutional tribunals provide an ideal forum to continue the domestic conversation about the acceptability of the ECHR's rulings.

Writing about supranational organizations in general, Jürgen Habermas says that "the interrelation between the rule of law and democracy would necessarily be dissolved if supranational constitutions were completely severed from the channels of democratic legitimation which are institutionalized within the constitutional state." Hence, he asserts, "liberal constitutions beyond the state, if they are to be anything more than a hegemonic legal façade, must remain tied at least indirectly to processes of legitimation within constitutional states." He continues, "Supranational constitutions rest at any rate on basic rights, legal principles, and criminal codes which are the product of prior learning processes and have been tried and tested within democratic nation-states."[37]

True, these dialogic checks on the ECHR may affect to a certain extent the uniformity in the interpretation of the convention. If such checks are activated, the case law of the ECHR will not be immediately accepted and followed by national courts in all instances. But uniformity is not the dominant value in the Strasbourg context. Actually, the contracting states have committed themselves to *different bills of rights* at this European level: although all of them have ratified the convention, it is up to them to ratify additional protocols that guarantee other rights. By choosing to sign some of the additional protocols but not others, they subject themselves to a more or less generous catalog of rights. Also, as previously mentioned, the ECHR often grants states a certain "margin of appreciation" in controversial areas where no consensus arises among European nations as to the correct interpretation and application of a convention right. The ECHR, moreover, in contrast to the ECJ, can publish dissenting and concurring opinions. This gives visibility to the interpretive divisions that human-rights issues can generate within the court itself. In this context of normative and interpretive pluralism, no great damage results if constitutional courts are allowed to express certain qualifications to the Strasbourg jurisprudence in connection with issues that are indeed deeply controversial.

In this regard, the formula established by the United Kingdom Human Rights Act 1998 to define the authority of the case law of the ECHR is useful. Section 2 of the act provides that when interpreting convention rights, the national courts "must take into account any judgment, decision, declaration or opinion of the European Court of Human Rights" that is relevant. The case law of the ECHR must be taken seriously, but it is not strictly binding. A similar understanding seems to underlie section 4 of the Irish European Convention on Human Rights Act 2003, which provides that courts "shall, when interpreting the Convention provisions, take due account of the principles laid down by [the] declarations, decisions, advisory opinions, opinions and judgments" of the EHCR. The German Constitutional Court, in turn, has also emphasized the importance of ECHR case law in interpreting the fundamental rights set out in the

German Basic Law but has not gone so far as to ascribe to such case law a strictly binding effect on domestic courts.[38]

CONCLUSION

Both legal certainty and democratic principles, I have argued, press in favor of a centralized system of judicial review of legislation under the European Convention on Human Rights. With this chapter, we have completed our examination of the external forces that may undermine the Kelsenian model. If we are convinced that the cluster of arguments developed in parts 1 and 2 of this book offer a sufficiently strong case in favor of centralizing legislative review in a constitutional court, we should be skeptical of attempts to introduce a very decentralized system under supranational norms. The Kelsenian model, whatever its shortcomings, has proved to be a satisfactory arrangement for the European countries that are parliamentary democracies and that belong to the civil-law tradition. There is room for some adjustments, but the basic architecture is sound.

Indeed, it would be paradoxical if the moment of triumph of Kelsen's idea, with the establishment of constitutional courts in so many European countries at the end of the twentieth century, were the beginning of their domestic decline as a result of supranational developments. In these two final chapters I have offered some proposals to reorient those developments. As we gain historical perspective, the idea of a constitutional court is likely to be regarded as the most notable contribution of twentieth-century European public law to modern constitutionalism. There is no compelling reason to believe that it is no longer a useful institutional scheme for the decades to come, even though pragmatic adaptations to the new circumstances are certainly necessary.

Afterword

THIS BOOK HAS BEEN a long argument to support the European preference for constitutional courts. I have tried to highlight the potential virtues of the centralized model of judicial review in the particular context of parliamentary democracies that belong to the civil-law tradition.

When European scholars nowadays read *Marbury v. Madison,* however, they cannot fail to be attracted by its powerful logic. After all, is it not the case that Europeans share the premises from which Chief Justice John Marshall derived his famous conclusion? His central argument, as everybody knows, boiled down to this. First, the constitution is law. Second, the constitution has a higher rank in the legal hierarchy than ordinary legislation. Third, it is the judiciary's function to decide cases according to the law—all the relevant law. Fourth, when different norms that belong to the same legal system collide, judges must decide which one is to be applied, according to the classical criteria of *lex posterior, lex specialis,* and *lex superior.* The conclusion seems to follow quite naturally: judges are empowered to disregard a piece of legislation for purposes of resolving a specific controversy if they conclude that it violates the constitution.

All these premises are endorsed in Europe. For a long time, constitutions may have belonged to the political sphere and been excluded from the legal domain. In Europe today, however, there is no doubt that they are part of the law, no matter how different they are in many respects from ordinary legislation. Their supremacy over ordinary law, moreover, cannot be denied. Constitutions are harder to amend than ordinary law because it is taken for granted that they are to prevail over the latter in the event of a conflict. As to the role of the judiciary, there does not seem to be any deep disagreement either. Judges in Europe are expected to resolve disputes according to the law, *lex superior* being one of the rules they have traditionally employed for these purposes. Why shouldn't this rule be used by judges when they confront clashes between ordinary legislation and the constitution? Even for Europeans, the "natural" option, it seems, would be to have a decentralized system of legislative review. The establishment of a constitutional court with a monopoly over legislative review has an element of artificiality. The burden of the argument, one could say, rests with the Europeans: What reasons can they adduce to support an institutional arrangement that deviates from what seems to be dictated by those shared premises?

Throughout the book, I have been sympathetic to the European case in favor of constitutional courts. I believe that the burden of the argument can be sufficiently satisfied. Though I have acknowledged the weaknesses of the centralized model at many junctures, the overall tone has been optimistic; the model is basically in good order, despite the partial reforms that need to be introduced. A different story could have been told, however, on the basis of the same materials I have worked with. According to this alternative narrative, the logic of *Marbury v. Madison* would exert an irresistible gravitational pull that would attract European systems toward a decentralized model. Constitutional courts would have been necessary at an intermediate transitional stage to guarantee that the constitutions would be taken seriously by political actors and to ensure that fundamental values would permeate the whole legal system. Once this goal has been achieved, however, the ordinary judiciary should fully enter the constitutional realm. The constitutional courts' monopoly would start to be a little embarrassing. Ordinary judges could now scrutinize statutes directly themselves, working under the jurisprudential guidance of the court—not only in relatively "clear" cases but also in the "hard" ones. According to this alternative narrative, the very success of constitutional courts would have planted the seeds of their own destruction—or at least of their radical transformation. From this perspective, the supranational developments discussed in chapters 11 and 12 would point in the right direction, toward a larger role for ordinary courts in the business of checking the conformity of laws to higher standards. The *Simmenthal* decision, in particular, would represent modernity, whereas the Kelsenian preference for the constitutional court's monopoly would be a residue of a complicated European past.

For a while, I was attracted to this more radical view about the future of constitutional courts in Europe. My friend and colleague Mattias Kumm, in our many fruitful conversations about this matter, has often insisted on the provisional character of the centralized model. As I have reflected on these issues in the course of my project, however, I have had my doubts about such a provocative theory. I think that the centralized model still has much to recommend it for a parliamentary system that operates within the civil-law tradition. Time will tell, though, which of the two narratives is closer to the truth. Meanwhile, constitutional scholars will benefit from the existing contrast between the European and the American models. A richer understanding of each system will be obtained as we continue discussing their respective strengths and weaknesses. I hope that this book makes a useful contribution to this fascinating subject—from a European perspective, admittedly.

NOTES

INTRODUCTION
1. 5 U.S. (1 Cranch) 137 (1803).
2. For a general view of this contrast, one should consult the classic study by Mauro Cappelletti, *Judicial Review in the Contemporary World* (Indianapolis, Ind.: Bobbs-Merrill, 1971), especially pages 45–96, as well as Allan-Randolph Brewer-Carías, *Judicial Review in Comparative Law* (Cambridge, U.K.: Cambridge University Press, 1989). See also Louis Favoreu, "Constitutional Review in Europe," in *Constitutionalism and Rights: The Influence of the United States Constitution Abroad,* ed. Louis Henkin and Albert Rosenthal (New York: Columbia University Press, 1990), 38–62. For more updated descriptions of the systems of constitutional review that exist in European countries, see Dominique Rousseau, *La justice constitutionnelle en Europe* (Paris: Montchrestien, 1998); Eliseo Aja, ed., *Las tensiones entre el Tribunal Constitucional y el Legislador en la Europa actual* (Barcelona: Ariel, 1998); Wojciech Sadurski, ed., *Constitutional Justice, East and West: Democratic Legitimacy and Constitutional Courts in Post-Communist Europe; A Comparative Perspective* (The Hague: Kluwer Law International, 2002); and Marco Olivetti and Tania Groppi, eds., *La giustizia costituzionale in Europa* (Milan: Giuffrè, 2003). Interesting reports on the relationship between judicial review and the legislative process in various countries can be found in Christine Landfried, ed., *Constitutional Review and Legislation: An International Comparison* (Baden-Baden, Germany: Nomos Verlagsgesellschaft, 1988). An illuminating theory of the role of constitutional courts in Europe can be found in Alec Stone Sweet, *Governing with Judges: Constitutional Politics in Europe* (Oxford: Oxford University Press, 2000). For a good treatment of the different historical contexts in which the American and the

European models emerged and evolved, see Marian Ahumada Ruiz, *La jurisdicción constitucional en Europa* (Madrid: Civitas, 2005). For an overview of the different systems of constitutional review around the world, see Michel Fromont, *La justice constitutionnelle dans le monde* (Paris: Dalloz, 1996). Fromont questions the traditional distinction between centralized and decentralized models. He prefers to draw a contrast between concrete (subjective) review and abstract (objective) review. Other comparatists share this view. See, e.g., Alessandro Pizzorusso, "I sistemi di giustizia costituzionale: Dai modelli alla prassi," *Quaderni costituzionali* 3 (1982): 521–533, and Francisco Rubio Llorente, "Tendencias actuales de la jurisdicción constitucional en Europa," in *Estudios sobre jurisdicción constitucional,* by Francisco Rubio Llorente and Javier Jiménez Campo (Madrid: McGraw-Hill, 1998), 155–173. As I hope to show as we deal with several issues in this book, the distinction between centralized and decentralized models is still illuminating when comparing European constitutional courts with the American system of judicial review. Other factors must certainly be taken into account to enrich the comparative picture, however, as these scholars rightly point out.

CHAPTER 1. THE RISE OF CONSTITUTIONAL COURTS

1. It should be noted, however, that Germany at that time had a fragmentary system of constitutional review of a centralized character, which operated in the field of federalism and in connection with the constitutional conflicts that arose within the Länder. Two courts had responsibility over these matters: the Reichsgericht (Supreme Court of the German Reich) and the Staatsgerichtshof (a special court). The Supreme Court held in 1925, in a sort of *Marbury v. Madison* decision, that all courts could set aside legislation on constitutional grounds. A legislative proposal was drafted in 1926 to establish a more complete system of constitutional review. Under this proposal, the Staatsgerichtshof would act as a general constitutional court. The proposal anticipated some features that have become typical of the European model of judicial review after the Second World War: the ability of a qualified minority in parliament to challenge a law in the abstract and the duty of ordinary judges to send a question to the constitutional court when they conclude that the applicable statute is inconsistent with the constitution. The proposal was discussed in the parliament, but it was not enacted. For a detailed analysis of the system of judicial review in the Weimar Republic, see Pedro Cruz Villalón, *La formación del sistema europeo de control de constitucionalidad (1918–1939)* (Madrid: Centro de Estudios Constitucionales, 1987), 71–227. See also Donald Kommers, *The Constitutional Jurisprudence of the Federal Republic of Germany* (Durham, N.C., and London: Duke University Press, 1997), 4–7.

2. Georg Jellinek, for example, had already made some proposals in 1885 that went in the direction of concentrating in the Austrian Supreme Court

(Reichsgericht) some form of abstract review of legislation under the 1867 constitution. See Cruz Villalón, *La formación del sistema europeo*, 240–242. It should also be noted that the ability to attack a law in the abstract, which is a typical feature of the European model as conceived by Kelsen, had already been introduced in Venezuela (in 1858) and Colombia (in 1910). In these countries, citizens were granted standing to bring direct challenges against statutes they deemed unconstitutional.

3. Two articles by Kelsen are particularly important: "Judicial Review of Legislation: A Comparative Study of the Austrian and the American Constitution," *Journal of Politics* 4 (1942): 183–200, and "La garantie juridictionnelle de la Constitution (La justice constitutionnelle)," *Revue du droit public et de la science politique en France et à l'étranger* 45 (1928): 197–257. I will make frequent references to these texts.

4. Portugal's constitution of 1976, however, did not initially establish a constitutional court. Instead, a political organ, the Council of the Revolution, was created to review legislation with the support of an advisory body, the Constitutional Commission. It was not until 1982 that the constitution was amended to establish a constitutional court that replaced these institutions.

5. In the post-Communist European countries, the centralized model is absolutely dominant. See Herman Schwartz, *The Struggle for Constitutional Justice in Post-Communist Europe* (Chicago: University of Chicago Press, 2000), 22–48, and Wojciech Sadurski, *Rights Before Courts: A Study of Constitutional Courts in Postcommunist States of Central and Eastern Europe* (Dordrecht, The Netherlands: Springer, 2005), 40–58. It should be mentioned that during the Communist regime, two countries had already created constitutional courts: Yugoslavia (1963) and Poland (1982). Czechoslovakia had also amended its constitution in 1968 to establish a constitutional court, but the law to actually bring it into existence was never adopted. For a brief description of the structure and competences of these courts, see Allan-Randolph Brewer-Carías, *Judicial Review in Comparative Law* (Cambridge, U.K.: Cambridge University Press, 1989), 236–242. In general, the Marxist legal theory that prevailed in Communist countries was opposed to judicial review of legislation. This institution was thought to be part of the general principle of separation of powers, and this principle, in turn, was taken to belong to bourgeois societies. It was only in societies divided by class that governmental powers had to be divided and subjected to checks and balances; no such separation of powers was necessary in a classless society.

6. In Sweden and Finland, the constitution explicitly establishes the "clear mistake" rule: only when a statute is unconstitutional beyond any reasonable doubt may courts set it aside for purposes of deciding a case. See article 14, chapter 11 of the Swedish Instrument of Government and section 106 of the Finnish Constitution. There is no similar clause in the Constitution of Denmark, but in practice courts are very deferential. Thus, it was

not until 1999 that the Danish Supreme Court (Højesteret) rejected a
politically important statute as being contrary to the constitution. On the
system of constitutional review in the Nordic countries, see Jaakko Husa,
"Guarding the Constitutionality of Laws in the Nordic Countries: A Comparative Perspective," *American Journal of Comparative Law* 48 (2000):
345–382. It should also be noted that two countries that do not belong to
the European Union, Norway and Switzerland, also follow the American
model. In Norway, all courts can set aside legislation deemed unconstitutional. This power has rarely been used, however. In Switzerland, constitutional review is similarly decentralized, but federal statutes (as opposed to
federal executive regulations and regional laws) are immune from any kind
of judicial review. The system is mixed, moreover, since it combines constitutional review by all courts with the existence of a special procedure ("recourse of public law") that may lead the Federal Supreme Court (Tribunal
fédéral suisse) to invalidate a regional act with *erga omnes* effects. See
Brewer-Carías, *Judicial Review in Comparative Law,* 271–274. In 1936, a legislative initiative was discussed that would have extended judicial review to
federal legislation. The proposal was rejected, however, by the cantons and
by the people themselves in a referendum held in 1939. See Cruz Villalón,
La formación del sistema europeo, 68. The new constitution of 1999 (which
came into force in 2000) has not changed the situation in this regard.
Federal statutes are still shielded against judicial review.

7. In Ireland, there is no constitutional court, but judicial review is not com-
   pletely decentralized. Only some courts (the High Court and the Supreme
   Court of Ireland) have been bestowed with that power. The Irish Supreme
   Court also has the authority to rule on the validity of legislation before it is
   enacted, at the request of the president of the republic. See article 34 of the
   Irish Constitution.

8. In Greece, all the courts have the authority to set aside legislation if they
   conclude that it is unconstitutional. See article 93.4 of the Greek Constitution. But at the apex of the judicial pyramid there is the Special Highest
   Court, a sort of constitutional tribunal that resolves conflicts that arise between the supreme courts concerning the validity of statutes. See article
   100.1 of the Greek Constitution.

9. Cyprus used to have a constitutional court, which was established and
   regulated in its 1960 constitution. See articles 133–151. In 1964, however,
   Cyprus passed a law combining the functions of this court and those of the
   court of last resort in ordinary litigation into a single supreme court. See
   Mauro Cappelletti, *Judicial Review in the Contemporary World* (Indianapolis, Ind.: Bobbs-Merrill, 1971), 51 n. 18.

10. The Estonian Supreme Court is a court of cassation that also performs
    the functions of a constitutional tribunal. See article 149.3 of the Estonian
    Constitution. A special chamber within the court (the Constitutional Re-
    view Chamber) is responsible for constitutional matters, though some-

times the court decides a case en banc. The Supreme Court, moreover, can exercise legislative review in the abstract. For these purposes, proceedings can be initiated by the president, the legal chancellor, and local government councils. The system is relatively decentralized, since all the courts in Estonia can set aside legislation they deem unconstitutional. See articles 15 and 152 of the Estonian Constitution. Such a ruling, however, initiates a special procedure in which the Supreme Court reviews the constitutionality of the pertinent law. Once the Supreme Court has spoken to the issue, the lower-court judgment can then be appealed. So the decentralized character of the system is rather qualified. See *Constitutional Review Court Procedure Act* (March 13, 2002).

11. See article 120 of the Constitution of the Kingdom of the Netherlands.
12. As K. D. Ewing explains in "The Human Rights Act and Parliamentary Democracy," *Modern Law Review* 62 (1999): 92, the intention was that "Parliament should still hold the key."
13. Brewer-Carías, *Judicial Review in Comparative Law*, 156.
14. I have greatly benefited in this regard from the comprehensive study of Wojciech Sadurski, *Rights Before Courts*.
15. Overall, the monopoly that the constitutional court enjoys has been formally respected in the countries we are considering. We will see in chapter 10, however, that ordinary judges have sometimes undermined the court's authority by resorting to strained interpretations of statutes. In Central and Eastern Europe, the ordinary judiciaries in some countries have gone further; they have claimed the power to set side unconstitutional legislation, thus eroding the exclusivity that the constitutional court is supposed to have. See Sadurski, *Rights Before Courts*, 20–21.
16. Thus, in Germany, constitutional review of statutes that were enacted before the constitution came into force is basically in the hands of ordinary judges. (The court made this clear in an early decision in 1953. See Bundesverfassungsgericht [Federal Constitutional Court] 2 BVerfGE 124.) The Constitutional Court can only review those statutes through an abstract challenge or, indirectly, in the context of the complaints procedure or the procedure that allows the court to certify the continued applicability of old law as federal law. See articles 76, 80, 86, and 93 of the *Bundesverfassungsgerichtsgesetz* [Federal Constitutional Court Act]. In Spain, the court held in an early decision (decision no. 4/1981, February 2, 1981) that ordinary judges can disregard old statutes on their own authority. In case of doubt, however, they can choose to certify a question to the constitutional court. In Italy, the court assumed in its very first decision (decision no. 1/1956, June 5, 1956) the power to check preconstitutional legislation. It did not deny the concurrent power of judges, however. See Gustavo Zagrebelsky, *La giustizia costituzionale* (Bologna: il Mulino, 1988), 140–147. In contrast, the Austrian Constitutional Court (Verfassungsgerichtshof) has the exclusive power to check the validity of statutes that were enacted before

the constitution entered into force. The same is true in France and Belgium.

17. See article 204 of Portugal's constitution of 1976. Actually, the constitution of 1911 had already accorded ordinary judges the power of constitutional review. In this respect, the Portuguese framers of 1911 were influenced by Brazil's constitution of 1891, which had established an American-style system of judicial review. See Carlos Blanco de Morais, *Justiça constitucional,* vol. 1, *Garantia da Constitução e controlo da constitucionalidade* (Coimbra, Portugal: Coimbra Editora, 2006), 316.

18. See article 280.3 of the Portuguese Constitution. According to Portuguese scholars, the justification for this arrangement is related to the notion that laws benefit from a presumption of constitutional validity—a presumption that only the constitutional court is entitled to destroy. Thus, if an ordinary court disregards a legal provision in a particular case, its decision must be reviewed by the constitutional court to determine whether the provision is indeed at odds with the constitution. In contrast, there is no need for the court to intervene if the lower court has upheld the validity of the legal provision. See J. J. Gomes Canotilho, *Direito constitucional e teoria da Constituição* (Coimbra, Portugal: Livraria Almedina, 2002), 986.

19. See article 142 of the Belgian Constitution and article 95ter of the Luxembourg Constitution.

20. In France, the court's major task is constitutional review of legislation, but it also has jurisdiction over electoral matters and referenda. See articles 58, 59, 60, and 61 of the French Constitution.

Similarly, in Italy the central function of the court is constitutional review of legislation. It also rules on disputes between state organs, between the state and the regions, or between regions; it passes judgment on the permissibility of referenda; and it has jurisdiction over criminal charges brought against the president of the republic. See article 134 of the Italian Constitution, and *Legge costituzionale 11 marzo 1953,* no. 1. When the court sits as a criminal court, its fifteen regular members are supplemented by sixteen Italian citizens selected at random, specifically for the trial, from a list of forty-five people chosen every nine years by parliament sitting in joint session.

In Portugal, most of the court's decisions deal with the validity of legislation. But the court also has some other tasks of a heterogeneous character: verifying the death and declaring the permanent physical incapacity of the president of the republic and verifying cases in which the president is temporarily prevented from performing his or her functions; verifying forfeiture of the office of president of the republic; issuing rulings on the proper conduct and validity of electoral acts; verifying the death and declaring the incapacity to exercise the office of president of the republic of any presidential candidate; verifying the legality of the formation of political parties and ordering their abolition as required by law; verifying the legality of referenda; ruling on appeals concerning losses of parliamentary seats and elections; ruling on appeals in cases involving elections within, and decisions taken by, political parties; and receiving statements of assets and earnings, as well as declarations of incompatibility and impediment, from holders of political posts. See article 223 of the Portuguese Constitution and articles 6–11-A of the *Lei do Tribunal Constitucional, Lei 28/82, de 15 de Novembro.*

21. In Germany, the court has many other functions apart from constitutional review of legislation. The most important one, in terms of the number of cases it generates, is to decide constitutional complaints brought by individuals claiming that a public authority has violated their fundamental rights. Between 1951 and 2005, 157,233 applications were lodged with the court, of which 151,424 were constitutional complaints. (Information on the number of cases is available on the court's Web site, at http://www .bundesverfassungsgericht.de/en/organization.html.) The other questions it has jurisdiction over include the forfeiture of certain basic rights (of individuals who abuse their rights in order to combat the free democratic order); the prohibition of political parties; electoral disputes and the loss of legislative seats; the validity of decisions by investigatory parliamentary commissions; impeachment of the federal president; impeachment of judges; disputes between federal organs; federal-state disputes; constitutional disputes within states; questions concerning the domestic status of international laws; references from state courts that wish to deviate from earlier interpretations rendered by the federal or other state constitutional courts; and questions concerning the continuing validity of earlier law as federal law. See article 93 of the German Basic Law and article 13 of the *Bundesverfassungsgerichtsgesetz* [Federal Constitutional Court Act].

In Austria, the court is in charge of reviewing not only the constitutionality of statutes under the constitution but also the validity of administrative ordinances. It has jurisdiction, moreover, over the following items: pecuniary claims on governmental institutions; conflicts of competence between courts and administrative authorities; conflicts between courts; conflicts between states and between a state and the federation; questions concerning agreements between states and the federation; questions concerning the validity of international treaties; electoral disputes, loss of representative seats, and questions concerning popular initiatives, consultations, or referenda; impeachment and criminal accusations against high governmental officials; constitutional challenges to administrative decisions; and violations of international law. See articles 137–145 of the Austrian Constitution.

In Spain, the court has jurisdiction to review the constitutionality of legislation, but it can also decide constitutional complaints; conflicts between regions and between the state and the regions; conflicts between state organs; conflicts in the protection of local autonomy; and questions concerning the constitutionality of international treaties. See article 161 of the Spanish Constitution and article 2 of the *Ley Orgánica 2/1979, de 3 de octubre, del Tribunal Constitucional*. In practice, constitutional complaints generate the vast majority of decisions. In 2007, for example, the court received 10,013 applications, of which 98.3 percent were constitutional complaints. This figure reflects a more general trend during the past years. See Tribunal Constitucional de España, "Memoria 2007," http://www .tribunalconstitucional.es/memorias/2007/memorias07.html.

22. In Austria, abstract challenges can be filed by the federal government (against state statutes), a state government (against federal statutes), one-third of the House of Representatives or the Senate (against federal statutes), or one-third of a state parliament (against state statutes if the state constitution so provides). It is also possible for individuals to impugn a law that infringes personal rights, in so far as the law has become immediately operative for the applicant without the delivery of a judicial or administrative decision. (The challenge does not have an abstract character in this case.) See article 140.1 of the Austrian Constitution. In Belgium, challenges can be filed by the federal, regional, or communal governments; by any natural or legal person whose interests are affected; or by the presidents of the legislative assemblies at the request of two-thirds of their members. See article 2 of the *Loi spéciale du 6 janvier 1989 sur la Cour d'arbitrage*. In France, the challenges can only be brought before the promulgation of the statute, by the president of the republic, the prime minister, the president of the National Assembly, the president of the Senate, sixty deputies, or sixty senators. See article 61 of the French Constitution. In Germany, challenges can be instituted by the federal government, the state government, or one-third of the members of the House of Representatives. See article 93.2 of the German Basic Law. In Italy, challenges may be filed, on federalism grounds, by the state government (against a regional statute) and by a regional government against a state statute or a statute of another region. See article 127 of the Italian Constitution. In Portugal, challenges can be brought both before and after the promulgation of the statute. Preventive challenges may be filed (depending on the type of legal provision) by the president of the republic, the representatives of the republic in the regions, the prime minister, or one-fifth of the members of the Portuguese assembly. See article 278 of the Portuguese Constitution. After promulgation of the statute, challenges can be filed by the president of the republic, the president of the assembly, the prime minister, the ombudsman, the attorney general, one-tenth of the members of the assembly, or (in connection with regional controversies), by the representatives of the republic in the regions, the regional legislative assemblies, the presidents of the latter, the presidents of the regional governments, or one-tenth of the members of a regional legislative assembly. See article 281 of the Portuguese Constitution. In Spain, statutes can be challenged by the prime minister, the om-

budsman, fifty deputies, fifty senators, the regional governments, or the regional parliaments. See article 162.1 of the Spanish Constitution. The only country that does not have this mechanism is Luxembourg. In all these countries (except Austria, Germany, and Portugal), a deadline is established, after which no abstract challenges can be brought.

23. The various countries differ as to when the judge must certify a question to the constitutional court: Must the judge be of the opinion that the law is unconstitutional, or are mere doubts sufficient? In Germany, for example, mere doubts are not regarded as sufficient, whereas in Italy, Spain, Belgium, and Luxembourg, they are.

24. This mechanism exists in Austria (articles 89.2, 129c, and 140.1 of the Austrian Constitution), Belgium (article 142.3 of the Belgian Constitution), France (article 61.1 of the French Constitution), Germany (article 100 of the German Basic Law), Italy (article 1 of the *Legge costituzionale 9 febbraio 1948*, no. 1), Luxembourg (article 95ter of the Luxembourg Constitution), and Spain (article 163 of the Spanish Constitution). This mechanism does not exist in Portugal, where ordinary judges can set aside statutes on their own authority. It did not exist in France either, until a constitutional amendment enacted in July 2008 introduced it. See articles 29 and 30 of the *Loi constitutionnelle no. 2008-724 du 23 juillet 2008 de modernisation des institutions de la Ve République*, giving new content to articles 61 and 62 of the constitution. It should be noted that Austria, France, and Belgium present some special characteristics with regard to this sort of procedure. In Austria, only the highest courts (the Higher Administrative Court [Verwaltungsgerichtshof], the Supreme Court of Justice [Oberster Gerichtshof], an appellate court, an independent administrative tribunal, and the Independent Federal Asylum Tribunal) are authorized to use this power of referral when statutes are at stake. If, in contrast, an administrative ordinance is to be examined, all courts can raise a question. In France, any court can trigger this procedure, but the relevant supreme court (Court of Cassation [Cour de cassation] or the Council of State [Conseil d'État]) acts as a filter so that it is actually the supreme court that formally certifies the question to the Constitutional Council (Conseil constitutionnel). This mechanism, moreover, can only be used to impugn the validity of legislative provisions on the ground that they violate constitutionally guaranteed rights and liberties. It cannot be employed to attack legislation on other grounds. Finally, with respect to Belgium, all courts are empowered to certify questions to the Constitutional Court (Cour constitutionnelle), but the courts of last resort (in practice, the Court of Cassation [Cour de cassation] and the Council of State [Conseil d'État]) are under a stricter duty to do so: when one of the parties claims that the applicable law is unconstitutional, the highest courts must raise the pertinent question to the Constitutional Court, even if they think that the law is not invalid or that it is not necessary to get an

answer from the court. This stricter requirement was introduced in 1989. See article 26.2 of the *Loi spéciale du 6 janvier 1989 sur la Cour d'arbitrage.*

25. See article 93 of the German Basic Law, and articles 90–95 of the *Bundes- verfassungsgerichtsgesetz* [Federal Constitutional Court Act]; articles 161 and 162 of the Spanish Constitution and articles 41–58 of the *Ley Orgánica 2/1979, de 3 de octubre, del Tribunal Constitucional;* and article 144 of the Austrian Constitution and articles 82–88 of the *Verfassungsgerichtshofgesetz* [Constitutional Court Act]. In Germany and Spain, litigants must (as a general rule) first exhaust all the remedies that are available within the ordinary judiciary; only then is their complaint admissible. In Austria, in contrast, the complaint is normally brought against administrative deci- sions directly, without first going to the ordinary courts to seek redress. In both Austria and Germany, moreover, individuals can challenge a law directly before the court in some special circumstances. It should also be noted that in Spain, the ombudsman and the public prosecutor are also en- titled to lodge a complaint for violations of fundamental rights. They rarely do so, however. It is individuals that initiate this procedure in practice.

26. On this general tendency in Europe, see Francisco Rubio Llorente, "Ten- dencias actuales de la jurisdicción constitucional en Europa," in *Estudios sobre jurisdicción constitucional,* by Francisco Rubio Llorente and Javier Jiménez Campo (Madrid: McGraw-Hill, 1998), 155–173. Rubio Llorente at- tributes this trend to the pervasive culture of rights and to the difficulty of fully protecting fundamental rights if legislation is checked only in the abstract.

27. Similar proposals to change the system had already been made in the 1990s, but they were not adopted. For a description of these proposals and the debate they generated, see Dominique Rousseau, *Droit du contentieux constitutionnel* (Paris: Montchrestien, 2006), 73–78.

28. Sadurski, *Rights Before Courts,* 19.

29. We find this feature in the eight Western European countries we are focus- ing on; Luxembourg is the only exception. The Constitutional Court of Luxembourg (Cour constitutionnelle) can review statutes only in the con- text of constitutional questions raised by ordinary judges. Its decisions are not binding on all judges—only on those who raised the questions (as well as the other judges that may have to intervene later in the same case). So when the court holds that a statute is unconstitutional, the statute is not invalidated with general effects. See article 15 of the *Loi du 27 juillet 1997 portant organisation de la Cour constitutionnelle.* In Belgium, when the Con- stitutional Court reviews a statute in the context of a question certified by an ordinary judge, the statute is not eliminated from the system either. But the court does have the power to strike down a statute with general effects when it decides abstract challenges brought by public institutions or indi- viduals whose interests are at stake. See articles 8, 9, 10, and 28 of the *Loi spéciale du 6 janvier 1989 sur la Cour d'arbitrage.* Finally, it should be men-

tioned that in Portugal, when the Constitutional Court (Tribunal Constitucional) reviews the validity of statutes in the context of concrete cases
decided on appeal, the statutes are not invalidated with general effects.
However, if the court has ruled in three cases that a particular statute is
unconstitutional, a procedure of abstract review is then initiated, normally
at the request of the attorney general. The court can then decide to formally eliminate the statute from the legal system. See article 281.3 of the
Portuguese Constitution.

30. Referring to Austria's constitution of 1920, he said: "The decision of the
Constitutional Court by which a statute was annulled had the same character as a statute which abrogated another statute. It was a negative act of
legislation." Kelsen, "Judicial Review of Legislation," 187.

31. Until the 2008 constitutional reform, France was an important exception
to this general rule: normally, a statute in France could be reviewed by the
Constitutional Council only before it was promulgated. Once a statute had
passed this initial filter, it became immune from any further attacks. It
should be noted, however, that this general immunity granted to statutes
was already a qualified one. First, when reviewing the validity of a new statute that had not yet been promulgated, the court could examine the validity
of an earlier statute that had been modified, completed, or affected by the
new one. See Conseil constitutionnel decision no. 85-187 DC, January 25,
1985 (France). Second, when an administrative regulation that contradicted
an earlier statute was about to be enacted, the prime minister could first
ask the Constitutional Council to ascertain whether that statute invaded
the regulatory sphere that the constitution grants to the government. If the
court so declared, the new administrative regulation could then modify
that statute. See article 37 of the French Constitution.

32. In Germany, for example, the court sometimes moves beyond the particular objections put forth by petitioners. See Albrecht Weber, "Alemania,"
in *Las tensiones entre el Tribunal Constitucional y el Legislador en la Europa
actual,* ed. Eliseo Aja (Barcelona: Ariel, 1998), 69–70, and Francesca
Rescigno, "La giustizia costituzionale in Germania," in *La giustizia
costituzionale in Europa,* ed. Marco Olivetti and Tania Groppi (Milan:
Giuffrè, 2003), 111.

33. The degree of this asymmetry between decisions that invalidate and decisions that uphold the constitutionality of laws varies in the different countries. In Italy, for example, the asymmetry is rather strong: statutes are
never said to be "upheld," since they can always be attacked in the future
through new procedures; the court's decisions are therefore taken to have
binding effect only to the extent that they declare a statute unconstitutional. See Zagrebelsky, *La giustizia costituzionale,* 255–256, 293. A similar
view is espoused in Portugal. The only decisions that have *erga omnes*
effects are those that declare a statute unconstitutional, and only if they
are made in an abstract review procedure. See Luís Nunes de Almeida,

"Portugal," in *Las tensiones* (see note 32), 243–246. In Spain and Germany, in contrast, decisions upholding statutes have binding effects on all authorities: they are granted "general effects" in Spain (article 38.1 of the *Ley Orgánica 2/1979, de 3 de octubre, del Tribunal Constitucional*), and "force of law" in Germany (article 31.2 of the *Bundesverfassungsgerichtsgesetz* [Federal Constitutional Court Act]). The court itself, however, is not strictly bound by those decisions: it can overrule them in the future. This "reversibility" of constitutional holdings is generally favored by scholars. See, e.g., Javier Jiménez Campo, "El control de constitucionalidad de la ley en el Derecho español," in *Estudios sobre jurisdicción constitucional* (see note 26), 70.

34. For good summaries of the use of these various techniques by courts in different European countries, see the reports collected in *Las tensiones* (see note 32).

CHAPTER 2. HISTORICAL BACKGROUND

1. M. J. C. Vile, *Constitutionalism and the Separation of Powers* (Indianapolis, Ind.: Liberty Fund, 1998), 173.

2. See generally Michel Troper, *La séparation des pouvoirs et l'histoire constitutionnelle française* (Paris: Librairie Générale de Droit et de Jurisprudence, 1980), 43–68, 165–178, and Philippe Blachèr, *Contrôle de constitutionnalité et volonté générale* (Paris: Presses Universitaires de France, 2001), 209–215.

3. Title I of the constitution of 1791 provided for the enactment of a civil code to ensure legal equality. It also explicitly guaranteed the right of citizens to be eligible for public offices and employment without other distinctions than virtues and talents.

4. Mauro Cappelletti, *Judicial Review in the Contemporary World* (Indianapolis, Ind.: Bobbs-Merrill, 1971), 35.

5. Title II, article 12 of the Law of 16–24 August 1790 (my translation).

6. Charles de Secondat, baron de Montesquieu, *The Spirit of the Laws*, trans. and ed. Anne M. Cohler, Basia Carolyn Miller, and Harold Samuel Stone (Cambridge, U.K.: Cambridge University Press, 1989), 160.

7. The court was created by a decree of November 27–December 1, 1790.

8. See title III, chapter V, article 22 of the constitution of 1791.

9. Title II, article 13 of the Law of 16–24 August 1790 (my translation). This prohibition was soon constitutionalized. See title III, chapter V, article 3 of the constitution of 1791 and article 203 of the constitution of 1795. According to Troper, *La séparation des pouvoirs*, 174, the main reason for the rejection of judicial review of executive actions was that the legislative assembly had not enacted a code establishing in a complete and precise manner the limits that the administrative authorities had to respect. In the absence of such a code, courts would have overstepped the limited role that was expected of them if they had been allowed to check the actions of the executive branch.

10. The *tribunaux administratifs* were set up in 1953, and the *cours administra-*

tives d'appel in 1987. See John Bell, *Judiciaries within Europe: A Comparative Review* (Cambridge, U.K.: Cambridge University Press, 2006), 48.

11. For a good description of the origins and evolution of administrative justice in France, see J. W. F. Allison, *A Continental Distinction in the Common Law* (Oxford: Oxford University Press, 1996), 138–146.

12. See title II, article 10, of the Law of 16–24 August 1790 (my translation); title III, chapter V, article 3 of the constitution of 1791; and article 203 of the constitution of 1795.

13. Thus, title VII of the constitution of 1791 regulated the process of constitutional revision. Three successive legislatures had to agree on the proposed amendment. The final decision was in the hands of the Assembly of Revision, a special body composed of new ordinary legislators and 249 additional members to be elected in separate ad hoc elections.

14. See title VII, article 8 of the constitution of 1791.

15. On Sieyès's contributions to constitutional debates, see Pasquale Pasquino, *Sieyès et l'invention de la Constitution en France* (Paris: Odile Jacob, 1998).

16. Dominique Rousseau, *Droit du contentieux constitutionnel* (Paris: Montchrestien, 2006), 12.

17. See ibid., 13, and Allan-Randolph Brewer-Carías, *Judicial Review in Comparative Law* (Cambridge, U.K.: Cambridge University Press, 1989), 252.

18. Brewer-Carías, *Judicial Review in Comparative Law*, 118–119.

19. For a similar point, see Wojciech Sadurski, *Rights Before Courts: A Study of Constitutional Courts in Postcommunist States of Central and Eastern Europe* (Dordrecht, The Netherlands: Springer, 2005), 44.

20. For a description of this evolution, see Cappelletti, *Judicial Review in the Contemporary World*, 12–16.

21. Gustavo Zagrebelsky, *La giustizia costituzionale* (Bologna: il Mulino, 1988), 172.

22. Hans Kelsen, "La garantie juridictionnelle de la Constitution (La justice constitutionnelle)," *Revue du droit public et de la science politique en France et à l'étranger* 45 (1928): 224–225.

23. Ibid., 226.

24. For references, see Rousseau, *Droit du contentieux constitutionnel*, 13, and Alec Stone, *The Birth of Judicial Politics in France: The Constitutional Council in Comparative Perspective* (Oxford: Oxford University Press, 1992), 33–40.

25. Charles Eisenmann, *La justice constitutionnelle et la Haute cour constitutionnelle d'Austriche* (Paris: Economica; Aix-en-Provence: Presses Universitaires d'Aix-Marseille, 1986), 105–107.

CHAPTER 3. A TRADITIONAL JUSTIFICATION

1. See, e.g., Hans Kelsen, "Judicial Review of Legislation: A Comparative Study of the Austrian and the American Constitution," *Journal of Politics* 4 (1942): 183–200, especially page 186; Charles Eisenmann, *La justice*

172 NOTES TO PAGE 21

constitutionnelle et la Haute cour constitutionnelle d'Austriche (Paris: Economica; Aix-en-Provence: Presses Universitaires d'Aix-Marseille, 1986), 291–293; and Mauro Cappelletti, *Judicial Review in the Contemporary World* (Indianapolis, Ind.: Bobbs-Merrill, 1971), 55–66.

2. A division of labor of this sort can be found in Austria, Belgium, France, Italy, Luxembourg, and Portugal, for instance. In other countries there is even greater division: in Germany and Spain, for example, there are five supreme courts, each specialized in a particular field of the law. In Germany, these courts are the supreme court that deals with civil and criminal law (which sits in Karlsruhe, except for the criminal sections, which sit in Leipzig), the supreme court for administrative law (which sits in Berlin), the supreme court for tax law (which sits in Munich), the supreme court for labor law (which sits in Erfurt), and the supreme court for social law (which sits in Kassel). In Spain, the five courts are nominally chambers (*salas*) of a single supreme court in Madrid. As a matter of fact, however, each chamber acts as a separate court, against whose decisions there is no further appeal (except for the complaints that can be brought to the constitutional court if fundamental rights have been violated). These chambers deal with civil law (Sala 1), criminal law (Sala 2), administrative law (Sala 3), labor and social law (Sala 4), and military matters (Sala 5).

3. Kelsen, "Judicial Review of Legislation," 186.

4. In Denmark and Norway, where constitutional review of legislation is decentralized, the judiciary is unified. In Finland and Sweden, in contrast, where review is also decentralized, the judiciary is divided between ordinary courts and administrative courts. Statutes are very rarely found to be unconstitutional, however, which makes the problem of divergence almost disappear. Incidentally, it is important to note that in those countries where the judiciary is unified under a single supreme court, it is possible to establish a centralized system of constitutional review without having to create a separate constitutional court: the existing supreme court can be granted the exclusive authority to review the validity of legislation, and other judges can be denied this power. The system is then centralized, but without a constitutional court. Allan-Randolph Brewer-Carías, *Judicial Review in Comparative Law* (Cambridge, U.K.: Cambridge University Press, 1989), mentions the examples of Papua New Guinea (180, 186), Panamá, Uruguay, and Paraguay (243–244).

5. See article 100.1 of the Greek Constitution. For a brief description of the system, see Brewer-Carías, *Judicial Review in Comparative Law,* 170–172.

6. Cappelletti, *Judicial Review in the Contemporary World,* 58.

7. Under the alternative decentralized system, Kelsen explained, "the decisions of the highest ordinary court, the so-called *Oberster Gerichtshof,* concerning the constitutionality of a statute or an ordinance, had no binding force upon the lower courts. The latter were not forbidden to apply a statute which the *Oberster Gerichtshof* had previously declared unconstitutional

and which it had, therefore, refused to apply in a given case." Kelsen, "Judicial Review of Legislation," 186.

8. For illuminating reports on the extent to which precedents are actually operative in civil-law countries, see Neil MacCormick and Robert Summers, eds., *Interpreting Precedents: A Comparative Study* (Aldershot, U.K.: Ashgate, 1997).

9. As Damaška observes, the attempt by the French revolutionaries to ensure that the legal opinions of higher courts would not be binding on lower courts did not succeed: "While formally free to disregard legal opinions of their superiors, judges continued to look to high courts for guidance. Although many factors conspired to preserve this deference to superiors, the attitude can most easily be explained as caused and nourished by recruitment, training, and promotion policies, all congenial to hierarchical organizations. Typically, the beginning of a career on the bench was also the beginning of the professional career for a young lawyer, fresh from a period of internship in the judicial apparatus. Rarely was a judge someone entering a second career. The first appointment (or election) was to the lowest court, a position carrying little prestige, and promotion depended at least in part on the approval of those who regularly reviewed lower courts' decisions. In this situation it is hardly surprising that assertion of independence on the part of lower judiciary, even where formally possible, remained quite aberrational. Firmly tied to the mast of civil service, lower judges could hear the seductive music of freedom as Ulysses heard the singing of the sirens." Mirjan Damaška, *The Faces of Justice and State Authority* (New Haven, Conn.: Yale University Press, 1986), 36–37.

10. On this difference, see Carlo Guarnieri and Patrizia Pederzoli, *The Power of Judges: A Comparative Study of Courts and Democracy* (Oxford: Oxford University Press, 2002), 78–97.

11. Damaška, *The Faces of Justice*, 37 n. 37.

12. See generally MacCormick and Summers, *Interpreting Precedents*.

13. See Acórdão do Tribunal Constitucional no. 810/93, December 7, 1993 (Portugal). The Portuguese Constitutional Court had to review the validity of article 3 of the civil code, which empowered the Supreme Court of Justice (Supremo Tribunal de Justiça) to fix doctrine "with general obligatory force" (*força obrigatória geral*). The court reasoned that judicial doctrines are not a source of law under the constitution. The judiciary cannot, therefore, generate legal rules that are binding on all. The highest courts, moreover, are not bound by their own doctrines: they are free to reconsider them in the future. To the extent that article 3 of the civil code violated these principles, it was declared unconstitutional. The court made it clear, however, that lower courts do not have a constitutionally protected liberty to disregard the judicial doctrines laid down by the highest courts. Judicial independence does not require that such liberty be accorded to them. It is therefore acceptable, the court asserted, for a statute to impose this kind of

obedience. This ruling beautifully reflects the deep tensions between old dogmas and pragmatic considerations in civil-law countries. Precedents cannot be classified as a source of law—to do so would be too radical a departure from the basic principles of the civil-law tradition. On the other hand, precedents are binding on lower courts; otherwise, legal certainty would be in danger. This unstable middle-ground solution to the underlying tensions was not accepted by Justice Maria da Assunção Esteves, who dissented. Speaking in the traditional voice that has been dominant in many European countries for many decades, she reasoned that requiring lower-court judges to follow the precedents established by the Supreme Court would offend the principle of judicial independence that the constitution guarantees.

14. Brewer-Carías, *Judicial Review in Comparative Law,* 128–131.

15. See John Henry Merryman, *The Civil Law Tradition* (Stanford, Calif.: Stanford University Press, 1985), especially chapters 5–9 and 13.

16. Kelsen proposed that a decision of the court regarding the constitutionality of a statute should be published in the same official journal in which the statute had been published. See Hans Kelsen, "La garantie juridictionnelle de la Constitution (La justice constitutionnelle)," *Revue du droit public et de la science politique en France et à l'étranger* 45 (1928): 249. This is the practice in most countries.

17. Kelsen was particularly worried about the risk of courts contradicting themselves when reviewing the constitutionality of statutes in concrete cases. He explained that before a constitutional tribunal was established in Austria, the Supreme Court of Justice could declare a law invalid in one case and sustain its validity in the next one. For this reason, he observed, when the Constitutional Court was later established in Austria, it was granted the power of general invalidation: "The decision of the court invalidated the statute or a special provision thereof not only for the concrete case but generally for all future cases." Kelsen, "Judicial Review of Legislation," 186. This is also the rule in most countries. As was already noted, however, Luxembourg, Belgium, and Portugal are exceptional in this regard. In both Luxembourg and Belgium, when the court decides a constitutional question certified by an ordinary judge, its decision has no general effects. If it holds that the statute is unconstitutional, the statute cannot be applied to the case, but it is not expelled from the legal system. However, in Belgium, the court's decision provides an opportunity for an abstract challenge to be filed. Similarly, in Portugal, when the court rules on the constitutionality of statutes in connection with concrete cases that are brought to it, its conclusions have no general effects. However, if the court rules in three cases that a particular statute is unconstitutional, a procedure of abstract review can then be initiated to invalidate the statute. In Belgium and Portugal, the drastic measure of formally eliminating a law can thus sometimes be deferred to a later moment, even if the court has already held that

the law is unconstitutional. Before that happens, of course, the court runs the risk of contradicting itself.

18. The Web sites of the supreme courts in the different European countries offer information about their workload. Just to mention some data that may be illustrative, the French Court of Cassation had to decide 20,354 civil cases and 8,468 criminal cases in 2007. See Cour de cassation, "Statistiques 2007," http://www.courdecassation.fr/institution_1/activite_cour _chiffres_58/statistiques_2007_11126.html. The court is composed of more than one hundred judges divided into six chambers: three civil chambers, a commercial chamber, a social chamber, and a criminal chamber. Similarly, the German Bundesgerichtshof (the supreme court in charge of civil and criminal matters) received 3,404 appeals in civil cases and 2,990 appeals in criminal cases in 2007. As of July 2008, it is composed of 127 judges divided into twelve civil sections, five criminal sections and eight special panels. See Bundesgerichtshof, *The Federal Court of Justice* (Karlsruhe, Germany, 2008), available at http://www.bundesgerichtshof.de/docs/ brochurebgh_2008.pdf. Since the heavy docket can only be handled by many judges organized in different panels, the court is likely to inadvertently contradict itself. Michele Taruffo and Massimo La Torre mention an extreme example of this. The Corte suprema di cassazione (the Italian court of last resort in civil and criminal matters) decides about 12,000 civil cases and 35,000 criminal cases every year. Not surprisingly, a study revealed that the court had contradicted itself no less than 864 times in five years when dealing with civil matters. See Michele Taruffo and Massimo La Torre, "Precedent in Italy," in *Interpreting Precedents* (see note 8), 144, 165.

19. Kelsen, "La garantie," 242. The deadline that Kelsen suggested was rather long, however—between three and five years after the promulgation of the statute.

20. See Pedro Cruz Villalón, *La formación del sistema europeo de control de constitucionalidad (1918–1939)* (Madrid: Centro de Estudios Constitucionales), 390.

21. Portugal is the most important example in this regard, since both types of review (a priori and a posteriori) can generally be used. See articles 278 and 281 of the Portuguese Constitution. Since the 2008 constitutional reform, France combines the two types of legislative review too. Other countries, in contrast, limit the scope of a priori review. In Austria, for example, it can only be used to examine legislation or administrative acts on federalism grounds. See article 138.2 of the Austrian Constitution. In Spain, only international treaties not yet ratified can be sent to the constitutional court for preventive review. See article 95.2 of the Spanish Constitution. Similarly, and as a matter of actual practice, the laws that are enacted in Germany to ratify international treaties can be challenged before promulgation. See Albrecht Weber, "Alemania," in *Las tensiones entre el Tribunal*

Constitucional y el Legislador en la Europa actual, ed. Eliseo Aja (Barcelona: Ariel, 1998), 62–63.

22. Kelsen, "La garantie," 218, 242–243. It is interesting to note that, apart from this pragmatic argument in favor of nonretroactivity, Kelsen offered a conceptual argument to reinforce it. He claimed that, for conceptual reasons, a statute cannot be taken to be void ab initio. The argument appears, for example, in Kelsen, "Judicial Review of Legislation," 189–191.

23. Kelsen himself mentioned this strategic consideration to justify exceptions to the general rule against retroactivity. See Kelsen, "Judicial Review of Legislation," 196, and Kelsen, "La garantie," 246. Actually, Austria's constitution of 1920 established that the statute declared unconstitutional was not to be applied to the case prompting judicial review. This exception still exists in the current constitution. See article 140.7 of the Austrian Constitution.

24. See Cappelletti, *Judicial Review in the Contemporary World,* 88–96. The Austrian Constitution, which established a rather categorical rule against retroactivity in its original 1920 version, was later amended to introduce more flexibility in this area. Article 140.7 now allows the court to give retroactive effect to its decisions declaring a statute unconstitutional. Brewer-Carías, *Judicial Review in Comparative Law,* 189–190, suggests that, given the internal logic of each system, the decentralized system is linked to retroactivity (though limited to the parties to the case to be decided), whereas the centralized model is linked to prospectivity. The argument for this conceptual connection is not easy to see, however. Kelsen himself thought that his own argument against retroactivity was valid *in both systems.* See Kelsen, "Judicial Review of Legislation," 189–191. And, vice versa, there are centralized systems where the Kelsenian thesis against retroactivity has been rejected. In Italy and Germany, for example, the general understanding, at least initially, was that the constitutional court's decisions striking down statutes had retroactive effect, since the assumption was that unconstitutional statutes were void ab initio. In any case, Brewer-Carías offers examples that illustrate how courts in different jurisdictions have applied flexible standards in this area in light of several pragmatic considerations. These examples suggest that courts do not find the conceptual arguments very compelling.

25. See article 140.5 of the Austrian Constitution. Originally (in 1920), the effects could be postponed for a maximum period of six months. The constitution was later amended in 1929, and the maximum period of delay was extended to one year. In 1992 the period was further extended: it is now eighteen months. The court resorts to this technique quite often. We also find it in other countries, such as France (see article 62 of the French Constitution), Belgium (see article 8 of the *Loi spéciale du 6 janvier 1989 sur la Cour d'arbitrage*), Hungary (see article 43.4 of the *Act XXXII of 1989 on the Constitutional Court*), Poland (see article 190.3 of the Polish Constitution),

Albania (see article 132.2 of the Albanian Constitution), Estonia (see article 58.3 of the *Constitutional Review Court Procedure Act,* March 13, 2002), and South Africa (see article 172.1.b of the South African Constitution). The Supreme Court of Canada has also accepted this technique. See its decision in *Schachter v. Canada,* [1992] 2 S.C.R. 679.

26. This rule was introduced in Austria's constitution of 1920. It currently figures in article 140.6.

27. Kelsen, "Judicial Review of Legislation," 198. Of course, when resorting to this technique, the constitutional court is no longer a mere "negative legislature." As Kelsen explains, in such cases the court acts both as a "negative legislature" (to the extent that it eliminates the statute it has found unconstitutional) and as a "positive legislature" (to the extent that it restores the old statute). Ibid., 199. It must be noted that, consistently with his theory that statutes are not void ab initio, Kelsen argued that the invalidation of the current statute cannot, by itself, make the earlier one effective again. Therefore, he said, an explicit clause must be introduced in the constitution in order to authorize the court to both eliminate the current statute and restore the applicability of the older one.

28. Kelsen, "La garantie," 244.

29. See article 282 of the Portuguese Constitution.

CHAPTER 4. THE JUSTIFICATION OF CONSTITUTIONAL REVIEW

1. Hans Kelsen, "La garantie juridictionnelle de la Constitution (La justice constitutionnelle)," *Revue du droit public et de la science politique en France et à l'étranger* 45 (1928): 253 (my translation).

2. The federalist-regionalist rationale is strong, for example, in Austria's constitution of 1920, Czechoslovakia's constitution of 1920, and Spain's constitution of 1931, which established constitutional courts. It was also present in the constitutions of Germany (1949) and Italy (1947) after the Second World War, and those of Portugal (1976), Spain (1978), and Belgium (1980). On the correlation between federalism and judicial review, see Martin Shapiro, "The Success of Judicial Review and Democracy," in *On Law, Politics, and Judicialization,* by Martin Shapiro and Alec Stone Sweet (Oxford: Oxford University Press, 2002), 149–183.

3. The French constitution of 1958 set up a political arrangement that departed from the parliamentary traditions of the country. It established a semi-presidential system under which the legislative powers of parliament were curtailed. The constitutional text defined the domain of matters that could be regulated by parliament (article 34) and provided that the rest were to be dealt with by the executive through administrative decrees (article 37). The constitutional court was created to police the boundary that defined the respective regulatory spheres of parliament and the executive. It was only later (especially after its important decision no. 71-44 DC, of July 16, 1971) that the court started to review legislation affecting

fundamental rights. See Dominique Rousseau, *Droit du contentieux consti-tutionnel* (Paris: Montchrestien, 2006), 63–73, and Alec Stone, *The Birth of Judicial Politics in France* (Oxford: Oxford University Press, 1992), 46–59. With respect to Belgium, the court was established to protect federalism, which was introduced in the country in 1980 through the creation of "re-gions" and "linguistic communities." The court was to resolve the legisla-tive conflicts that would inevitably arise. Actually, it was initially called the Cour d'arbitrage, a name that clearly expresses the function it was expected to carry out. It was only later that it received jurisdiction in the field of fun-damental rights. A constitutional amendment of July 15, 1988, extended the jurisdiction of the court to include the supervision of the observance of articles 10, 11, and 24 of the constitution, which guarantee the principles of equality and nondiscrimination and the rights and liberties in respect of education. See article 142 of the Belgian Constitution. What triggered this expansion was the decision to transfer to the regions the competences on education that were originally held by the state. The intervention of the court was thought to be desirable to ensure the respect of minority rights in the respective regions. See Francesca Rescigno, "La giustizia costituzio-nale in Belgio," in *La giustizia costituzionale in Europa,* ed. Marco Olivetti and Tania Groppi (Milan: Giuffrè, 2003), 259. In addition, the constitu-tional amendment of 1988 permitted "special" laws granting the court the authority to review compliance with other articles of the constitution. (Enactment of a "special" law requires the approval of a majority of each linguistic group in both chambers of parliament and an overall super-majority of two-thirds.) This facility was used in the special act of March 9, 2003. Title II (articles 8 to 32) of the constitution, as well as articles 170, 172, and 191, all of which protect fundamental rights, are now part of the body of constitutional provisions that the court can use to strike down stat-utes. Consistently with the broader jurisdiction that the court has been given, a May 2007 constitutional amendment changed the court's name to the more standard Cour constitutionnelle.

4. Bruce Ackerman, *We the People: Foundations* (Cambridge, Mass.: Harvard University Press, 1991).

5. For an interesting reading of Kelsen and his historical context, see Carlo Mezzanotte, *Corte costituzionale e legittimazione politica* (Rome: Tipografia Veneziana, 1984), 14–33.

6. Kelsen, "La garantie," 239–242. In his debate with Carl Schmitt on the ac-ceptability of judicial review, Kelsen acknowledged that if the constitution is too abstract, the presence of politics in constitutional adjudication be-comes excessive. See Hans Kelsen, *¿Quién debe ser el defensor de la Consti-tución?* (Madrid: Tecnos, 1995), 33–39. It should be mentioned, moreover, that Kelsen was basically an emotivist: he thought that one can rationally justify a course of action as a means to serve particular values, but one can-not rationally defend the choice of the values themselves or the choice of a

particular solution when different values collide. See Hans Kelsen, "What Is Justice?" in *What Is Justice? Justice, Law and Politics in the Mirror of Science* (Berkeley: University of California Press, 1957).

7. Actually, as Michel Rosenfeld, "Constitutional adjudication in Europe and the United States," *International Journal of Constitutional Law*, 2 (2004): 633–668, suggests, there seems to be a stronger consensus around fundamental values in contemporary Europe than in the United States, where constitutional issues are more divisive. He mentions the European consensus on the abolition of the death penalty as an example. Ibid., 667.

8. For a general treatment of these problems, see Jon Elster, *Ulysses Unbound: Studies in Rationality, Precommitment, and Constraints* (Cambridge, U.K.: Cambridge University Press, 2000).

9. Lawrence Sager, *Justice in Plainclothes: A Theory of American Constitutional Practice* (New Haven, Conn.: Yale University Press, 2004), 54–55.

10. Barry Friedman and Scott Smith, "The Sedimentary Constitution," *University of Pennsylvania Law Review* 147 (1998): 1–90.

11. Alexander Bickel, *The Least Dangerous Branch* (New Haven, Conn.: Yale University Press, 1962), 25.

12. Sager, *Justice in Plainclothes*, 75.

13. Ibid., 199.

14. Owen Fiss, *The Law as It Could Be* (New York and London: New York University Press, 2003), 11–12.

15. Ibid., 163.

16. See generally Neil K. Komesar, *Imperfect Alternatives: Choosing Institutions in Law, Economics, and Public Policy* (Chicago: University of Chicago Press, 1994).

17. Ronald Dworkin, *A Matter of Principle* (Cambridge, Mass.: Harvard University Press, 1985), 70–71.

18. See, e.g., Mark Tushnet, *Taking the Constitution Away from the Courts* (Princeton, N.J.: Princeton University Press, 1999).

19. Wojciech Sadurski, *Rights Before Courts: A Study of Constitutional Courts in Postcommunist States of Central and Eastern Europe* (Dordrecht, The Netherlands: Springer, 2005), 193–194. Although he is more critical of the courts when they have dealt with other rights, such as minority rights, his overall assessment is favorable. Ibid., 289.

CHAPTER 5. THE SPECIAL NATURE OF CONSTITUTIONAL DISCOURSE

1. There are currently two: Valéry Giscard d'Estaing and Jacques Chirac.

2. Initially, there were twenty-four judges on the court. The number was later reduced, first to twenty, and finally to sixteen. See Francesca Rescigno, "La giustizia costituzionale in Germania," in *La giustizia costituzionale in Europa*, ed. Marco Olivetti and Tania Groppi (Milan: Giuffrè, 2003), 97.

3. This was not always so. Until 1891, the court was obliged to decide all cases properly brought to it. In 1891, a limited discretionary jurisdiction

was established. By the 1920s, however, the court's workload had become so burdensome that Congress enacted the Judiciary Act of 1925, which drastically reduced the range and number of cases that fell within the court's obligatory jurisdiction. This law was to be the great divide between the court's traditional role and its modern one. In 1988, Congress further reduced the scope of obligatory jurisdiction. See Joel B. Grossman and Charles R. Epp, "Agenda Formation on the Policy Active U.S. Supreme Court," in *Constitutional Courts in Comparison: The U.S. Supreme Court and the German Federal Constitutional Court,* ed. Ralf Rogowski and Thomas Gawron (New York and Oxford: Berghahn Books, 2002), 109–111.

4. Richard Posner, "The Supreme Court 2004 Term—Foreword: A Political Court," *Harvard Law Review* 119 (2005): 79. Posner notes, in addition, that the U.S. Supreme Court can no longer control the lower courts by means of narrow, case-by-case determinations—the incremental method of the common law. It must instead act in a more legislative manner, laying down general rules or standards that will cover a large number of cases. Ibid., 35–37.

5. See generally Lech Garlicki, "Constitutional Courts versus Supreme Courts," *International Journal of Constitutional Law* 5 (2007): 44–68.

6. Even here, there is a potential source of conflict: if the constitutional court declares that a statute is valid only if it is interpreted in a certain way, what happens if the supreme court or other lower courts interpret the statute differently? Despite the institutional battles that this question has provoked, the answer seems quite obvious from a theoretical point of view. If the constitutional court has the authority to eliminate a statute from the legal system on constitutional grounds, it must be accorded the implied power to establish the constitutional conditions under which a statute can remain in the system. When the court holds that a particular reading of the statute would make the statute unconstitutional, there is no reason why ordinary judges should be entitled to disregard such a holding. If they read the statute in the manner that the court has disallowed, they would actually be applying an unconstitutional norm.

7. Garlicki, "Constitutional Courts versus Supreme Courts," 63.

8. The Italian Constitutional Court (Corte costituzionale) retained its jurisdiction, however, over crimes committed by the president of the republic.

9. In Germany, the court, which consists of two panels (senates), is further divided into six chambers with three judges each in order to handle most of the work. Between 1951 and 2001, only 5,237 decisions were made by the senates; the chambers rendered 109,366 decisions. For a description of the court's admission procedures, see Werner Heun, "Access to the German Federal Constitutional Court," in *Constitutional Courts in Comparison* (see note 3), 125–156. A similar pattern can be found in the Spanish Constitutional Court (Tribunal Constitucional de España). The court is divided into two panels (*salas*) with six judges each, and is further divided into four sec-

tions of three judges each. The vast majority of decisions are made by the sections.

10. Some proposals in this direction have been considered in Germany and Spain. See Pablo López Pietsch, "Objetivar el recurso de amparo: Las recomendaciones de la Comisión Benda y el debate español," *Revista española de derecho constitucional* 53 (1998): 115–151. The Spanish law that regulates the functions of the Spanish Constitutional Court (*Ley Orgánica 2/1979, de 3 de octubre, del Tribunal Constitucional*) was amended in May 2007 to make it easier for the court to reject complaints that do not pose an important issue.

11. Thus, Pedro Cruz Villalón, a former president of the Spanish court, has urged that a radical change be introduced in Spain (which would require amending the constitution). The complaints procedure, as currently conceived, should be abolished. Individuals would have access to the court only when they challenge the validity of a statute. See Pedro Cruz Villalón, "Tribuna abierta: Qué hacer con el amparo," *Actualidad jurídica Uría Menéndez* 15 (2006): 7–13. This is basically the way the complaints procedure works in Poland, for example. See Wojciech Sadurski, *Rights Before Courts: A Study of Constitutional Courts in Postcommunist States of Central and Eastern Europe* (Dordrecht, The Netherlands: Springer, 2005), 25.

12. For this general contrast between the "bureaucratic" model that is typical of civil-law countries and the "professional" model that is typical of the common law, see Carlo Guarnieri and Patrizia Pederzoli, *The Power of Judges: A Comparative Study of Courts and Democracy* (Oxford: Oxford University Press, 2002), 18–77.

13. Alexander Bickel, *The Least Dangerous Branch* (New Haven, Conn.: Yale University Press, 1962), 25.

14. The curricula vitae of the judges on the German Constitutional Court can be found on the court's website at http://www.bundesverfassungsgericht .de/en/judges.html.

15. In France, for example, according to Dominique Rousseau, the Constitutional Council (as of 2006) had ten members, most of whom (eight) had received legal training. They were perfectly informed of the governmental game, however, since a large majority (seven) had been ministers or had worked in ministerial cabinets. See Dominique Rousseau, *Droit du contentieux constitutionnel* (Paris: Montchrestien, 2006), 38–48. According to John Bell, *Judiciaries within Europe: A Comparative Review* (Cambridge: Cambridge University Press, 2006), 95–96, when one analyzes the sixty-two appointments from 1959 to 2004 in terms of governmental experience, one finds that nineteen constitutional judges had been ministers and a further fifteen had served as advisers in ministerial cabinets.

16. The other half must exhibit a specific legal background: professor of law at a Belgian university, magistrate with the Court of Cassation or the Council

of State, or legal secretary with the Constitutional Court. See article 34 of the *Loi spéciale du 6 janvier 1989 sur la Cour d'arbitrage*.

17. See Bell, *Judiciaries within Europe*, 95–96.

18. See, e.g., Christine Landfried, "Constitutional Review and Legislation in the Federal Republic of Germany," in *Constitutional Review and Legislation: An International Comparison*, ed. Christine Landfried (Baden-Baden, Germany: Nomos Verlagsgesellschaft, 1988), 149.

19. Hans Kelsen, "La garantie juridictionnelle de la Constitution (La justice constitutionnelle)," *Revue du droit public et de la science politique en France et à l'étranger* 45 (1928): 227.

20. Francis Delpérée, for example, in *Le droit constitutionnel de la Belgique* (Brussels: Bruylant; Paris: L.G.D.J., 2000), 109, defends the presence of former members of parliament on the Belgian Constitutional Court against the charge that the court will be unduly influenced by partisan spirit. He thinks it reasonable to require half the members of the court to be acquainted with the methods and concerns of the legislators given that the court's only task is to review parliamentary enactments. An interesting question arises: Should a constitutional judge abstain from participating in a case in which someone challenges the validity of a statute that was enacted when that judge was a legislator? There are sometimes explicit rules on this, with opposite solutions. In Belgium, a judge cannot recuse himself or herself merely on such grounds. See article 101.2 of the *Loi spéciale du 6 janvier 1989 sur la Cour d'arbitrage*. The same is true in Germany. See article 18.3 of the *Bundesverfassungsgerichtsgesetz* [Federal Constitutional Court Act]. In Austria, in contrast, the judge must abstain in such a case. See article 12.4 of the *Verfassungsgerichtshofgesetz* [Constitutional Court Act].

21. Charles Eisenmann, *La justice constitutionnelle et la Haute cour constitutionnelle d'Austriche* (Paris: Economica; Aix-en-Provence: Presses Universitaires d'Aix-Marseille, 1986), 294.

22. For a general description of these issues, see Peter E. Quint, *The Imperfect Union: Constitutional Structures of German Unification* (Princeton, N.J.: Princeton University Press, 1997).

23. Ibid., 314.

24. See Sadurski, *Rights Before Courts*, xiv–xv, 14.

25. The Belgium Constitutional Court, for example, is of the "pure" type. As already indicated, the law establishes that half the court's members must have had political experience as members of parliament. They need not be lawyers.

26. Christopher Eisgruber, *Constitutional Self-Government* (Cambridge, Mass.: Harvard University Press, 2001), 67.

27. See articles 31, 33, 34.4, and 54 of the *Loi spéciale du 6 janvier 1989 sur la Cour d'arbitrage*.

28. Delpérée, *Le droit constitutionnel de la Belgique*, 108.

29. Enzo Cheli (a former justice of the Italian Constitutional Court), for example, argues that checking legislation under a constitution is such an atypical function that it requires an atypical institution to carry it out. See *Il giudice delle leggi: La Corte costituzionale nella dinamica dei poteri* (Bologna: Il Mulino, 1996), 15–16.

30. See Corte costituzionale della Repubblica italiana, "What is the Constitutional Court?" (page 2), http://www.cortecostituzionale.it/versioni_in _lingua/eng/lacortecostituzionale/cosaelacorte/pag_02.asp.

31. Robert Alexy, *A Theory of Constitutional Rights* (Oxford: Oxford University Press, 2002). For an illuminating comment on Alexy's theory, see Mattias Kumm, "Constitutional Rights as Principles: On the Structure and Domain of Constitutional Justice," *International Journal of Constitutional Law* 2 (2004): 574–596.

32. See the Italian Constitution, *Disposizioni transitorie e finali* VII.

33. See Carlo Mezzanotte, *Corte costituzionale e legittimazione politica* (Rome: Tipografia Veneziana, 1984), 126–131.

34. It may be argued that the Constitutional Council is not the only body in France that applies such unwritten principles. Before the court was born, the Council of State (the supreme court in charge of administrative law) had already started to appeal to general principles in order to enrich the body of law against which administrative decisions are to be reviewed. It should be noted, however, that like the Constitutional Council, the Council of State is special: it was created as an institution separate from the ordinary judiciary. It could develop its own jurisprudence, with a different style, precisely because it was specialized in a particular field that required a different, less formalist approach than the one that ordinary courts followed. It is revealing, in this connection, to contrast the ease with which the French Council of State has developed general principles that the administration is required to respect, with the caution that English courts have traditionally exhibited when reviewing administrative decisions as a result of their more legalistic attitude as ordinary courts. See J. W. F. Allison, *A Continental Distinction in the Common Law* (Oxford: Oxford University Press, 1996), 170–189.

35. There is an interesting analogy with the votes taken within a legislative assembly. Jon Elster, *Ulysses Unbound: Studies in Rationality, Precommitment, and Constraints* (Cambridge, U.K.: Cambridge University Press, 2000), 93 n. 12, explains that the first French constituent assembly after the 1789 revolution did not record the number of votes for and against the proposals that were made. The identification of majority vote with the general will had this practical implication.

36. See Mitchel de S.-O. L'E. Lasser, *Judicial Deliberations: A Comparative Analysis of Judicial Transparency and Legitimacy* (Oxford: Oxford University Press, 2004). Lasser distinguishes between a French "discursive bifurcation" and an American "unification." Whereas there is a strong separation

in France between the final judicial opinion and the official documents that express the more political internal deliberations of the court, the American practice fuses the two into a highly argumentative opinion.

37. This is the situation in Germany, for example. Dissenting opinions were first explicitly introduced in 1970, but only for the Constitutional Court. See article 30.2 of the *Bundesverfassungsgerichtsgesetz* [Federal Constitutional Court Act]. Actually, the court had already published dissents before the law codified the practice, which went against the German tradition on the matter. See Francesca Rescigno, "La giustizia costituzionale in Germania," in *La giustizia costituzionale in Europa* (see note 2), 100–101. The case of Spain is interesting. The publication of dissenting opinions was first introduced by the constitution of 1978, in connection with the Constitutional Court (article 164.1). Later, in 1985, a statute extended the practice to ordinary courts. See article 260 of the *Ley Orgánica 6/1985, de 1 de julio, del Poder Judicial*.

38. It has to be acknowledged, however, that a decentralized system could introduce a similar "dualistic device": it could prohibit ordinary courts from publishing dissenting opinions except when the constitutional validity of a statute was being decided. Interestingly, Ireland, which has a quasi-decentralized system, has a rule of this kind, but with the opposite content: dissenting opinions are allowed, except when the Supreme Court rules on the constitutionality of a statute. See articles 34.4.5 and 26.2.2 of the Irish Constitution.

39. This is so in Italy, France, Austria, and Belgium, for example. In Italy, a general constitutional revision was discussed in 1997 to reform governmental institutions. One of its innovations was the introduction of dissenting opinions. The general reform was not approved in the end, however.

40. See, e.g., Philippe Blachèr, *Contrôle de constitutionnalité et volonté générale* (Paris: Presses Universitaires de France, 2001), 166–167, and Rousseau, *Droit du contentieux constitutionnel*, 475, 511. Rousseau explains that, sometimes, the governmental majority in France is constrained by the Constitutional Council in the name of certain jurisprudential principles and rules that the current majority helped generate when it was in the opposition and challenged statutes. Ibid., 480. This theme is explored in Louis Favoreu, *La politique saisie par le droit* (Paris: Economica, 1988). For a similar emphasis on the importance of consistency, see Gustavo Zagrebelsky, *La giustizia costituzionale* (Bologna: il Mulino, 1988), 59. Zagrebelsky gives the example of the Italian court's adherence to an earlier ruling on divorce. The court did so out of coherence, despite the partial change in its composition.

41. In Germany, six out of the sixteen members of the Constitutional Court must be chosen from any of the five federal supreme courts. See article 2.3 of the *Bundesverfassungsgerichtsgesetz* [Federal Constitutional Court Act]. The vast majority of legal assistants that work for the court, moreover, are

ordinary judges who interrupt their normal careers for about three or four years. See Joachim Wieland, "The Role of the Legal Assistants at the German Federal Constitutional Court," in *Constitutional Courts in Comparison* (see note 3), 198. In Portugal, six members of the Constitutional Court that are appointed by the assembly or co-opted must be selected from among the judges of the other courts. See article 222.2 of the Portuguese Constitution. In Spain, two of the twelve members of the court are appointed by the General Council of the Judiciary, which in practice means that they are recruited from among ordinary judges.

42. For an account of this transformation, see Sylvia Snowiss, *Judicial Review and the Law of the Constitution* (New Haven, Conn.: Yale University Press, 1990), and Larry Kramer, *The People Themselves: Popular Constitutionalism and Judicial Review* (New York: Oxford University Press, 2004).

43. That the constitutional court has been granted the authority to invalidate legislation is absolutely clear, from a legal point of view, in all European countries. This is so in France too, although the history of the French Constitutional Council has been more complex. As was already noted, its original task was to police the boundary between the sphere of legislation and the sphere of executive regulation. When in its historic decision on the right of association of July 16, 1971, the court held that the preamble to the constitution was also justiciable and that, therefore, fundamental rights and liberties had to be protected against ordinary legislation, the court assumed a new function that the framers had not contemplated. This judicial move, however, received ex post facto political legitimation when the constitution was later amended in 1974 to permit the parliamentary opposition (sixty deputies or sixty senators) to challenge statutes. Obviously, the opposition is not going to be worried about statutes invading the regulatory domain that pertains to the executive. Its objections against statutes will instead be more substantive and usually related to fundamental rights. So the 1974 amendment was a retroactive political foundation for the power of constitutional review that the court had assumed in 1971. See Rousseau, *Droit du contentieux constitutionnel*, 66–73. The 2008 amendment, which allows the ordinary judiciary to certify questions to the court when legislation seems to breach constitutionally guaranteed rights and liberties, is an even more explicit and clear source of authority for the court's power of legislative review.

44. The Portuguese Constitution, for example, declares in article 288(l) that it is not possible to amend the constitution to eliminate the scrutiny of legal provisions for active unconstitutionality and unconstitutionality by omission. In Austria, it is usually understood that only a total revision of the constitution, which requires a referendum—and not an ordinary constitutional amendment that is simply passed by a parliamentary supermajority —can abolish constitutional review. See Heinz Schäffer, "Austria," in *Las*

tensiones entre el Tribunal Constitucional y el Legislador en la Europa actual,
ed. Eliseo Aja (Barcelona: Ariel, 1998), 40.

45. 17 U.S (4 Wheat.) 316 (1819).

46. Posner, "The Supreme Court 2004 Term," 79–80.

47. Burt Neuborne, "Hommage à Louis Favoreu," *International Journal of
Constitutional Law* 5 (2007): 25.

48. Jeremy Waldron, "The Core of the Case against Judicial Review," *Yale
Law Journal* 115 (2006): 1381.

49. Eisgruber, *Constitutional Self-Government,* 208.

50. Christopher Zurn, *Deliberative Democracy and the Institutions of Judicial
Review* (New York: Cambridge University Press, 2007), 282.

CHAPTER 6. THE STRUCTURE OF THE CONSTITUTIONAL CONVERSATION

1. See, for instance, the classification of political regimes drawn by Arend
Lijphart in his book *Patterns of Democracy: Government Forms and Performance in Thirty-six Countries* (New Haven, Conn., and London: Yale University Press, 1999), especially pages 116–142. In Central-Eastern Europe,
most countries have opted for a parliamentary democracy with a relatively
weak presidency. Poland, with a semi-presidential system, is the most
notable exception. See Wojciech Sadurski, *Rights Before Courts: A Study of
Constitutional Courts in Postcommunist States of Central and Eastern Europe*
(Dordrecht, The Netherlands: Springer, 2005), 91–92.

2. Alec Stone Sweet, *Governing with Judges: Constitutional Politics in Europe*
(Oxford: Oxford University Press, 2000), 52–53.

3. Ibid., 53–55. Concerning the German political system, David Currie,
The Constitution of the Federal Republic of Germany (Chicago and London:
University of Chicago Press, 1994), 173, observes that "federalism thus
compensates in substantial measure for the lack of structural separation
between the central legislature and executive powers."

4. Gustavo Zagrebelsky, *El derecho dúctil: Ley, derechos, justicia* (Madrid:
Trotta, 1995), 58–65.

5. Not surprisingly, Kelsen was sympathetic to the idea of centralizing constitutional review of earlier statutes given the risk for legal certainty. He
noted, in particular, that the constitutions enacted after the First World
War announced new general principles that were at odds with those that
had inspired previous legislation. As an example, he referred to the constitutional principle of sex equality, which could affect important parts of
earlier laws. It seemed preferable to have the constitutional court give a
unified answer to the controversies that were likely to arise. Hans Kelsen,
"La garantie juridictionnelle de la Constitution (La justice constitutionnelle)," *Revue du droit public et de la science politique en France et à l'étranger*
45 (1928): 235–236.

6. As noted in chapter 1, Portugal is exceptional within the group of European
countries with constitutional courts, in that ordinary judges may set aside

statutes on their own authority. Therefore, before the Portuguese Constitutional Court speaks on the validity of a statute, lower courts have had the opportunity to express their opinions by ruling on the matter.

7. See article 39.2 of the French Constitution.

8. See Louis Favoreu, "The Constitutional Council and Parliament in France," in *Constitutional Review and Legislation: An International Comparison*, ed. Christine Landfried (Baden-Baden, Germany: Nomos Verlagsgesellschaft, 1988), 92–93, 105.

9. In Luxembourg and Belgium, administrative regulations are excluded from the field of legal provisions that the constitutional court is authorized to control. Only parliamentary statutes can be examined. In Italy and Spain, the court's jurisdiction is rather limited when it comes to administrative regulations: it is basically in connection with the conflicts that arise between the state and the regions that such jurisdiction can be exercised. In Germany, the authority of the court is more expansive: it can test the validity of administrative regulations against any constitutional norm. It can do so in abstract review procedures, however, not in concrete review ones, because ordinary courts may disregard administrative regulations on their own authority. Similarly, the court in Portugal can check the validity of such regulations against the constitution. A more extreme solution is found in Austria. Under the inspiration of Hans Kelsen, Austria established a completely centralized system to review the validity of administrative regulations on both constitutional and ordinary legal grounds. Kelsen thought that there is a sort of natural frontier between general rules, on the one hand, and individual acts of application of those rules, on the other, making it advisable to centralize judicial review of general rules (whether statutes or regulations) in the hands of the constitutional court. Kelsen, "La garantie," 230.

10. Francisco Rubio Llorente, "Tendencias actuales de la jurisdicción constitucional en Europa," in *Estudios sobre jurisdicción constitucional*, by Francisco Rubio Llorente and Javier Jiménez Campo (Madrid: McGraw-Hill, 1998), 156. For a similar view, see Luis María Díez-Picazo, "Dificultades prácticas y significado constitucional del recurso de amparo," *Revista española de Derecho constitucional* 40 (1994): 35–37.

11. Some Italian scholars, for example, believe that the fact that the Italian Constitutional Court can review legislation, but not concrete decisions made by the executive branch or by the ordinary judiciary, is an important gap in the Italian system of constitutional justice. In this regard, they view the complaints procedure of the German-Spanish sort as a desirable mechanism to introduce. See, e.g., Gustavo Zagrebelsky, *La giustizia costituzionale* (Bologna: il Mulino, 1988), 104, 175. In a press conference on January 20, 2005, the former president of the court Valerio Onida pointed to the absence of the complaints procedure as a deficiency of the current arrangement in Italy. See Valerio Onida, "Introduzione del Presidente Valerio

Onida" (press conference, Palazzo della Consulta, Rome, Italy, January 20, 2005), 21, available at http://www.cortecostituzionale.it/documenti/download/pdf/Relazione breve _Onida_.pdf. It should be noted that the failed constitutional revision that was discussed in 1997 would have expanded the court's jurisdiction to include complaints for violation of rights.

12. It is possible, of course, to have a decentralized system in which public institutions can initiate abstract review procedures. In Ireland, for example (as noted in chapter 1), there is no special constitutional court, but the president of the republic can petition the Supreme Court to examine the constitutionality of a statute before it is enacted. Similarly, in some states in the United States it is possible to get abstract advisory opinions from the state supreme courts.

13. When commenting on the American system of judicial review, Kelsen observed that the question whether a statute is constitutional "can only arise incidentally when a party maintains that the application of the statute in a concrete case is an illegal violation of its interests because the statute is unconstitutional. Hence it is in principle only the violation of a party-interest which puts in motion the procedure of the judicial review of legislation." He found this system deficient: "The interest in the constitutionality of legislation is, however, a public one which does not necessarily coincide with the private interest of the parties concerned. It is a public interest which deserves protection by a special procedure in conformity with its special character." Hans Kelsen, "Judicial Review of Legislation: A Comparative Study of the Austrian and the American Constitution," *Journal of Politics* 4 (1942): 193. Kelsen mentions a federal law of the United States (the Judiciary Act of August 24, 1937) that allows the federal government to intervene in any action between private parties whenever the constitutionality of any act of Congress affecting the public interest is brought in question. The law also grants the government the right to appeal to the U.S. Supreme Court from a decision declaring a federal statute unconstitutional and seeks to preclude the granting of injunctions by a single judge to restrain the enforcement of an act of Congress on constitutional grounds. But Kelsen notes the asymmetry of the American system as far as the protection of public interest is concerned: "All this is provided for by the Act of 1937 only to defend the validity of statutes enacted by Congress, to render more difficult a judicial decision by which a federal statute is declared unconstitutional, *not to promote the annulment of unconstitutional statutes.*" Ibid., 194 (emphasis added).

14. Kelsen, "La garantie," 247.

15. This familiar element within the European model was not introduced until after the Second World War, however. Kelsen was an earlier advocate of the idea, which he linked to the need to protect minorities against abuses by the parliamentary majority. Ibid., 247. His proposal was not accepted, though. A similar legislative proposal was discussed but not enacted dur-

ing the Weimar Republic in Germany. See Pedro Cruz Villalón, *La forma-ción del sistema europeo de control de constitucionalidad (1918–1939)* (Madrid: Centro de Estudios Constitucionales, 1987), 204.

16. See information provided in chapter 1.

17. Other institutions in France can also challenge statutes in the abstract, but they have never done so—or only rarely. According to Dominique Rousseau, *Droit du contentieux constitutionnel* (Paris: Montchrestien, 2006), 183–185, the president of the republic has never used his power to challenge statutes. (Some presidents have brought international treaties to the court, however, in order to dispel doubts about their compatibility with the constitution.) As far as the prime minister is concerned, he has challenged statutes in a few cases. (He has more often, however, requested that the court issue a declaration to the effect that a statute invades the regulatory domain of the executive so that a new regulation can then be validly enacted by the government.) The president of the National Assembly, who also has standing to challenge statutes, has only done so twice, in connection with legislative procedural matters. Finally, the president of the Senate used to attack statutes more often before 1974. The Senate was then an important counterweight to the Gaullist government. After 1974, however, when the parliamentary opposition was accorded standing to bring challenges, the president of the Senate no longer had to play the role of constitutional counterweight. In his or her capacity as senator, the president of the Senate generally prefers to join a challenge brought by colleagues (if they belong to the president's party).

18. Christopher Zurn, *Deliberative Democracy and the Institutions of Judicial Review* (New York: Cambridge University Press, 2007), 289.

19. Stone Sweet, *Governing with Judges*, 61–91.

20. Ibid., 74.

21. Mentioned in Philippe Blachèr, *Contrôle de constitutionnalité et volonté générale* (Paris: Presses Universitaires de France, 2001), 168 n. 3.

22. Rousseau, *Droit du contentieux constitutionnel*, 72, 478.

23. Dieter Grimm, "Constitutional Adjudication and Democracy," in *Liber Amicorum in Honour of Lord Slynn of Hadley*, vol. 2, *Judicial Review in International Perspective*, ed. Mads Andenas and Duncan Fairgrieve (The Hague: Kluwer Law International, 2000), 111.

24. Erhard Blankenburg, "Mobilization of the German Federal Constitutional Court," in *Constitutional Courts in Comparison: The U.S. Supreme Court and the German Federal Constitutional Court*, ed. Ralf Rogowski and Thomas Gawrop (New York and Oxford: Berghahn Books, 2002), 171.

25. See Wojciech Sadurski, *Rights Before Courts: A Study of Constitutional Courts in Postcommunist States of Central and Eastern Europe* (Dordrecht, The Netherlands: Springer, 2005), 95. According to Carlos Blanco de Morais, *Justiça constitucional*, vol. 2, *O contencioso constitucional Português entre o modelo misto e a tentação do sistema de reenvio* (Coimbra, Portugal:

Coimbra Editora, 2006), 160–161, scarcely more than thirty challenges against enacted laws were lodged by the parliamentary minorities between 1983 and 2004. A large portion of the challenges were filed by the Communist Party before 1999. Afterward, the party no longer had the required number of seats (one tenth of the deputies) to avail itself of this mechanism.

26. Interestingly, one of Kelsen's French students, Charles Eisenmann, writing in 1928, criticized the Austrian system in its original form because ordinary judges deciding concrete cases were not allowed at that time to certify constitutional questions to the court. (This mechanism was introduced in 1929, but for the supreme courts only; it was later extended to the courts of appeal in 1975.) Eisenmann justified his criticism on the grounds that a statute could be artificially protected against review through a *marchandage politique*. See Charles Eisenmann, *La justice constitutionnelle et la Haute Cour Constitutionnelle d'Austriche* (Paris: Economica; Aix-en-Provence: Presses Universitaires d'Aix-Marseille, 1986), 188–189. This sort of criticism, of course, applied with equal force to the system that existed in France until the 2008 constitutional reform.

27. The French Constitution gives standing to sixty deputies or sixty senators. This means that the minor political forces have no power of referral.

28. This risk of immunity, however, did not exist in France when it came to "organic laws" (which regulate certain basic matters that the constitution enumerates) and parliamentary bylaws, for these types of laws *must* be sent to the court for constitutional review. It should also be mentioned that the court has sometimes examined the validity of statutory provisions on its own motion. Thus, a unanimous parliament in 1982 enacted a law that established, among other things, gender quotas for the electoral lists drawn by political parties. Certain unrelated provisions of the law were challenged, but the court decided not to confine its attention to them. It went further and examined the clauses on the quotas, and struck them down on its own motion. See Conseil constitutionnel decision no. 82-146 DC, November 18, 1982 (France).

29. *Loi no. 2004-228 du 15 mars 2004 encadrant, en application du principe de laïcité, le port de signes ou de tenues manifestant une appartenance religieuse dans les écoles, collèges et lycées publics* (France).

30. Zagrebelsky, *La giustizia costituzionale*, 505–507.

31. See Donald Kommers, *The Constitutional Jurisprudence of the Federal Republic of Germany* (Durham, N.C., and London: Duke University Press, 1997), 530 n. 59.

32. See Tribunal Constitucional decision no. 45/1989, February, 20, 1989 (Spain).

33. In Austria, for example, it is the federal or the state governments, not their respective parliaments, that are entitled to appear before the court to defend a federal or a state statute. See article 63 of the *Verfassungsgerichts-*

hofgesetz [Constitutional Court Act]. Most legislation (more than 95 percent), however, is initiated by the government. See Heinz Schäffer, "Austria," in *Las tensiones entre el Tribunal Constitucional y el legislador en la Europa actual,* ed. Eliseo Aja (Barcelona: Ariel, 1998), 13. The same is true in Italy: the president of the government is a party to the procedure and is expected to defend the statute. As in Austria, the government is the principal originator of legislation. When a regional statute is questioned, the president of the government of the region is notified so that he can defend its constitutionality. See article 25 of *Legge costituzionale 11 marzo 1953,* no. 87 (Italy) and Zagrebelsky, *La giustizia costituzionale,* 228–232. Similarly, in France the government takes charge of the defense of the impugned law. Although the court must notify the president of the republic, the prime minister, and the presidents of the two parliamentary chambers about the challenge (see article 18 of the *Ordonnance no. 58-1067 du 7 novembre 1958 portant loi organique sur le Conseil constitutionnel*), in practice, it is only the executive, through its Secrétariat général du Gouvernement, that comes to the law's defense. Its allegations, by the way, are now published in the *Journal Officiel* (this practice started in 1994), where the brief of the challengers is also published. See Rousseau, *Droit du contentieux constitutionnel,* 35. In Spain, the government and the two chambers of the national parliament are notified by the court; when a regional statute is challenged, so are the regional executive and the regional parliament. In addition, the Fiscal General del Estado, who presides over public prosecutors, is also notified when an ordinary judge certifies a constitutional question to the court. See articles 34 and 37 of the *Ley Orgánica 2/1979, de 3 de octubre, del Tribunal Constitucional* (Spain). In practice, however, very rarely does the national parliament participate in the proceedings—the executive, the principal source of legislative projects, does. The participation of the regional parliaments, in contrast, is more frequent. In Germany, the law gives both chambers of the parliament, as well as the federal government and the government of the Länder, the right to participate in the procedure of constitutional review. When the legislation at stake has been enacted by a Land, the Land's parliament is also entitled to intervene. See article 77 of the *Bundesverfassungsgerichtsgesetz* [Federal Constitutional Court Act]. In Portugal, when the court deals with abstract review proceedings, it must give notice to the specific body that issued the contested legal provision. See article 54 of *the Lei do Tribunal Constitucional, Lei 28/82, de 15 de Novembro.* With respect to the jurisdiction of the court to hear appeals in concrete review cases, the law establishes that the public prosecutor's office is obliged to file such an appeal under certain circumstances, such as when a lower court has refused to apply a law on constitutional grounds. See article 72. In such cases, the court will not notify the body that issued the law, for its decision will not have general effects but only *inter partes* effects. See Luis Nunes de Almeida, "Portugal," in *Las tensiones* (see above, this note),

214. In Belgium, both the government and the legislature are notified of the challenges and questions that are lodged before the Constitutional Court so that they can take part in the proceedings. See articles 76 and 77 of the *Loi spéciale du 6 janvier 1989 sur la Cour d'arbitrage.*

34. See 28 U.S.C. § 2403. The attorney general of the United States, moreover, must give notice to the Senate if he or she refrains from defending the constitutionality of any federal law. See 2 U.S.C. § 288k(b).

35. In Hungary, for example, the death penalty was abolished as a result of an *actio popularis.* See Sadurski, *Rights Before Courts,* 6.

36. Zagrebelsky, *La giustizia costituzionale,* 225–226, mentions, in this regard, budgetary laws, electoral laws, and temporal laws. He criticizes the fact that in Italy, abstract review is possible only with respect to regional conflicts. It would be advisable, he asserts, to extend this type of procedure to cover other matters by granting standing to a special prosecutor, parliamentary groups, or even the people.

37. See Adrian Vermeule, "Veil of Ignorance Rules in Constitutional Law," *Yale Law Journal* 111 (2001): 427.

38. Actually, Frederick Schauer has offered good epistemic reasons to prefer decision making according to general rules to particularistic decision making in many contexts. See Frederick Schauer, *Profiles, Probabilities, and Stereotypes* (Cambridge, Mass.: Harvard University Press, 2003).

39. 372 U.S. 335 (1963).

40. Alec Stone Sweet and Martin Shapiro, "Abstract and Concrete Review in the United States," in *On Law, Politics, and Judicialization* (Oxford: Oxford University Press, 2002), 370.

41. 397 U.S. 254 (1970).

42. Owen Fiss, *The Law as It Could Be* (New York and London: New York University Press, 2003), 218–219.

43. Alexis de Tocqueville, *Democracy in America,* trans. Henry Reeve (1835; New York: Vintage Books, 1990), 1:102.

44. In France, Germany, and Spain, for example, the abortion controversy was brought to the constitutional court in abstract review procedures. It is not obvious that the discussion was epistemically impoverished as a result.

CHAPTER 7. OVERCOMING JUDICIAL TIMIDITY

1. Some of these differences were briefly mentioned, without elaboration, by Mauro Cappelletti, *Judicial Review in the Contemporary World* (Indianapolis, Ind.: Bobbs-Merrill, 1971), 82–83.

2. Interestingly, the same mechanism (the writ of certiorari) that makes it possible for the U.S. Supreme Court to focus on issues that have constitutional implications and thus become a quasi-constitutional tribunal also makes it possible for the court to decline to hear a particular constitutional case, a passive reaction that is hard for a constitutional court of the European type to engage in.

3. See, for instance, *Byrd v. Raines,* 521 U.S. 811 (1997), in which the U.S. Supreme Court denied standing to six members of Congress who challenged the constitutionality of the Line Item Veto Act on separation-of-power grounds. In their concurring opinion, Justices David Souter and Ruth Bader Ginsburg argued that it is preferable for courts to adjudicate constitutional issues brought by private parties than by political actors or institutions: "While it is true that a suit challenging the constitutionality of this Act brought by a party from outside the Federal Government would also involve the Court in resolving the dispute over the allocation of power between the political branches, it would expose the Judicial branch to a lesser risk. Deciding a suit to vindicate an interest outside the Government raises no specter of judicial readiness to enlist on one side of a political tug of war." In this context, they referred to Alexis de Tocqueville's observations to the effect that American courts censure laws in connection with private interests so that legislation is protected from "the daily aggressions of party spirit."

4. With respect to the practice of the Italian Constitutional Court, for example, see Paolo Bianchi, *La creazione giurisprudenziale delle tecniche di selezione dei casi* (Turin, Italy: G. Giappichelli editore, 2000), 215–336.

5. *Jones v. United States,* 526 U.S. 227, 239 (1999) (quoting *United States ex rel. Attorney General v. Delaware & Hudson Co.,* 213 U.S. 366, 408 [1909]).

6. Frederick Schauer, "*Ashwander* Revisited," *Supreme Court Review,* 1995, 88.

7. See generally William Kelley, "Avoiding Constitutional Questions as a Three-Branch Problem," *Cornell Law Review* 86 (2001): 831–898, especially pages 857–858 and 864. Kelley explains that there has been an important historical shift in the way the avoidance canon has been applied in the United States. Until the early twentieth century, the avoidance canon was about preferring a reading of the statute that met constitutional scrutiny to another reading that was actually unconstitutional. Later, however, it was about avoiding an interpretation that merely raised constitutional doubts. Ibid., 839–840. For a similar account of the distinction between the classical and the modern avoidance canon, see Adrian Vermeule, "Saving Constructions," *Georgetown Law Journal* 85 (1997): 1945–1977. Note that the classical understanding of the doctrine is the only one that, for structural reasons, constitutional courts are authorized to engage in, as we will see.

8. When the Supreme Court of the United States has to decide cases in which the relevant legislation is *state* legislation, however, its position is different. Because, as a federal court, it is not the supreme interpreter of state law, it is more difficult for the court to apply the avoidance canon in such cases.

9. This overconstitutionalization of the law has some repercussions on the question whether constitutional rights can bind private individuals. For a sharp analysis of this matter, see Mark Tushnet, "The Issue of State Action/Horizontal Effect in Comparative Constitutional Law," *International Journal of Constitutional Law* 1 (2003): 79–98, especially pages 84–88.

10. There is no important theoretical difference between the two formulas. Sometimes, however, there is a practical difference. In Italy, for example, only the Constitutional Court's decisions declaring a statute unconstitutional are formally recognized by the legal system to have *erga omnes* effects. Ordinary judges are accordingly bound by the court's holding about the interpretation of the statute only if the court asserts that the statute is *unconstitutional* if it is interpreted in a certain way (or unless it is interpreted in a certain way). This limitation does not exist in other countries, such as Spain or Germany. On this difference, see Francisco Javier Díaz Revorio, *Las sentencias interpretativas del Tribunal Constitucional* (Valladolid, Spain: Editorial Lex Nova, 2001), 80–81, 99–112.

11. Incidentally, it should be mentioned that, precisely because the scope of the attack is unlimited when abstract challenges are filed, in most countries these actions can be brought only by a limited set of institutions. This is so in order to "protect" statutes: when there is no particular case that justifies the process of review, only some agents are authorized to dispute their validity in the abstract and on the basis of a constitutional ground. See Luis Javier Mieres, *El incidente de constitucionalidad en los procesos constitucionales (Especial referencia al incidente en el recurso de amparo)* (Madrid: Civitas, 1998), 191–192.

12. Alexander Bickel, *The Least Dangerous Branch* (New Haven, Conn.: Yale University Press, 1962). For a more recent defense of some forms of avoidance, see Cass Sunstein, *One Case at a Time: Judicial Minimalism on the Supreme Court* (Cambridge, Mass.: Harvard University Press, 1999). Different techniques of avoidance were enumerated by Justice Louis D. Brandeis in his concurring opinion in *Ashwander v. Tennessee Valley Authority,* 297 U.S 288, 346 (1936).

13. Bruce Ackerman, *The Future of Liberal Revolution* (New Haven, Conn.: Yale University Press, 1992), 107–112.

14. Thus, Donald Kommers explains that although the German Constitutional Court "lacks a storehouse of 'passive virtues' by which it might for prudential reasons avoid a ruling on a constitutional issue," it can nevertheless exercise self-restraint. "The court occasionally makes an ally of time, delaying decision until the controversy loses its urgency or is settled by political means, prompting the initiating party ultimately to withdraw the case." *The Constitutional Jurisprudence of the Federal Republic of Germany* (Durham, N.C., and London: Duke University Press, 1997), 54–55.

15. Wojciech Sadurski, *Rights Before Courts: A Study of Constitutional Courts in Postcommunist States of Central and Eastern Europe* (Dordrecht, The Netherlands: Springer, 2005), 244–245, offers an interesting example from Poland. A controversial law on "lustration" was enacted to allow the removal of judges who had collaborated with the Communist regime. The law provided that statutes of limitation would not apply until a specified date (December 31, 2000). This provision was challenged by the president, and the

court overturned it on purely procedural grounds. The National Council of the Judiciary, it held, should have been consulted during the legislative process. In this manner, the court effectively avoided facing the substantive issues that lustration posed.

16. In Portugal, for example, the constitution provides that if a statute is declared unconstitutional in a procedure of a priori review, the parliament can override that judgment through a two-thirds supermajority. See article 279.2 of the Portuguese Constitution. There has been debate in Portugal concerning the legitimacy of this device, however. See Carlos Blanco de Morais, *Justiça constitucional*, vol. 2, *O contencioso constitucional Português entre o modelo misto e a tentação do sistema de reenvio* (Coimbra, Portugal: Coimbra Editora, 2005), 94–100. It should be noted that before the Portuguese Constitutional Court was established in 1982, the Council of the Revolution was in charge of legislative review. Given the political nature of that institution, it was understandable that the parliament was authorized to override its decisions through a qualified majority. The override mechanism was maintained, however, when the new court replaced the council. Many scholars think that the mechanism should then have been abolished. In any case, the legislative assembly at the national level has never resorted to it. Only a regional legislature (that of the autonomous region of Açores) did so once. See Tribunal Constitucional decision no. 151/93, February, 3, 1993 (Portugal). The same type of mechanism exists in Romania: the decisions of the Constitutional Court in abstract a priori procedures can be overridden by a majority of two-thirds of each legislative chamber. This has not yet happened. A similar arrangement existed in Poland until 1997; the parliament successfully overruled the court eleven times. See Sadurski, *Rights Before Courts*, 79–80.

17. Alec Stone Sweet, *Governing with Judges: Constitutional Politics in Europe* (Oxford: Oxford University Press, 2000), 52–55.

18. Louis Favoreu, "Constitutional Review in Europe," in *Constitutionalism and Rights: The Influence of the United States Constitution Abroad*, ed. Louis Henkin and Albert Rosenthal (New York: Columbia University Press, 1990), 48–49.

19. See, e.g., Dominique Rousseau, *La justice constitutionnelle en Europe* (Paris: Montchrestien, 1998), 24, and Michel Fromont, *La justice constitutionnelle dans le monde* (Paris: Dalloz, 1996), 2. Interestingly, European developments under fascism and communism had an impact on the American mind, too: they suggested the need to keep and strengthen those institutions that could serve as checks on popular politics. The activism of the Warren court, for example, may have to be understood in this context. On this correlation, see Larry Kramer, *The People Themselves* (New York: Oxford University Press, 2004), 221–222.

20. Thus, the first articles of the constitutions of Germany and Italy refer to fundamental rights. In Portugal, Spain, Belgium, and Luxembourg, the

bill of rights is placed immediately after some introductory provisions that deal with general principles. The rules on the organization of the state come afterward. Austria and France present special cases, however. In Austria, no new constitution was drafted after the Second World War. Instead, the constitution of 1920, which did not include a bill of rights, was reenacted. (Since no agreement had been reached by the framers in 1920 as to the content of the catalog of rights, a reference was made in the constitution to earlier statutes that guaranteed some liberties.) With respect to France, the preamble to the constitution solemnly proclaims the people's commitment to rights. It explicitly mentions the Declaration of the Rights of Man and of the Citizen of 1789 and some additional principles that figure in the preamble to the 1946 constitution. The articulated text of the constitution, however, does not include a bill of rights.

21. The Italian Constitutional Court, for instance, sounds a familiar note when it asserts that "the twentieth century was a period shaken by wars and deeply marked by authoritarian political experiences and the repression of democratic institutions. In the wake of this experience," it explains, "there emerged a growing awareness that safeguarding the basic rights established in constitutions and the constitutional balance of powers meant being able to exert control even over the highest expression of the will of representative organs, including parliaments, and thus on the laws themselves." Corte costituzionale della Repubblica italiana, "What is the Constitutional Court?" (page 7), http://www.cortecostituzionale.it/versioni_in _lingua/eng/lacortecostituzionale/cosaelacorte/pag_07.asp.

22. Georg Vanberg, *The Politics of Constitutional Review in Germany* (Cambridge, U.K.: Cambridge University Press, 2005), 95–115.

23. An analogy can be drawn with the creation of administrative courts in France. To a significant degree, it was the emergence of a powerful, very centralized administrative state in France that led the French to believe that a specific branch of law, public law, had to be created in order to tame the government. In contrast, the English had to deal with a less centralized government, and ordinary law and ordinary courts were accordingly regarded as sufficient. For this contrast, see J. W. F. Allison, *A Continental Distinction in the Common Law* (Oxford: Oxford University Press, 1996), 42–108.

24. In Greece, for example, it was an 1847 decision by the Supreme Court that established the power of judicial review—the constitution was silent on the matter. This power was exercised with caution, however. The court first held that the substantive content of legislation could not be scrutinized. It later changed its position and came to accept substantive review, but it required an "evident" contradiction between the statute and the constitution. See Allan-Randolph Brewer-Carías, *Judicial Review in Comparative Law* (Cambridge, U.K.: Cambridge University Press, 1989), 168. In Japan too, where a decentralized system of constitutional review was established,

courts have been extremely deferential. Writing in 1989, Brewer-Carías noted that only three laws had been declared unconstitutional in Japan since the Second World War. Ibid., 175.

25. The Greek Constitution, for instance, explicitly gives the power of constitutional review to ordinary courts (article 93.4). So does the Portuguese Constitution (article 204). It is interesting to note that in both countries, there was first a decision by the judiciary assuming the power of constitutional review. It was later (in 1927 and 1911, respectively) that the constitutions explicitly codified this power. See Brewer-Carías, *Judicial Review in Comparative Law*, 168, and Fromont, *La justice constitutionnelle dans le monde*, 15. Similarly, in Sweden and Finland, the constitution explicitly bestows upon judges the power of constitutional review. See article 14, chapter 11 of the Swedish Instrument of Government and section 106 of the Finnish Constitution.

26. Gustavo Zagrebelsky, *La giustizia costituzionale* (Bologna: il Mulino, 1988), 484.

27. *Legge costituzionale 9 febbraio 1948*, no. 1, article 1 (Italy). On the rationale of this rule, see Zagrebelsky, *La giustizia costituzionale*, 202–205.

28. Luís Nunes de Almeida, "Portugal," in *Las tensiones entre el Tribunal Constitucional y el Legislador en la Europa actual*, ed. Eliseo Aja (Barcelona: Ariel, 1998), 217–219.

29. Blanco de Morais, *Justiça constitucional*, 2:983.

30. See article 14, chapter 11 of the Swedish Instrument of Government and section 106 of the Finnish Constitution. On the practice of constitutional review in these countries, see Jaakko Husa, "Guarding the Constitutionality of Laws in the Nordic Countries: A Comparative Perspective," *American Journal of Comparative Law* 48 (2000): 345–382.

31. James Bradley Thayer, "The Origin and Scope of the American Doctrine of Constitutional Law," *Harvard Law Review* 7 (1893): 136–137.

32. Carlo Mezzanotte, *Corte costituzionale e legittimazione politica* (Rome: Tipografia Veneziana, 1984), 138.

33. Enzo Cheli, *Il giudice delle leggi* (Bologna: il Mulino, 1996), 32–44; Zagrebelsky, *La giustizia costituzionale*, 494–501.

34. The Web site of the French Constitutional Council (http://www.conseil -constitutionnel.fr) offers information about the opinions that have examined the constitutionality of laws, indicating whether such laws were upheld or invalidated (either totally or partially). On the high rate of declarations of unconstitutionality in France, see Louis Favoreu, "The Constitutional Council and Parliament in France," in *Constitutional Review and Legislation: An International Comparison*, ed. Christine Landfried (Baden-Baden, Germany: Nomos Verlagsgesellschaft, 1988), 94–95, and Stone Sweet, *Governing with Judges*, 63. The available data support Favoreu's conclusion that "the proportion of nullification compared to the total number

of cases decided is undoubtedly higher in France than in other countries."
Favoreu, "The Constitutional Council and Parliament in France," 95.

35. Thomas Gawron and Ralf Rogowski, "Implementation of German Federal
Constitutional Court Decisions," in *Constitutional Courts in Comparison:
The U.S. Supreme Court and the German Federal Constitutional Court,* ed.
Ralf Rogowski and Thomas Gawron (New York and Oxford: Berghahn
Books, 2002), 244. The calculation is based on the 1951–1987 period.

36. Erhard Blankenburg, "Mobilization of the German Federal Constitutional
Court," in *Constitutional Courts in Comparison* (see note 35), 160.

37. Indeed, it is so pronounced that some criticisms have recently been voiced
against the court for spending too much time reviewing the validity of ordinary judicial opinions to the detriment of the necessary checks that the
legislature must be subjected to. A former minister of justice recently published an important article in the most widely read national newspaper,
claiming that if the court goes on like this, exhibiting so much passivity
toward the legislature, the very existence of the court will be questioned.
See Juan Antonio Ortega Díaz-Ambrona, "La hora del Tribunal Constitucional," *El País* (Madrid), August 3, 2007. Things could improve in the future, however, since a recent legal reform has been introduced in Spain
whose aim is to encourage the court to focus its attention on the procedures of constitutional review of legislation. See *Ley Orgánica 6/2007, de
24 de mayo.* The complaints against administrative and judicial decisions,
which are filed every year in overwhelming numbers, are to be disposed
of more easily, through quicker procedures, so that enough institutional
energy is preserved for the truly central task the court was established to
carry out—legislative review.

38. Georges Vedel, preface to *Droit du contentieux constitutionnel,* by Dominique Rousseau (Paris: Montchrestien, 2006), 9.

39. Cappelletti, *Judicial Review in the Contemporary World,* 62–64, mentions
the experiences in three countries (Germany, during the Weimar Republic;
Italy, from 1948 until 1956, when the Constitutional Court was finally established; and Japan, since the Second World War) as evidence that ordinary judges in the civil-law tradition do not have the requisite mentality
to address constitutional issues. In the United States, in contrast, many
judges—not only those that sit on the U.S. Supreme Court—have political
experience and strong policy views. As Robert Kagan explains, "Many
agree to enter the judiciary because they see it as an opportunity to put
their personal stamp on the development of the law." Robert A. Kagan,
"Constitutional Litigation in the United States," in *Constitutional Courts
in Comparison* (see note 35), 48.

40. This point has been made by Charles Eisenmann, *La justice constitutionnelle et la Haute cour constitutionnelle d'Austriche* (Paris: Economica; Aix-en-
Provence: Presses Universitaires d'Aix-Marseille, 1986), 227. On similar
grounds, Zagrebelsky, *La giustizia costituzionale,* 320, and Cheli, *Il giudice*

delle leggi, 65, are in favor of introducing in Italy the Austrian-German technique of deferring the invalidating effects of the court's decisions. As was explained in chapter 3, the Austrians adopted this device in the 1920 constitution. In Germany, the court started the practice of sometimes declaring a law to be "incompatible" with the constitution, without annulling it. The legislature is thus asked to repair the statute when the court cannot do so directly. Meanwhile, the law cannot generally be enforced in pending cases. The *Bundesverfassungsgerichtsgesetz* was later amended to explicitly authorize this practice (see article 31.2). For a description of this technique, see Albrecht Weber, "Alemania," in *Las tensiones* (see note 28), 77–80.

CHAPTER 8. THE DEMOCRATIC OBJECTION TO CONSTITUTIONAL REVIEW

1. The expression is from Alexander Bickel, *The Least Dangerous Branch* (New Haven, Conn.: Yale University Press, 1962), 16: "The root difficulty is that judicial review is a counter-majoritarian force in our system." For a fascinating account of the history of this debate in the United States in the modern era, see Barry Friedman, "The Birth of an Academic Obsession: The History of the Countermajoritarian Difficulty, Part Five," *Yale Law Journal* 112 (2002): 153–259. Friedman persuasively shows that the various positions held by constitutional theorists on this topic have been the product of a historically contingent set of circumstances. At the end of his article, he suggests, quite rightly, that theoretical work on judicial review should transcend immediate political preference. Ibid., 256–259.

2. See generally Jeremy Waldron, *Law and Disagreement* (Oxford: Oxford University Press, 2001). A more recent presentation of his views on judicial review can be found in his article "The Core of the Case against Judicial Review," *Yale Law Journal* 115 (2006): 1346–1406.

3. The German Basic Law, for example, requires a parliamentary supermajority of two-thirds for a state of defense to be declared (article 115a). In a similar spirit, Bruce Ackerman in the United States has proposed an emergency constitutional regime that requires an increasing supermajority for Congress to declare and renew a state of emergency. Bruce Ackerman, *Before the Next Attack: Preserving Civil Liberties in an Age of Terrorism* (New Haven, Conn.: Yale University Press, 2006), 80–83.

4. For example, in Germany (article 23.1 of the German Basic Law), Luxembourg (article 37 of the Luxembourg Constitution), and Ireland (article 29 of the Irish Constitution), a parliamentary supermajority is required for the country to join the European Union (or other supranational organizations) or to ratify treaties that affect its structure and competences.

5. Luigi Ferrajoli, *Derechos y garantías: La ley del más débil* (Madrid: Trotta, 1999).

6. Aharon Barak, *The Judge in a Democracy* (Princeton, N.J.: Princeton University Press, 2006), 33–35.

7. Ronald Dworkin, *Freedom's Law* (Cambridge, Mass.: Harvard University Press, 1996), 24–26.

8. Jürgen Habermas, *Between Facts and Norms: Contributions to a Discourse Theory of Law and Democracy* (Cambridge, Mass.: MIT Press, 1996), 263.

9. Dworkin, *Freedom's Law,* 32.

10. Ibid., 32.

11. Ibid., 32–33.

12. Bruce Ackerman, *We the People: Foundations* (Cambridge, Mass.: Harvard University Press, 1991), 262, and Bruce Ackerman "The Living Constitution" (2006 Oliver Wendell Holmes Lectures), *Harvard Law Review* 120 (2007): 1805.

13. Jed Rubenfeld, *Freedom and Time: A Theory of Constitutional Self-Government* (New Haven, Conn.: Yale University Press, 2001).

14. Dominique Rousseau, *La justice constitutionnelle en Europe* (Paris: Montchrestien, 1998), 40–48; Dominique Rousseau, *Droit du contentieux constitutionnel* (Paris: Montchrestien, 2006), 492–495; and Michel Fromont, *La justice constitutionnelle dans le monde* (Paris: Dalloz, 1996), 132.

15. Rousseau, *Droit du contentieux constitutionnel,* 495.

16. Philippe Blachèr, *Contrôle de constitutionnalité et volonté générale* (Paris: Presses Universitaires de France, 2001), 175–195.

17. Conseil constitutionnel decision no. 85-197 DC, August 23, 1985 (France).

18. Lawrence Sager, *Justice in Plainclothes: A Theory of American Constitutional Practice* (New Haven, Conn.: Yale University Press, 2004), 203.

19. Ibid., 203.

20. Ibid., 205.

21. Ibid., 139.

22. Ibid., 207 (emphasis added).

23. John Rawls, *A Theory of Justice,* rev. ed. (Cambridge, Mass.: Harvard University Press, 1999), 201.

24. Waldron, "The Core of the Case," 1393. Thus, referring to the respective institutional advantages of the legislature and the judiciary, he asserts: "If one institution or the other was clearly superior at determining what rights people really have, then that would weigh very heavily indeed in favor of that institution." His claim, however, is that we do not have good reasons to think that judicial review of legislation is better on instrumental grounds. Therefore, he concludes, we must resort to noninstrumental considerations, which refer to the intrinsic merits of the different institutions and procedures.

25. This is not to exclude the need to strengthen the direct participation of citizens in deliberative bodies. For interesting proposals in this connection, see Bruce Ackerman and James Fishkin, *Deliberation Day* (New Haven, Conn.: Yale University Press, 2004).

26. Frederick Schauer, "The Supreme Court 2005 Term—Foreword: The

Court's Agenda—And the Nation's," *Harvard Law Review* 120 (2006): 4–64.

27. Owen Fiss, "Between Supremacy and Exclusivity," in *The Least Examined Branch: The Role of Legislatures in the Constitutional State,* ed. Richard W. Bauman and Tsvi Kahana (Cambridge, U.K.: Cambridge University Press, 2006), 452–467.

28. Dominique Rousseau, for instance, believes that since the process of constitutional interpretation should always be open to future revisions, it is legitimate for the parliament to enact a statute that is similar to an earlier one that had been held unconstitutional by the court. A certain period of time (some years) must have elapsed, however. See Rousseau, *Droit du contentieux constitutionnel,* 168. In a similar vein, Christine Landfried maintains that the arguments used by the court to strike down a statute should bind the legislature only as long as the assumptions of the judges hold true in social reality. Parliament should therefore have more self-confidence and consider the possibility of enacting new laws despite the existing constitutional doctrines. See Christine Landfried, "Constitutional Review and Legislation in the Federal Republic of Germany," in *Constitutional Review and Legislation: An International Comparison,* ed. Christine Landfried (Baden-Baden, Germany: Nomos Verlagsgesellschaft, 1988), 166–167.

29. Thus, a parliamentary supermajority is required in Austria (article 44 of the Austrian Constitution), Germany (article 79 of the German Basic Law), Portugal (article 286 of the Portuguese Constitution), Belgium (article 195 of the Belgian Constitution), Luxembourg (article 114 of the Luxembourg Constitution) and Spain (articles 167 and 168 of the Spanish Constitution). In France, a supermajority is also required, but if people participate directly in a referendum, a simple parliamentary majority is then sufficient. See article 89 of the French Constitution. In Italy, an absolute majority is necessary in a second vote by both houses of the Italian parliament; a referendum is to be held if requested by one-fifth of the members of a legislative chamber, 500,000 citizens, or five regional councils; no such referendum is to be held, however, if the amendment was approved by two-thirds of each legislative chamber. See article 138 of the Italian Constitution.

30. Barry Friedman, "The Politics of Judicial Review," *Texas Law Review* 84 (2005): 257–337.

31. Barry Friedman, "The Importance of Being Positive: The Nature and Function of Judicial Review," *University of Cincinnati Law Review* 72 (2004): 1297.

CHAPTER 9. DEMOCRATIC CHECKS ON COURTS

1. Pedro Cruz Villalón, *La formación del sistema europeo de control de constitucionalidad (1918–1939)* (Madrid: Centro de Estudios Constitucionales, 1987), 411–412. Villalón notes that the Constitutional Court of

Czechoslovakia (under the constitution of 1920) had weak links with the democratic branches, since four of its seven members were appointed by the highest courts. Interestingly, this must have contributed, he asserts, to the establishment of a supermajority requirement on the court pursuant to which at least five judges had to hold that a statute was unconstitutional in order to invalidate that statute.

2. In France and Germany, for example, the executive is responsible for many judicial appointments, but independent commissions are in place to tame the influence of politics. See John Bell, *Judiciaries within Europe: A Comparative Review* (Cambridge, U.K.: Cambridge University Press, 1996), 52–62, 113–125.

3. European Charter on the Statute for Judges, section 1.3.

4. Ibid., section 2.1 (emphasis added).

5. Eight judges of the Austrian Constitutional Court (including the president and vice president) are appointed by the president of the republic on the recommendation of the federal government, and the other six are appointed on the recommendation of the House of Representatives and the Senate (article 147 of the Austrian Constitution). In Belgium, the twelve judges are appointed by the king from a double list of candidates proposed alternately by the House of Representatives and the Senate (articles 31 and 32 of the *Loi spéciale du 6 janvier 1989 sur la Cour d'arbitrage*). In France, three judges are appointed by the president of the republic, three by the president of the National Assembly, and three by the president of the Senate (article 56 of the French Constitution). In Germany, half the judges are elected by the House of Representatives and the other half by the Senate (article 94 of the German Basic Law). In Italy, five judges are appointed by the president, five by the parliament in joint session, and five by the ordinary and administrative supreme courts (Court of Cassation, Council of State, and Court of Accounts) (article 135.1 of the Italian Constitution). In Portugal, ten judges are appointed by the assembly, and three are co-opted by those ten (article 222.1 of the Portuguese Constitution). In Spain, four judges are selected by the House of Representatives, four by the Senate, two by the government, and two by the General Council of the Judiciary (article 159.1 of the Spanish Constitution). Luxembourg is a special case: the court is composed of the president of the Superior Court of Justice, the president of the Administrative Court, two counselors of the Court of Cassation and five magistrates nominated by the grand duke, upon the joint opinion of the Superior Court of Justice and the Administrative Court (article 95ter of the Luxembourg Constitution). With respect to the courts in Central-Eastern Europe, the appointment process is also very political. There are basically three models: the parliament makes the appointments exclusively; it selects the judges together with the executive; or a quota of seats on the court is filled by different bodies (normally the president, the parliament, and a body representing the judiciary). Estonia is a special

case: the members of the Constitutional Review Chamber are appointed by the parliament at the proposal of the president of the National Court. See Wojciech Sadurski, *Rights Before Courts: A Study of Constitutional Courts in Postcommunist States of Central and Eastern Europe* (Dordrecht, The Netherlands: Springer, 2005), 15–16, 26.

6. See, for instance, the criticism voiced by Alfred Rinken in connection with Germany in "The Federal Constitutional Court and the German Political System," in *Constitutional Courts in Comparison: The U.S. Supreme Court and the German Federal Constitutional Court,* ed. Ralf Rogowski and Thomas Gawron (New York and Oxford: Berghahn Books, 2002), 74.

7. Richard Posner, "The Supreme Court 2004 Term—Foreword: A Political Court," *Harvard Law Review* 119 (2005): 79.

8. John Ferejohn and Pasquale Pasquino, "Constitutional Courts as Deliberative Institutions: Towards an Institutional Theory of Constitutional Justice," in *Constitutional Justice, East and West,* ed. Wojciech Sadurski (The Hague, London, and New York: Kluwer Law International, 2003), 31–32. Sadurski, *Rights Before Courts,* 43–44, notes, however, that the judges on the constitutional courts were not so "purified" of their old ideologies; nor were ordinary judges so hopelessly immersed in the preceding period of dictatorship. In Poland, for instance, all the judges of the Supreme Court were appointed anew after the transition of 1989.

9. It is worth mentioning that Kelsen did not offer this kind of argument to defend his proposal that the members of the constitutional court should be elected by the parliament. He instead reasoned, first, that since the court is a "negative legislature," and since the legislative power is in principle in the hands of the parliament, the latter should elect the constitutional justices. "Since the Constitution conferred upon the Constitutional Court a legislative function, *i.e.,* a function which, in principle, was reserved to the Parliament, the Austrian Constitution of 1920 provided that the members of the Constitutional Court had to be elected by the Parliament and not like other judges, to be appointed by the administration." Hans Kelsen, "Judicial Review of Legislation," *Journal of Politics* 4 (1942): 187. This argument is not very convincing, though, for there are important differences between the parliament's repeal of a statute and the court's invalidation of it, as we saw in chapter 2. A second argument that Kelsen offered was more pragmatic. Kelsen thought it advisable that the court be granted the monopoly over reviewing not only statutes but also administrative regulations. Of the two branches he had in mind to appoint the judges of the court—the legislature and the executive—he believed that it was better to rely on the legislature. He thought that it was more dangerous for the executive to violate the constitution than for the parliament to do so, for "by a misuse of [its] powers the administration could easily suppress the parliament and thus eliminate the democratic basis of the State." Ibid., 188. So it was more important to guarantee the independence of the court vis-à-vis the executive than

against the parliament. A third argument was tied to federalism: the participation of the second parliamentary chamber (the senate) in the appointment process was necessary in order to make the court a neutral arbiter between the federation and the member states. See Charles Eisenmann, *La justice constitutionnelle et la Haute cour constitutionnelle d'Austriche* (Paris: Economica; Aix-en-Provence: Presses Universitaires d'Aix-Marseille, 1986), 177.

10. The term is nine years in France (article 56 of the French Constitution), twelve years in Germany (article 4 of the *Bundesverfassungsgerichtsgesetz* [Federal Constitutional Court Act]), nine years in Italy (article 135.3 of the Italian Constitution), nine years in Portugal (article 222.3 of the Portuguese Constitution), and nine years in Spain (article 159.3 of the Spanish Constitution). It should be noted that in Germany judges must retire when they reach sixty-eight years of age, even if their twelve-year term has not yet expired.

11. Gustavo Zagrebelsky, *La giustizia costituzionale* (Bologna: il Mulino, 1988), 77 (my translation).

12. For a general view of the debate, see Sanford Levinson, *Our Undemocratic Constitution* (New York: Oxford University Press, 2006), 123–139.

13. Ronald Dworkin, *Is Democracy Possible Here? Principles for a New Political Debate* (Princeton, N.J.: Princeton University Press, 2006), 158.

14. In some countries, this limitation was not originally established. In Germany, for example, the *Bundesverfassungsgerichtsgesetz* first provided that members of the Federal Constitutional Court be chosen for renewable eight-year terms (except for the eight federal judges required to be elected to the court, who enjoyed their terms until retirement age). The law was amended in 1970 to provide for single twelve-year terms for all justices, with no possibility of reelection. See Donald Kommers, *The Constitutional Jurisprudence of the Federal Republic of Germany* (Durham, N.C., and London: Duke University Press, 1997), 20–21. In Portugal, the terms were renewable until the constitution was amended in 1997. It should also be mentioned that in Spain, the judges of the Constitutional Court cannot be reappointed *immediately* after their term has expired, but they can be reappointed after three years. See article 16 of *Ley Orgánica 2/1979, de 3 de octubre, del Tribunal Constitucional*.

15. Sadurski, *Rights Before Courts,* 14.

16. Eisenmann, *La justice constitutionnelle,* 176–177.

17. Christopher Eisgruber, *Constitutional Self-Government* (Cambridge, Mass.: Harvard University Press, 2001), 67.

18. Alessandro Pizzorusso, "Constitutional Review and Legislation in Italy," in *Constitutional Review and Legislation,* ed. Christine Landfried (Baden-Baden, Germany: Nomos Verlagsgesellschaft, 1988), 113.

19. Mary Volcansek, *Constitutional Politics in Italy: The Constitutional Court* (New York: St. Martin's Press, 2000), 8, 24, makes this point in connec-

tion with the Italian Constitutional Court. It is interesting to note, in this regard, that when the German government in the late 1960s introduced a bill providing for both dissenting opinions and twelve-year terms with the possibility of reelection, the Social Democrats in the parliament wisely insisted on a single fixed term of twelve years and conditioned support of dissenting opinions on the acceptance of this proposal. See Kommers, *The Constitutional Jurisprudence,* 21.

20. Ferejohn and Pasquino, "Constitutional Courts as Deliberative Institutions," 21–36.

21. Thus, Manfried Welan, "Constitutional Review and Legislation in Austria," in *Constitutional Review and Legislation* (see note 18), 71, explains that the absence of dissenting opinions in Austria has contributed to the low public visibility of the Austrian Constitutional Court.

22. Adrian Vermeule, "Veil of Ignorance Rules in Constitutional Law," *Yale Law Journal* 111 (2001): 419.

23. In Austria, the judges serve on the Constitutional Court until the age of retirement, at seventy (article 147.6 of the Austrian Constitution). The same rule applies in Belgium (*Loi du 6 janvier 1989 relative aux traitements et pensions des juges, des référendaires et des greffiers de la Cour d'arbitrage*) and Luxembourg (article 95ter of the Luxembourg Constitution).

24. In Belgium, each chamber of the legislature selects six judges by a two-thirds majority. In Germany, each chamber appoints eight judges by the same supermajority. In Italy, five judges (out of fifteen) are selected by both houses sitting in joint session, by a two-thirds majority vote in the first three ballots and three-fifths in all subsequent ballots. In Portugal, ten judges (out of thirteen) are selected by the assembly by a two-thirds majority. In Spain, each house selects four judges (out of twelve) by a three-fifths majority. In contrast, no supermajority is required in Austria for the six justices (out of fourteen) appointed by the two legislative chambers. In practice, however, the appointments are made on the basis of a broad consensus irrespective of current majorities. According to Manfried Welan, "This is obviously the reason for the virtual absence of public and open attacks against the Constitutional Court from the Big Parties." See Welan, "Constitutional Review and Legislation in Austria," 65. It should be noted that the tendency to select moderate judges is stronger when each judicial nominee is individually supported by a legislative supermajority. If, instead, a bargain is struck among the political parties, such that each party is entitled to freely designate its own candidate or group of candidates with no substantive checks from the other parties, the risk is higher that more extreme judges will be appointed. This kind of deal, moreover, makes each judge on the court more dependent on the particular political force that supported his or her candidacy. For a criticism of this practice in Italy, see Zagrebelsky, *La giustizia costituzionale,* 74–75. Spanish practices on judicial appointments can also be criticized on these grounds.

25. Alexis de Tocqueville, *Democracy in America,* trans. Henry Reeve (1835; New York: Vintage Books, 1990), 1:100–101.

26. Hans Kelsen, "La garantie juridictionnelle de la Constitution (La justice constitutionnelle)," *Revue du droit public et de la science politique en France et à l'étranger* 45 (1928): 206. It should be noted that in Austria, statutes and constitutional amendments were passed, and are still passed, by the same organ: the parliament. The only difference lies in the required majority (simple majority versus supermajority of two-thirds). Moreover, the parliament is always free to enact a law explicitly as a constitutional clause so that it prevails over any other constitutional clause it may conflict with. Pedro Cruz Villalón rightly connects Kelsen's theory to this unbounded domain of constitutional norms, which is a peculiar characteristic of the Austrian legal system. Cruz Villalón, *La formación del sistema europeo,* 406.

27. Eisenmann, *La justice constitutionnelle,* 98. He devotes many pages of his book to criticize natural law theories. See ibid., 24–92.

28. For a good exposition and criticism of this thesis, see Michel Troper, "The Logic of Justification of Judicial Review," *International Journal of Constitutional Law* 1 (2003): 111–114.

29. Louis Favoreu, "Les décisions du Conseil constitutionnel dans l'affaire des nationalisations," *Revue du droit public et de la science politique en France et à l'étranger* 98 (1982): 419.

30. Georges Vedel, "Schengen et Maastricht. (À propos de la décision n°. 91-294 DC du Conseil constitutionnel du 25 juillet 1991)," *Revue française de droit administratif* 8 (1992): 173, quoted in Troper, "The Logic of Justification of Judicial Review," 113.

31. See Dominique Rousseau, *Droit du contentieux constitutionnel* (Paris: Montchrestien, 2006), 502–503.

32. See Conseil constitutionnel decision no. 2003-469 DC, March 26, 2003 (France).

33. See Conseil constitutionnel decision no. 2000-429 DC, May 30, 2000 (France).

34. See articles 167 and 168 of the Spanish Constitution, and article 44 of the Austrian Constitution.

35. This authority of the court to strike down constitutional amendments that have been approved by a mere supermajority of the parliament, without referendum, is especially important in Austria given the tendency of the two largest political parties to form coalitions and to agree on constitutional matters. Since the two big parties together reach the parliamentary supermajority of two-thirds that is required to change the constitution through the easy procedure, they have often enacted as "constitutional laws" a set of norms they would normally have approved as ordinary statutes. In this way, they have attempted to immunize their parliamentary enactments against judicial review. Sometimes, moreover, they have reenacted, as "constitutional laws," earlier statutes that had been struck down

by the court. As Manfried Welan puts it, the two big parties have thus assumed a "King Midas" role and have turned questionable legal regulations
into uncontestable ones. See Welan, "Constitutional Review and Legislation in Austria," 72. In this context, it is understandable that the court has
insisted on the proposition that, though there are no limits to constitutional reform in Austria, the more onerous procedure must be followed
when the basic principles of the constitution are at stake. For a description
of the situation in Austria concerning these matters, see Marco Olivetti,
"La giustizia costituzionale in Austria (e in Cecoslovacchia)," in *La giustizia
costituzionale in Europa,* ed. Marco Olivetti and Tania Groppi (Milan: Giuffrè, 2003), 61–64, and Heinz Schäffer, "Austria," in *Las tensiones entre el
Tribunal Constitucional y el Legislador en la Europa actual,* ed. Eliseo Aja
(Barcelona: Ariel, 1998), 40–42.

36. For references, see Kommers, *The Constitutional Jurisprudence,* 48, and
    David Currie, *The Constitution of the Federal Republic of Germany* (Chicago
    and London: University of Chicago Press, 1994), 26, 171–172. Thus, in the
    Klass case, the court passed judgment on the validity of a constitutional
    amendment limiting the right of privacy and communications. The court
    upheld it over the vigorous dissent of three judges, who would have struck
    it down. See Bundesverfassungsgericht [Federal Constitutional Court]
    [1970] 30 BVerfGE 1 (Germany). Some years later, in June 1993, the Ger-
    man Basic Law was reformed to restrict the right of asylum. The court af-
    firmed the validity of that amendment, too. See Bundesverfassungsgericht
    [Federal Constitutional Court] [1996] 94 BVerfGE 49.
37. Corte costituzionale decision no. 1146/1988, December 15–29, 1988 (Italy).
38. Zagrebelsky, *La giustizia costituzionale,* 119.
39. See J. J. Gomes Canotilho, *Direito constitucional e teoria da Constituição*
    (Coimbra, Portugal: Livraria Almedina, 2002), 1063. Interestingly, how-
    ever, this provision was itself amended in 1989 to make it possible for the
    Portuguese economic system to comply with the norms of the European
    Community. In particular, the principle of collective ownership of means
    of production, which originally figured in the protected list, was with-
    drawn from it, and the constitutional clause that originally declared the ir-
    reversibility of the nationalizations that had been carried out between 1974
    and 1976 was repealed. The Constitutional Court was not asked to pass
    judgment on the validity of this controversial amendment, and the govern-
    ment thus encountered no obstacles in the pursuit of its privatization pro-
    gram. As a result of these events, the view has prevailed in Portugal that
    article 288 can itself be amended. This does not necessarily mean, how-
    ever, that there are no limits to constitutional change. Prominent scholars
    have argued that even if article 288 can be amended, there are some funda-
    mental principles that are so strongly linked to the very identity of the con-
    stitution that no revision may breach them. See Carlos Blanco de Morais,

Justiça constitucional, vol. 1, *Garantia da Constituição e controlo da constitu-cionalidade* (Coimbra, Portugal: Coimbra Editora, 2006), 65–83.

40. See, for instance, Jeff Rosen, "Was the Flag Burning Amendment Uncon-stitutional?" *Yale Law Journal* 100 (1990): 1073–1092, and Walter Murphy, "Merlin's Memory: The Past and Future Imperfect of the Once and Future Polity," in *Responding to Imperfection: The Theory and Practice of Constitu-tional Amendment,* ed. Sanford Levinson (Princeton, N.J.: Princeton Uni-versity Press, 1995), 163–190.

41. In its 1975 decision on abortion, 39 BVerfGE 1, the German Constitutional Court invoked the intangible principle of human dignity to protect the fe-tus. Accordingly, it disqualified a law that would have allowed a woman to terminate her pregnancy during the first three months. The court held that the state had the constitutional duty to criminalize abortion, except for cer-tain special situations in which important fundamental interests of the woman are at stake. During the process of German unification, however, the constitution was amended to authorize for a provisional period (until December 31, 1992) the maintenance of East German laws. This provision shielded the more liberal abortion law that existed in the East. Afterward, a new abortion law was enacted for a unified Germany, similar in many respects to the statute that had been invalidated in 1975. The law was chal-lenged on constitutional grounds, but the court in its 1993 decision, 88 BVerfGE 203, reconsidered its earlier jurisprudence. In particular, it moved away from a general requirement of the criminalization of abortion. So human dignity is an intangible principle under the German Basic Law, but its implications for the abortion controversy have been worked out by the court through interaction with the political process. Another example of this type of interaction concerns the court's 2002 decision, 104 BVerfG 337, holding that Muslim butchers may be permitted to perform ritual slaughters in exception to the general rules that protect animals. This deci-sion was of fundamental importance in setting the parameters of religious accommodation, and it provoked debate on the desirability of inserting a general animal-protection clause into the German Basic Law. The constitu-tion was finally amended, and article 20a now imposes on the state the duty to protect natural sources of life and animals. For commentary on the court's decision and the amendment it triggered, see Christine Langenfeld, "Developments: Germany," *International Journal of Constitutional Law* 1 (2003): 1, 141–147.

42. In 2001, for example, the Italian Constitution was modified to promote gender parity in electoral bodies (article 117). In decision no. 49/2003, Feb-ruary 10–13, 2003, the Italian Constitutional Court acknowledged that this change had altered the constitutional framework that ordinary legislation had to respect. Consequently, the court went on to qualify an earlier deci-sion (decision no. 422/1995, September 6–12, 1995) that had been critical of gender quotas. In the same vein, article 111 of the constitution was

amended in 1999 to make the criminal process more adversarial than the court had prescribed in an earlier judgment (decision no. 361/1998, October 26–November 2, 1998).

CHAPTER 10. DECENTRALIZING TENDENCIES IN THE SYSTEM

1. There is an explicit legal provision in Spain, for example, that tells judges not to refer a question to the court if it is possible to interpret the statute so that it no longer violates the constitution. See article 5.3 of the *Ley Orgánica 6/1985, de 1 de julio, del Poder Judicial,* enacted in 1985. In Italy, the system has clearly evolved in this direction. Initially, ordinary judges were not required to read legislation in light of the constitution before certifying a question to the court. Nowadays, they clearly are. See Gustavo Zagrebelsky, *La giustizia costituzionale* (Bologna: il Mulino, 1988), 204–205, 516–517. In a press conference given on February 9, 2006, Annibale Marini, who was then president of the court, reminded ordinary judges of this interpretive duty. See Annibale Marini, "La giustizia costituzionale nel 2005" (press conference, Palazzo della Consulta, Rome, Italy, February 9, 2006), 11, available at http://www.cortecostituzionale.it/documenti/download/pdf/ Conferenza_stampa_2006_Marini_.pdf.

2. The German Constitutional Court did so, for instance, in a leading 1973 decision, the *Princess Soraya* case, 34 BVerfGE 269. Article 253 of the Bürgerliches Gesetzbuch [Civil Code] provided that damages could only be awarded in delict for nonpecuniary injuries in cases where statute so authorized. The court, however, held that judges had the duty to protect the constitutional right of privacy and were therefore required to award damages for nonpecuniary losses to victims of a violation of that right, even in the absence of a specific statutory authorization. See Donald Kommers, *The Constitutional Jurisprudence of the Federal Republic of Germany* (Durham, N.C., and London: Duke University Press, 1997), 124–128.

3. For interesting examples of judicial decisions that clearly distinguish between the initial stage of interpreting the statute, on the one hand, and the final stage of repairing the statute once its constitutional defects have been ascertained, on the other, see the decision of the Supreme Court of Canada in *Vriend v. Alberta,* [1998] 1 S.C.R. 493, and the decision of the Constitutional Court of South Africa in *National Coalition for Gay and Lesbian Equality v. Minister of Home Affairs,* 2000 (2) S.A. 1 (CC). Of course, when a law has been applied for a long time and ordinary courts (especially the supreme courts) have generated an interpretive gloss, the constitutional court should assume that the meaning of that law is the one that results from that gloss. The legislature, after all, has acquiesced to that reading by not amending the law. The Italian Constitutional Court, for example, has established the doctrine of *diritto vivente,* according to which the court must review legislation under the constitution on the assumption that the legislation means what the Supreme Court of Cassation (Corte suprema di

cassazione) has said it means through its case law, when the latter is clear and stable. Through this doctrine, by the way, the court tried to pacify its earlier battles with the Supreme Court of Cassation. See Zagrebelsky, *La giustizia costituzionale*, 285–288. The Portuguese Constitutional Court has also held that for purposes of constitutional review, it should understand a law to mean what ordinary courts have actually interpreted it to mean. See Luís Nunes de Almeida, "Portugal," in *Las tensiones entre el Tribunal Constitucional y el Legislador en la Europa actual*, ed. Eliseo Aja (Barcelona: Ariel, 1998), 234. Interestingly, the German Constitutional Court, when checking the validity of a statutory provision in a concrete review procedure, is authorized to ask the relevant supreme courts to provide it with information as to how they have interpreted that provision in their case law. See article 82.4 of the *Bundesverfassungsgerichtsgesetz* [Federal Constitutional Court Act].

4. Zagrebelsky, *La giustizia costituzionale*, 167–168.

5. Ibid., 145.

6. The Spanish Constitutional Court, for example, has criticized ordinary judges (including judges on the Supreme Court) for having resorted to strained interpretations of the applicable statutes. *Contra legem* interpretations of statutes are unacceptable, the court has held, even if they are driven by the need to preserve constitutional values. See, e.g., Tribunal Constitucional decision no. 138/2005, May 26, 2005 (Spain). On the need to limit ordinary judges in this connection, see Javier Jiménez Campo, "Sobre la cuestión de inconstitucionalidad," in *Estudios sobre jurisdicción constitucional*, by Francisco Rubio Llorente and Javier Jiménez Campo (Madrid: McGraw-Hill, 1998), 94.

7. See Danny Nicol, "Statutory Interpretation and Human Rights after *Anderson*," *Public Law*, Summer 2004, 274–282, and Aileen Kavanagh, "The Elusive Divide between Interpretation and Legislation under the Human Rights Act of 1998," *Oxford Journal of Legal Studies* 24 (2004): 259–285. An interesting case to illustrate this problem is *Ghaidan v. Godin-Mendoza*, decided by the House of Lords, June 21, 2004, [2004] UKHL 30.

8. See, e.g., Konrad Hesse, *Escritos de Derecho constitucional* (Madrid: Centro de Estudios Constitucionales, 1992), 33–54.

9. See Konrad Zweigert and Hein Kötz, *An Introduction to Comparative Law* (Oxford: Clarendon Press, 1998), 265–268.

10. See *Probstmeier v. Germany*, and *Pammel v. Germany*, respectively, both decided on July 1, 1997, in *Reports of Judgments and Decisions* 1997-IV (ECHR).

11. See Dominique Rousseau, *La justice constitutionnelle en Europe* (Paris: Montchrestien, 1999), 108–109. The Spanish Constitutional Court, for example, has clearly held that the judge must refer the second statute to the court for its review. See Tribunal Constitucional decision nos. 23/1988, February 22, 1988, 158/1993, May 6, 1993, and 18/2003, January 30, 2003 (Spain). The same rule applies in Italy. See Zagrebelsky, *La giustizia costi-*

tuzionale, 327. In Belgium, the law explicitly provides that a new procedure must be initiated in such cases. The law establishes that when the court strikes down a particular statute, a new six-month term commences during which an action can be brought to the court for the annulment of any other statute that has the same object. See article 4.1 of the *Loi spéciale du 6 janvier 1989 sur la Cour d'arbitrage.*

12. Such a reform would be easy to introduce in Portugal. As has been noted in previous chapters, Portugal represents an exceptional case in that it allows all courts to ignore laws they take to be unconstitutional. The Constitutional Court, however, has jurisdiction to examine on appeal any judicial decision on these matters. In particular, the public prosecutors' office is obliged to appeal lower-court decisions holding a statute invalid. See article 280.3 of the Portuguese Constitution. This means that, in the end, the intervention of the Constitutional Court is needed to license the nonapplication of a statute in a particular lawsuit. Interestingly, however, an exception has been introduced: the public prosecutor is allowed "to abstain from filing an appeal on decisions taken within the guidelines already established in the case law of the Constitutional Court for the issue in question." Article 72.4 of *Law of the Constitutional Court,* Law no. 28/82 [*Lei do Tribunal Constitucional, Lei 28/82, de 15 de Novembro*]. That is to say, lower-court judges can decide themselves to set aside a piece of legislation, and the Constitutional Court will not be asked to intervene to confirm whether their decision is right, when the case law of the Constitutional Court is sufficiently clear. It would not be difficult to interpret this clause as applying to statutes that are similar to others that had already been declared unconstitutional. There is no firm position among scholars on this point, however. (I am indebted to Tiago Fidalgo de Freitas for this clarification.)

13. See article 33 of the Canadian Charter of Rights and Freedoms (Constitutional Act 1982). Some rights are beyond the reach of this mechanism, though: democratic rights (the right to vote), mobility rights, and linguistic rights. For an evaluation of this model of constitutionalism, under which the Parliament of Canada has the last word, see Stephen Gardbaum, "The New Commonwealth Model of Constitutionalism," *American Journal of Comparative Law* 49 (2001): 707–760.

CHAPTER 11. THE IMPACT OF THE EUROPEAN COURT OF JUSTICE

1. For an overview of the evolution that led to the establishment of these three pillars, and to several rearrangements within each of them, see Paul Craig and Gráinne de Búrca, *E.U. Law: Texts, Cases, and Materials* (Oxford: Oxford University Press, 2008), 1–37. It should be noted that, as of this writing, the Treaty of Lisbon, which was signed on December 13, 2007, has not yet been ratified by all member states. Although this treaty will change E.C. law in various ways, the legal doctrines and the judicial architecture that I examine in this chapter will not be affected at the foundational level.

2. There are actually three E.C. judicial bodies in Luxembourg: the European Court of Justice (ECJ) (which was originally the only court), the Court of First Instance (which was established in 1988), and the Civil Service Tribunal (which was established more recently, in 2004). They are all part of the so-called Court of Justice of the European Communities. In the text, I focus on the ECJ, since this is the only court that currently has the authority to render preliminary rulings, which play a key role, as we will see.

3. The "general version" of the preliminary reference is regulated in article 234 of the E.C. treaty (and article 150 of the Euratom treaty). Apart from this general version, there are two other types. One is the preliminary reference that operates in the context of articles 61–69 of the E.C. treaty, which deals with visas, asylum, immigration, and other policies concerning the free movement of persons. This type of preliminary ruling can only be sought by a national court against whose decisions there is no judicial remedy in national law. The other type was introduced by article 35 of the Treaty on European Union and covers police and judicial cooperation in criminal matters under the third pillar. The ECJ can give preliminary rulings on the interpretation and validity of certain measures adopted under this pillar, but only if the member state accepts the ECJ's jurisdiction by making a declaration to this effect. The member state has the further choice whether a preliminary ruling can be sought by any court or only by a court against whose decisions there is no judicial remedy in national law. In the text, I discuss only the "general" procedure regulated by article 234 of the E.C. treaty. For a detailed description of all these mechanisms, see Craig and de Búrca, *E.U. Law*, 460–501.

4. Actually, the ECJ has held that national courts cannot set aside E.C. acts on their own authority, even if they conclude that the acts are invalid. If a national court concludes that an E.C. act is invalid, the court must petition the ECJ to pass judgment on that act. See Case 314/85, *Foto-Frost v. Hauptzollamt Lübeck Ost*, 1987 E.C.R. 4199.

5. Craig and de Búrca, *E.U. Law*, 460.

6. Case 6/64, *Costa v. ENL*, 1964 E.C.R. 585.

7. Joseph Weiler, "The Transformation of Europe," in *The Constitution of Europe* (Cambridge, U.K.: Cambridge University Press, 1999), 10–101.

8. Case 106/77, *Amministrazione delle Finanze dello Stato v. Simmenthal S.p.A*, 1978 E.C.R. 629.

9. Ibid., par. 24 (emphasis added).

10. The Italian Constitutional Court, for example, finally endorsed the *Simmenthal* doctrine in the *Granital* case, decision 170/1984, June 5, 1984.

11. On the different and complex ways in which domestic legal systems have incorporated this basic principle of E.C. law, see Anne-Marie Slaughter, Alec Stone Sweet, and J. H. H. Weiler, *The European Court and National Courts: Doctrine and Jurisprudence* (Oxford: Hart Publishing, 1998).

12. Although these arguments are rather underdeveloped in the court's deci-

sion, they are more explicit in the opinion by Advocate General Gerhard Reischl.

13. Case 106/77, *Simmenthal,* pars. 23, 26.

14. There is an additional way to criticize the ECJ's efficiency argument. Since it requires some digression, I present it here. The ECJ saw no efficiency problem when it later held, in the *Foto-Frost* case, that when a national court believes that a legal provision enacted by the European Community (or even an administrative or executive decision of the European Community) is invalid under E.C. law, the court cannot simply set the provision aside, but must instead send a preliminary question to the ECJ. This important doctrine gives the ECJ a monopoly when it comes to determining that an E.C. act is invalid. "National courts have no jurisdiction themselves to declare that acts of Community institutions are invalid." Case 314/85, Foto-Frost, par. 20. One of the rationales for this centralized arrangement is uniformity and legal certainty, exactly the same values that figure so prominently in the classical justification of the Kelsenian model of constitutional review at the domestic level. As the ECJ said in its *Foto-Frost* decision, "Divergences between courts in the Member States as to the validity of Community acts would be liable to place in jeopardy the very unity of the Community legal order and detract from the fundamental requirement of legal certainty." Ibid., par. 15. This centralization is very strict, moreover, as strict as the Kelsenian system typically is. In a later case, *Gaston Schul Douane-expediteur B.V.,* the ECJ made clear that the national court is not exempted from the duty to raise a question to the ECJ, even in the extreme case in which the E.C. act to be scrutinized for its validity is very similar to another act that has already been held invalid by the ECJ. The national court is still required to seek a ruling from Luxembourg on a question relating to the validity of the provisions of a regulation "even where the Court has already declared invalid analogous provisions of another comparable regulation." Case C-461/03, *Gaston Schul Douane-expediteur B.V. v. Minister van Landbouw,* 2005 E.C.R. I-10513, par. 25. This means, of course, that the national court will have to stay the proceedings (although it can decree interim measures, see Cases C-143/88 and C-92/89, *Zuckerfabrik Süderdithmarschen AG v Hauptzollamt Itzehoe and Zuckerfabrik Soest GmbH v Hauptzollamt Paderborn, 1991 E.C.R. I-415*) and therefore wait until the ECJ rules on the validity of the relevant E.C. act. The ECJ, however, asserted: "Reducing the length of the proceedings cannot serve as justification for undermining the sole jurisdiction of Community Courts to rule on the validity of Community law." Case C-461/03, Gaston Schul, par. 23. (It should be noted that the average time that the ECJ needs to issue its ruling is currently 20.4 months.) The ECJ was probably right in *Foto-Frost:* it is more efficient for the ECJ to be the only court that can decide that an E.C. act is invalid, and to do so through a single decision that has general effects, than to allow all the different national courts to decide for themselves

whether to set aside the E.C. act in question. (See, however, the conclusions by Advocate General Dámaso Ruiz-Jarabo in the *Gaston Schul* case. He claimed that it is too rigid for the ECJ to insist on its monopoly when the act to be reviewed is very similar to one that has already been declared invalid.)

15. In its decision, the ECJ noted that the treaty "provides that any court or tribunal of a Member State is entitled to make a reference to the Court whenever it considers that a preliminary ruling on a question of interpretation or validity relating to Community law is necessary to enable it to give judgment," Case 106/77, *Simmenthal,* par. 19, and it concluded: "The effectiveness of that provision would be impaired if the national court were prevented from forthwith applying Community law in accordance with the decision or the case-law of the Court." Ibid., par. 20. Advocate General Gerhard Reischl was more explicit in his opinion: if the national court needs clarification, it must refer the case to the ECJ, not the national constitutional court.

16. See, for example, the references raised some years ago by the constitutional courts of Belgium and Austria in the cases C-93/97, *Federation Belge des Chambres Syndicales de Médecins ASBL v. Flemish Government,* 1998 E.C.R. I-4837, and C-143/99 *Adria-Wien Pipeline GmbH and Wietersdorfer & Peggauer Zementwerke GmbH v. Finanzlandesdirektion für Kärnten,* 2001 E.C.R. I-8365. For a more recent preliminary reference by the Belgian Constitutional Court, see C-303/05, *Advocaten voor de Wereld VZW v. Leden van de Ministerraad,* 2007 E.C.R. I-3633. See also Corte costituzionale decision no. 102/2008, February 13, 2008 from Italy.

17. Balancing is quite prominent in the jurisprudence of the ECJ in this area. On the reasoning of the court, see Joxerramon Bengoetxea, Neil MacCormick, and Leonor Soriano, "Integration and Integrity in the Legal Reasoning of the European Court of Justice," in *The European Court of Justice,* ed. Gráinne de Búrca and Joseph Weiler (Oxford: Oxford University Press, 2001), 43–85.

18. Because the member states have been transferring more and more powers to the European Community, the actions of the European Community need to be constrained by fundamental rights. In the 1970s, the ECJ started to recognize fundamental rights as unwritten "general principles" of E.C. law and drew inspiration from the common constitutional traditions of the member states and from various international instruments, the most relevant of which is the European Convention on Human Rights. For a general view of this evolution, see Bruno de Witte, "The Past and Future Role of the European Court of Justice in the Protection of Human Rights," in *The E.U. and Human Rights,* ed. Philip Alston, Mara Bustelo, and James Heenan (Oxford: Oxford University Press, 1999), 859–897. States are also bound by the fundamental rights that flow from E.C. law, but only when they are acting within the scope of application of E.C. law.

See Craig and de Búrca, *E.U. Law*, 395–402. It must be noted, incidentally, that the Charter of Fundamental Rights of the European Union, which was proclaimed in the Nice summit of December 2000 and was included in the failed treaty to establish a "Constitution for Europe," has increased the visibility of E.C. fundamental rights among national judges. (The new Treaty of Lisbon, signed on December 13, 2007, formally incorporates the charter into E.U. law.)

19. The ECJ's decision in Case C-224/01, *Köbler v. Republik Österreich*, 2003 E.C.R. I-10239, is a good step to reinforce this duty. Under the *Köbler* doctrine, a member state can be liable for damages caused by grave infringements of E.C. law stemming from a court's decision. One of the relevant factors in determining whether there has been a serious breach of E.C. law is "non-compliance by the court in question with its obligation to make a reference for a preliminary ruling under the third paragraph of Article 234 EC." Ibid., par. 55. And the court added: "In any event, an infringement of Community law will be sufficiently serious where the decision concerned was made in manifest breach of the case-law of the Court in the matter." Ibid., par. 56.

20. The ECJ announces on its Web site that its decisions are binding on all the national courts of the member states. The Web site includes a page with answers to frequently asked questions. Question 8 reads: "Are national courts obliged to follow the interpretation of the Court of Justice?" And the answer is: "Yes. Whenever the Court decides that a Community act is incompatible with the treaties, or whenever it gives an interpretation of Community law, that decision is *legally binding* and the national court which made the reference and all the other courts in the Member States are obliged to follow that ruling. The national courts are therefore bound by the interpretation of the Court. The same is true for all other public authorities." Curia, "FAQ: Your Questions about the Court of Justice of the European Communities," http://curia.europa.eu/en/instit/services/dpi/faq1.htm (question 8). The textbooks that European students read in law school, moreover, insist on the binding character of the ECJ's doctrines. As Karen Alter has explained, the role of E.C.-law experts in strengthening the authority of the ECJ has historically been of great significance. These experts started to create associations to promote knowledge of E.C. law and to spread the belief in the authority of the ECJ. One of their strategies was to publicize and criticize national judicial decisions that departed from the ECJ's case law. See Karen Alter, *Establishing the Supremacy of European Law: The Making of an International Rule of Law in Europe* (Oxford: Oxford University Press, 2001), 58.

21. These exceptions were defined by the ECJ in Case 283/81, *CILFIT v. Ministry of Health*, 1982 E.C.R. 3415.

22. Various proposals have been made to deal with the ECJ's excessive workload, which is a consequence of the increasing number of preliminary

references brought to it. See Alan Dashwood and Angus Johnston, eds., *The Future of the Judicial System of the European Union* (Oxford: Hart Publishing, 2001), and Paul Craig, "The Jurisdiction of the Community Courts Reconsidered," in *The European Court of Justice* (see note 17), 177–214. There seems to be a general consensus that in the near future, national judges will have to share more responsibility in the interpretation of E.C. law so that the ECJ can focus on the most important and controversial questions. See Thomas de la Mare, "Article 177 in Social and Political Context," in *The Evolution of E.U. Law*, ed. Paul Craig and Gráinne de Búrca (Oxford: Oxford University Press, 1999), 228–233.

23. Joseph Weiler, "Epilogue: The Judicial Après Nice," in *The European Court of Justice* (see note 17), 225.

24. On this bifurcation, see Mitchel Lasser, *Judicial Deliberations: A Comparative Analysis of Judicial Transparency and Legitimacy* (Oxford: Oxford University Press, 2004), 103–141, 203–238.

25. Sometimes, however, the ECJ does not offer national judges sufficient guidance. For a criticism of the ECJ on this ground, see Julio Baquero, "De la cuestión prejudicial a la casación europea: Reflexiones sobre la eficacia y la uniformidad del Derecho de la Unión," *Revista española de Derecho Europeo* 13 (2005): 35–58.

26. Daniel Sarmiento, *Poder judicial e integración europea: La construcción de un modelo jurisdiccional para la Unión* (Madrid: Civitas, 2004), 294–338.

27. Case C-368/95, *Vereinigte Familiapress Zeitungsverlags und vertriebs GmbH v. Heinrich Bauer Verlag*, 1997 E.C.R. I-3689.

28. Ibid., par. 29.

29. In France, for example, Dominique Rousseau has suggested that the French Constitutional Council should include E.C. law as part of the *bloc de la constitutionnalité* that it must guarantee against ordinary legislation. Actually, in some decisions, the court has already taken E.C. law into account in determining the validity of French statutes. See Dominique Rousseau, *Droit du contentieux constitutionnel* (Paris: Montchrestien, 2006), 115–122, 204–207. The Italian Constitutional Court can invalidate statutes under E.C. law in the context of abstract challenges (in connection with legislative conflicts between the state and the regions or between regions). For an updated description, see Federico Sorrentino, "Il diritto europeo nella giurisprudenza della Corte costituzionale: Problemi e prospettive," available at http://www.cortecostituzionale.it/informazione/eventi/eventi .asp?anno=2006. Ricardo Alonso García has suggested some types of cases in which the intervention of the Spanish Constitutional Court to strike down a statute in violation of E.C. law would be appropriate. See Ricardo Alonso García, *El juez español y el Derecho comunitario* (Madrid: Consejo General del Poder Judicial, 2003), 53–60. In an important report released in February 2006, the Spanish Consejo de Estado, in its capacity as an advisory body of the government, has advocated reforms that would allow the

Constitutional Court to determine the validity of Spanish statutes under
E.C. law, as a complementary mechanism to the *Simmenthal* arrangement.
The report, together with doctrinal commentary on it, can be found in
Francisco Rubio Llorente and José Álvarez Junco, eds., *El informe del
Consejo de Estado sobre la reforma constitucional: Texto del informe y debates
académicos* (Madrid: Consejo de Estado y Centro de Estudios Políticos y
Constitucionales, 2006), 116–117.

30. See article 23 of the Statute of the Court of Justice.

31. Thomas de la Mare has rightly emphasized the relevance of this participation, on the basis of discourse theory. If the court is to issue a ruling that
will be binding on all member states, the latter should be allowed to take
part in the procedure that will yield the ruling. See Thomas de la Mare,
"Article 177 in Social and Political Context," 240–249.

32. See article 104.3 of the Rules of Procedure of the Court of Justice.

33. See article 223 of the E.C. treaty.

34. Case C-450/93, *Kalanke v. Freie Hansestadt Bremen,* 1995 E.C.R. I-3051.

35. For some ideas and proposals, see Mattias Kumm and Victor Ferreres
Comella, "The Primacy Clause of the Constitutional Treaty and the Future
of Constitutional Conflict in the European Union," *International Journal
of Constitutional Law* 3 (2005): 473–492, and Aida Torres Pérez, *Conflicts
of Rights in the European Union: A Theory of Supranational Adjudication*
(Oxford: Oxford University Press, 2009).

36. In this regard, the French version of the centralized model of judicial review, until its recent reform in 2008, made it more difficult for the Constitutional Council to intervene in a conversation with the ECJ. The court
could review statutes only in abstract review proceedings, and only before
they were promulgated. In contrast, the German Constitutional Court, for
example, could speak to E.C. legal issues in the context of concrete cases.
On this difference, see Karen Alter, *Establishing the Supremacy of European
Law.*

37. Dieter Grimm, "The European Court of Justice and National Courts: The
German Constitutional Perspective after the *Maastricht* Decision," *Columbia Journal of European Law* 3 (1997): 238, 241.

CHAPTER 12. THE IMPACT OF THE EUROPEAN COURT OF
HUMAN RIGHTS

1. The convention guarantees the right to life (article 2); the right to liberty
and security (article 5); the right to a fair trial (article 6); the principle of
legality in criminal matters (article 7); the right to respect for private and
family life (article 8); freedom of thought, conscience, and religion (article
9); freedom of expression (article 10); freedom of assembly and association
(article 11); and the right to marry (article 12) and prohibits torture (article
3) and slavery and forced labor (article 4). In connection with these rights,
moreover, the convention guarantees the right to an effective national

remedy in case of violation (article 13) and the right not to be discriminated against (article 14). Several protocols have been adopted: protocol 1 protects the rights to property, education, and free elections; protocol 4 prohibits imprisonment for debt, the expulsion of nationals, and the collective expulsion of aliens, and guarantees freedom of movement; protocol 6 abolishes the death penalty, except in time of war or of imminent threat of war; protocol 7 establishes procedural safeguards relating to expulsion of aliens, the right to appeal in criminal matters, compensation for wrongful conviction, the right not to be tried or punished twice, and equality between spouses; protocol 12 sets out a general prohibition against discrimination; and protocol 13 abolishes the death penalty in all circumstances.

2. For an overview of the Strasbourg system for the protection of fundamental rights, see D. J. Harris, M. O'Boyle, and C. Warbrick, *Law of the European Convention on Human Rights* (London: Butterworths, 1995), 1–36, and P. van Dijk and G. J. H van Hoof, *Theory and Practice of the European Convention on Human Rights* (The Hague: Kluwer Law International, 1998), 1–69.

3. This was a result of protocol 11.

4. The court is divided into five sections, whose composition is geographically and gender balanced. Within each section, a chamber of seven judges is selected to deliver the judgments. (Committees of three judges in each section, however, dispose of applications that are clearly inadmissible.) In addition, the Grand Chamber, composed of seventeen judges, can render judgments and deals with cases of special importance. Thus, when a case pending before a chamber "raises a serious question affecting the interpretation of the Convention or the protocols," or "where the resolution of a question before the Chamber might have a result inconsistent with a judgment previously delivered by the Court," the chamber may relinquish jurisdiction in favor of the Grand Chamber, unless one of the parties objects. Article 30 of the European Convention on Human Rights. Also, when a judgment by a chamber has been delivered in a case, either party may (within a period of three months) request that the case be referred to the Grand Chamber. The request is accepted, in exceptional cases, if "the case raises a serious question affecting the interpretation or application of the Convention or the protocols thereto, or a serious issue of general importance." Ibid., article 43. When such a request is granted, the whole case is reheard.

5. These and other figures can be obtained from the ECHR's Web site, at http://www.echr.coe.int/ECHR/EN/Header/Reports+and+Statistics/ Reports/Annual+Reports.

6. See European Court of Human Rights, "Statistics 2008," http://www.echr .coe.int/NR/rdonlyres/A63F2A14-2C68-41F3-BFEF-49D3BF9D8C63/0/ Statistics2008.pdf. At the Third Summit of the Council of Europe in Warsaw in May 2005, it was decided that a "group of wise persons" should

meet to consider the steps that could be taken to ensure the system's workability. The report by the group was released in 2006. *Report of the Group of Wise Persons to the Committee of Ministers*, CM(2006)203 (2006), available at http://www.coe.int/t/cm/documentIndex_en.asp. The report suggests, among other things, the creation of a judicial committee that would be attached to the court, in charge of all cases that can be decided on the basis of well-established case law. The committee would declare certain applications either manifestly well founded or manifestly ill founded. In this way, the court would be relieved of a large number of cases and would be able to focus on its essential role.

7. The ECHR said: "The Convention is not part of the domestic law of the United Kingdom, nor does there exist any constitutional procedure permitting the validity of laws to be challenged for non-observance of fundamental rights. There thus was, and could be, no domestic remedy in respect of the applicants' complaint that the leasehold reform legislation itself does not measure up to the standards of the Convention and its Protocols. The Court, however, concurs with the Commission that Article 13 [of the Convention] does not go so far as to guarantee a remedy allowing a Contracting State's laws as such to be challenged before a national authority on the ground of being contrary to the Convention or to equivalent domestic legal norms." *James and Others v. United Kingdom*, February 21, 1986, par. 85, Series A no. 98 (ECHR). See also *Holy Monasteries (The) v. Greece*, December 9, 1994, par. 90, Series A no. 301-A (ECHR).

8. *Vermeire v. Belgium*, November 29, 1991, pars. 25, 26, and 27, Series A no. 214-C (ECHR).

9. For an overview of the various ways in which the different domestic legal systems have dealt with the European Convention on Human Rights, see Jörg Polakiewicz, "The Status of the Convention in National Law," in *Fundamental Rights in Europe: The European Convention on Human Rights and Its Member States, 1950–2000*, ed. Robert Blackmun and Jörg Polakiewicz (Oxford: Oxford University Press, 2001), 31–53. A more recent volume on this topic is Helen Keller and Alec Stone Sweet, eds., *A Europe of Rights: The Impact of the ECHR on National Legal Systems* (Oxford: Oxford University Press, 2008).

10. See articles 120 and 94, respectively, of the Constitution of the Kingdom of the Netherlands. According to Tim Koopmans, *Courts and Political Institutions* (Cambridge, U.K.: Cambridge University Press, 2003), 83–84, courts in the Netherlands, as a result of their power of judicial review of legislation under the convention, use a more assertive tone nowadays when they consider the constitutionality of a statute. Even if they cannot set aside the statute on constitutional grounds, they do express legal criticism of it.

11. Article 55 of the French Constitution awards international treaties a superior rank to statutes. The Constitutional Council has held that it is not part of its task, but that of ordinary judges, to review the conformity of

legislation with international treaties. Accordingly, ordinary judges can set aside statutes on the grounds that they violate convention rights. See Conseil constitutionnel decision no. 74-54 DC, January 15, 1975 (France). An illuminating description of the context in which this decision was made can be found in Noëlle Lenoir, "The Constitutional Council and the European Convention of Human Rights: The French Paradox," in *Liber Amicorum in Honour of Lord Slynn of Hadley*, vol. 2, *Judicial Review in International Perspective*, ed. Mads Andenas and Duncan Fairgrieve (The Hague: Kluwer Law International, 2000), 145–175.

12. For a systematic analysis of this constitutional clause, see Alejandro Saiz Arnaiz, *La apertura constitucional al Derecho internacional y europeo de los derechos humanos: El artículo 10.2 de la Constitución española* (Madrid: Consejo General del Poder Judicial, 1999).

13. The authority of international treaties vis-à-vis national legislation stems from article 96 of the Spanish Constitution. The Constitutional Court's doctrine on this issue can be found in its decision no. 28/1991, February 14, 1991 (Spain).

14. The 2006 *Report of the Group of Wise Persons to the Committee of Ministers*, which was mentioned in note 6, recommends a mechanism that would allow national courts to request an opinion by the ECHR on legal questions relating to the interpretation of the convention. Such a request, however, would be very different from the preliminary references that can be sent to the ECJ under E.C. law. First, only the constitutional courts and the courts of last instance would be allowed to ask the ECHR. Second, the requests would be optional. Third, the opinions given by the ECHR would not be binding.

15. See Laurence R. Helfer and Anne-Marie Slaughter, "Toward a Theory of Effective Supranational Adjudication," *Yale Law Journal* 107 (1997): 273–391.

16. For an assessment of the ECHR's jurisprudence in this area, with some comparative references to the different doctrinal framework set out by the U.S. Supreme Court, see Victor Ferreres Comella, "Freedom of Expression in Political Contexts: Some Reflections on the Case Law of the European Court of Human Rights," in *Political Rights under Stress in 21st Century Europe*, ed. Wojciech Sadurski (Oxford: Oxford University Press, 2006), 84–119.

17. Hans Kelsen, "La garantie juridictionnelle de la Constitution (La justice constitutionnelle)," *Revue du droit public et de la science politique en France et à l'étranger* 35 (1928): 237.

18. As has already been mentioned, the 2006 *Report of the Group of Wise Persons to the Committee of Ministers* suggests a mechanism that would allow the constitutional courts or the courts of last instance to request an advisory opinion by the ECHR. If this proposal were enacted, it would be easier for the constitutional court to derive a particular ruling from the case law

of the ECHR, for purposes of deciding whether a piece of national legislation is in conformity with the convention.

19. See *Verfassungsnovelle Bundesgesetzblatt* [Federal Constitutional Amendment] 1964/59. Pursuant to this act, the European Convention on Human Rights has the rank of constitutional law in Austria. The main reason for the inclusion of the convention in the Austrian Constitution was to modernize its bill of rights. Initially, the only rights that were protected were those enumerated in a statute of December 21, 1867, and some other old laws the constitution refers to in article 149. There is an interesting Austrian precedent for this "constitutionalization" of an international treaty in the field of human rights. Article 149 of the 1920 constitution incorporated several clauses of the Treaty of Saint-Germain, signed after the First World War, some of which protected fundamental liberties. Thus, in an important decision rendered on October 19, 1925, the Constitutional Court used articles 66 and 67 of that treaty (which protected individuals against religious discrimination) to declare the invalidity of an old law that had been enacted under the empire requiring the directors of primary schools to be professors capable of imparting religious teaching of the confession that was dominant among students. A Protestant professor who was denied his candidacy to the directorship of a school in Vienna successfully challenged the law before the Constitutional Court. See Charles Eisenmann, *La justice constitutionnelle et la Haute cour constitutionnelle d'Austriche* (Paris: Economica; Aix-en-Provence: Presses Universitaires d'Aix-Marseille, 1986), 248.

20. See, e.g., Guy Carcassonne, "Faut-il maintenir la jurisprudence issue de la décision n° 74-54 DC du 15 janvier 1975?" *Les cahiers du Conseil constitutionnel* 7 (1999): 141–153; Dominique Rousseau, *Droit du contentieux constitutionnel* (Paris: Montchrestien, 2006), 120, 233–234; Francis Delpérée, "Présentation de la Cour d'arbitrage de Belgique," *Les cahiers du Conseil constitutionnelle* 12 (2002): 97–98.

21. See article 72.3 of the *Lei do Tribunal Constitucional, Lei 28/82, de 15 de Novembro*.

22. Note that the move I am here favoring would be similar in spirit to the strategy that the Italian Constitutional Court followed in the past, in the context of the European Community, in order to assert its exclusive authority (within Italy) to review the conformity of Italian legislation with E.C. law. As will be recalled, the Italian Constitutional Court argued that an Italian statute that infringes E.C. law is, for that reason alone, invalid under the constitution. As we saw, the ECJ (in the *Simmenthal* decision) destroyed this monopoly and granted all courts the power of review. A similar move in the area of the European Convention on Human Rights, however, would be accepted by the ECHR. The contracting states must ensure that human rights are respected, but they have discretion to select the appropriate means to achieve this result. As was mentioned earlier, there is no equivalent to the *Simmenthal* doctrine in Strasbourg.

23. In countries where the convention has the same rank as an ordinary stat-
    ute, judges are often asked to read national legislation in light of the con-
    vention. In Germany, for example, the Constitutional Court held in a
    landmark decision of 1987 that the legislature must be presumed not to
    have wished to deviate from the convention "insofar as it has not clearly
    declared otherwise." Bundesverfassungsgericht [Federal Constitutional
    Court] [1987] 74 BVerfGE 358. See Andreas Zimmermann, "Germany,"
    in *Fundamental Rights in Europe* (see note 9), 339.
24. Article 36.2 of the European Convention on Human Rights.
25. Ibid., article 22.
26. Ibid., article 23.1.
27. When the convention was being discussed and negotiated, some represen-
    tatives even proposed not having a court and relying on the Committee
    of Ministers exclusively. Since only clear violations of basic human rights
    would have to be countered, they believed, there would be no need to create
    a body in charge of interpreting the convention to cover the more contro-
    versial issues of an evolving society. On the different views that were ex-
    pressed at the foundational moment concerning the role of the ECHR, see
    Danny Nicol, "Original Intent and the European Convention on Human
    Rights," *Public Law,* Spring 2005, 152–172.
28. See generally Howard Charles Yourow, *The Margin of Appreciation Doctrine
    in the Dynamics of European Human Rights Jurisprudence* (The Hague:
    Kluwer International, 1996).
29. *Open Door and Dublin Well Woman v. Ireland,* October 29, 1992, Series A
    no. 246-A (ECHR); *Tysiac v. Poland,* March 20, 2007, no. 5410/03, ECHR
    2007.
30. *Pretty v. United Kingdom,* April 29, 2002, no. 2346/02, ECHR 2002-III.
31. *Fretté v. France,* February 26, 2002, no. 36515/97, ECHR 2002-I. See, how-
    ever, *E.B. v. France* [GC], January 22, 2008, no. 43546/02, ECHR 2008.
32. *Evans v. United Kingdom* [GC], April 10, 2007, no. 6339/05, ECHR 2007.
33. *Von Hannover v. Germany,* June 24, 2004, no. 59320/00, ECHR 2004-VI.
34. Ibid., par. 76.
35. *Hirst v. United Kingdom (No. 2)* [GC], October 6, 2005, no. 74025/01, ECHR
    2005-IX.
36. Ibid. (joint dissent of Wildhaber, Costa, Lorenzen, Kovler, and Jebens),
    pars. 6, 9.
37. Jürgen Habermas, *The Divided West* (Cambridge, U.K., and Malden, Mass.:
    Polity Press, 2006), 140.
38. See Bundesverfassungsgericht [Federal Constitutional Court] [2004] 111
    BVerfG 307 (*Görgülü* case) (Germany). For a good description of the case
    and commentary, see Matthias Hartwig, "Much Ado about Rights: The
    Federal Constitutional Court Confronts the European Court of Human
    Rights," *German Law Journal* 6 (2005): 869–894.

INDEX

abortion debate, 35, 43, 70, 107, 114, 150
abstract review, xv, 8, 66–70, 73, 161n.2,
166–167n.22, 169n.31, 169n.33; advantages of, 67, 69; countries allowing,
64, 67; criticisms of, 67–70; deadlines for, 85, 167n.22; E.C. law and,
216n.29, 217n.36; European Convention on Human Rights and,
142; parliamentary opposition and,
61–62, 65; political issues and, 75–
76
academics, 40–41, 44, 45
access to court. *See* standing
Ackerman, Bruce, 30, 76, 91, 199n.3
acte clair doctrine, 129, 130
actio popularis, 67
activism. *See* judicial activism
administrative tribunals, 13, 21, 183n.34,
196n.23, 202n.5
Adria-Wien Pipeline case (E.C.R., 2001),
214n.16
*Advocaten voor de Wereld VZW v. Leden
van de Ministerraad* (E.C.R., 2007),
214n.16
advocates general, 130, 132
affirmative action, 136
Albanian Constitution, 177n.25
Alexy, Robert, 47

Alonso García, Ricardo, 216–217n.29
American model. *See* decentralized
system; United States
American Revolution, 11
Amsterdam, Treaty of (1997), 136
a posteriori review, 16, 17, 24, 58
a priori review, 7, 16–17, 24–25; abstract
review and, 68; disadvantages of,
58–59; invalidation consequences
of, 85; legislative override and, 77
Argentina, 23
Ashwander v. Tennessee Valley Authority
(U.S., 1936), 194n.12
asylum rights, 77, 105, 107n.36
attorney general, 66
Austria, 21, 131, 167n.24; historical judicial review in, 25, 160–161n.2; political
party coalitions in, 206–207n.35;
supreme courts' division of labor in,
172n.2
Austrian Constitution (1920), 31, 167n.24,
169n.30, 175n.21, 176n.23, 176n.25,
177n.1, 177n.26, 199n.40, 205n.24;
amendment process, 106, 185n.44,
201n.29, 206n.26; European Convention on Human Rights and, 145; post–
Second World War reenactment of,
196n.20

sures for expansion of, 116–118; secrecy of individual votes and, 102; statutory conformity vs. incompatibility and, 115–116; straining of, 113, 115, 116–118, 119, 120, 146, 163n.15; unalterable principles and, 107; U.S. Constitution and, 51–53; U.S. Supreme Court and, 53, 54, 73, 99. *See also* precedent

Ireland, 4, 99n.4, 152, 184n.38, 188n.12

Israeli Supreme Court, 87

Italian Constitution (1947), 4, 42, 177n.2; abstract values and, 47–48; amendment process, 106–107, 201n.29; fundamental rights and, 195n.20; legislation prior to, 83; on link with international organizations, 125

Italian Constitutional Court, 5, 57, 183n.29; abstract-concrete review and, 67; acceptance of cases by, 193n.4; access to, 60, 61, 65, 80–81, 166n.22, 167n.23; activism and, 83, 113; binding decisions and, 169n.33; case-consideration time delays and, 117; constitutional amendment checks by, 106–107; creation of (1956), 4, 42, 48, 100, 177n.2; *diritto vivente* doctrine, 209–210n.3; dissents and, 184n.39; E.C. law and, 125, 127, 132, 212n.10, 216n.29, 221n.22; first decision of, 80–81; functions of, 6; fundamental rights and, 29, 47, 48, 78, 196n.21; government corruption case and, 38–39; judge numbers, 37; judges' professional backgrounds, 41, 42; judges' ruling secrecy, 204–205n.19; judges' selection, 103, 202n.5; judges' term limits, 100, 101; jurisdictional limits of, 187n.9, 187n.11; monopoly within judicial system of, 125; objections to creation of, 80; ordinary judges and, 113, 167n.23, 198n.39, 209n.1, 209–210n.3, 210–211n.11; precedent and, 184n.40, 209–210n.3; retroactivity and, 176n.24; special position of, 46; statute defense and, 191n.33; unconstitutionality findings and, 194n.10, 199n.40

Italian Council of State, 202n.5

Italian Court of Accounts, 202n.5

Italian Court of Cassation, 202n.5, 209–210n.3

Italy, 57, 172n.2

Japan, 23, 195n.39, 196–197n.24

Jellinek, Georg, 160–161n.2

Judges, ordinary: abstract principles and, 47, 48; American judicial review and, 51, 58; American trust in, 11, 12; constitutional complaints jurisdiction and, 39; constitutional court precedents as guide for, 119–121, 130; constitutional court service by, 185n.41; constitutional interpretation attempts by, 50, 111, 112–121, 122; constitutional question initiation and, 7, 8, 36, 63–64, 65, 73, 80–81, 167nn.23–24, 168n.29; criteria for, 39, 40; dualist judicial structure and, 81–82, 112–113, 156; E.C. law review powers of, 111, 122, 125, 127–130, 131–132, 133, 136–137, 138; European constricted role of, xiv, xv, 6, 10, 11–13, 14–15, 22, 58, 113; European Convention on Human Rights and, 143; European independence of, 22; French historical distrust of, 12–14, 15, 16; historic timidity of, 85; international treaties and, 142; nonpolitical recruitment of, 98–99; objectivity of, 33, 34; Portuguese special judicial review powers, 6, 7–8, 81, 186–187n.6, 194n.10; precedent and, 22–23, 133; selection of, 98–99, 100; strained interpretations and, 163n.15; tenure of, 100–110

judicial activism, xv, 71–85, 95–96; dangers of passivity and, 71–75; factors in, 78–79, 83; flexibility of remedies and, 84–85; international treaties and, 142, 150; legal certainty protections and, 85; ordinary judges and, 113; vectors of, 84–85

judicial independence, 22, 23; appointment process and, 96, 98–99, 134–135, 203–204n.9; life tenure and, 101–102; opinion publication and, 48; precedent and, 174n.13; secrecy of dissents and, 102, 135

judicial review, xiii–xvi; abstract-concrete